GOOD JUDGMENT: THE EUROPEAN COURT OF JUSTICE AS A CONTEXT-CONSCIOUS LAWMAKER

Courts are context conscious. They interpret and apply the law in ways which are mindful of societal demands and potential implications. Case facts, institutional structures, political interest, and economic stakes bear on legal reasoning and case outcomes. This book elaborates the concept of good judgment, a term invoking in equal parts legal expertise, prudence, common sense, and political savoir faire, to investigate how much and in what circumstances they do so. The analysis focuses on the European Court of Justice and its free movement case-law. The framework and theory, however, are relevant to courts and case-law everywhere. This is a compelling and intriguing examination of the Court and its shaping of a key tenet of EU law.

Good Judgment

The European Court of Justice as a Context-Conscious Lawmaker

Urška Šadl

•HART•
OXFORD • LONDON • NEW YORK • NEW DELHI • SYDNEY

HART PUBLISHING

Bloomsbury Publishing Plc

Kemp House, Chawley Park, Cumnor Hill, Oxford, OX2 9PH, UK

1385 Broadway, New York, NY 10018, USA

29 Earlsfort Terrace, Dublin 2, Ireland

HART PUBLISHING, the Hart/Stag logo, BLOOMSBURY and the Diana logo are trademarks of Bloomsbury Publishing Plc

First published in Great Britain 2024

A catalogue record for this book is available from the British Library.

A catalogue record for this book is available from the Library of Congress.

ISBN: HB: 978-1-50996-812-1
ePDF: 978-1-50996-814-5
ePub: 978-1-50996-813-8

Typeset by Compuscript Ltd, Shannon

Good Judgment

The European Court of Justice as a Context-Conscious Lawmaker

Urška Šadl

•HART•
OXFORD • LONDON • NEW YORK • NEW DELHI • SYDNEY

HART PUBLISHING

Bloomsbury Publishing Plc

Kemp House, Chawley Park, Cumnor Hill, Oxford, OX2 9PH, UK

1385 Broadway, New York, NY 10018, USA

29 Earlsfort Terrace, Dublin 2, Ireland

HART PUBLISHING, the Hart/Stag logo, BLOOMSBURY and the Diana logo are trademarks of Bloomsbury Publishing Plc

First published in Great Britain 2024

A catalogue record for this book is available from the British Library.

A catalogue record for this book is available from the Library of Congress.

ISBN: HB: 978-1-50996-812-1
ePDF: 978-1-50996-814-5
ePub: 978-1-50996-813-8

Typeset by Compuscript Ltd, Shannon

Acknowledgements

AMONG MY COLLEAGUES at the European University Institute, I found role models, mentors, and friends. My PhD students brought new ideas and endless joy. iCourts gave me the confidence to walk the empirical walk. The Judging Under the Influence team played epically. Daniel built IUROPA with unmatched chivalry. Niels taught me Stata repeatedly, patiently, lovingly. Lee and Keren taught me judicial behaviour. Mikael taught me everything. Hans dared me to think hard and then harder. Angela could tell the real from the unreal. I could always be real with Stephanie and Carolina. Juan's kindness was transformative. Suvi's wicked sense of humour saved me from myself. My family loved me in hard times. Laura Clough from Pangram edited the text. Sasha Jawed and Tom Adams from Hart made it happen. Martijn said he would read 'a book like that.' For all this, I am grateful.

This book is for Yannis and Stella, the bravest.

Respectfully, U.

Acknowledgement of the funding

The research is funded by Danmarks Frie Forksningsfond Sapere Aude Research Leader Grant N. 8046-00019A.

Contents

PART II
THE MECHANICS OF GOOD JUDGMENT

PART III
THE MECHANISMS OF GOOD JUDGMENT

List of Tables and Figures

Tables

Figures

1

Introduction

SUMMARY

GOOD JUDGMENT IS a phrase evoking in equal parts legal expertise, prudence, common sense, and political savoir faire in the context of adjudication. For the purposes of the present analysis, good judgment describes a distinct form of context-conscious judging, which upholds conflicting claims to reconcile the law's demands for equality, consistency, coherence, and legal certainty, with societal demands, political circumstances, and economic implications. As a heuristic tool, it offers a new lens to observe and explain the decision-making strategy and role of the European Court of Justice. Chapter one presents the claim, the motivation, and the contribution, distinguishing the book from the existing literature. It concludes with the outline of individual chapters.

A. THE MAIN CLAIM

Courts are context conscious. They interpret and apply the law in ways which are mindful of societal demands and potential implications. Case facts, institutional structures, political interest, and economic stakes bear on legal reasoning and case outcomes. This book elaborates the concept of good judgment, a term invoking in equal parts legal expertise, prudence, common sense, and political savoir faire, to investigate how much and in what circumstances they do so.

Good judgment is a form of context-conscious judging which allows the European Court of Justice (the Court) to uphold conflicting claims by departing from the typical structure of rational justification and model law application in three distinct ways: the Court can censure Member State policies but adopt Member State friendly outcomes; it can limit unfavourable outcomes and interpretations so as to reduce their practical effect; and it can uphold free movement rights while conditioning and deferring key terms of their application to the national courts and administrations. In so doing, the Court (ideally) ensures individual rights protection, workable solutions, legally correct outcomes, and the effectiveness of its rulings.

The analysis approaches good judgment empirically and conceptually, combining case annotation (hand coding) and simple statistics from 1538 free movement of goods and 1091 free movement of persons judgments, decided from 1954 to 2022, with qualitative legal analysis. It identifies general trends and patterns in case-law, dissects specific conflicts underlying disputes, and unpacks individual instances in which the Court upholds conflicting claims. The findings suggest that context shapes the law when the political and economic stakes are sufficiently high. This varies according to the type of good judgment, policy area, and historical period, its share extending from 5 per cent to over 60 per cent.

Concretely, the share of good judgment in the free movement of persons has steadily increased while the share of good judgment in the free movement of goods has steadily decreased over time as the opposition to the latter has softened and the hostility toward the former has sharpened. This development has been particularly clear in the past two decades, reflecting variance in support for different aspects of European integration. Moreover, the participation of Member State governments in salient cases decided by the Grand Chamber almost doubles the probability of good judgment compared to the cases decided by the Grand Chamber without the participation of the Member States. Member State observations submitted in cases decided by smaller formations or in Chambers do not significantly affect the probability of good judgment.

Good judgment is furthermore unrelated to the status of the applicants (gender, family, or worker status, and whether they are natural or legal persons). In contrast, legal issues like residence rights, and trade, import, or fiscal restrictions significantly increase the probability of good judgment. The same trend is visible in cases where free movement of goods interacts with other freedoms and policy areas, like agriculture, or in the absence of harmonising legislation. While residence rights for economically inactive European citizens have been particularly contentious in recent years, state protectionism behind trade and fiscal restrictions, notably agriculture, accounted for intense litigation in the early integration period. Further qualitative analysis additionally emphasises the pivotal effect of national efforts to control immigration, curb the access of non-nationals to the national social security systems, close the domestic market to foreign products, or exempt traditional manufacture from market forces.

The insight that the Court has always responded to political and economic conflict by upholding conflicting claims complements the existing literature, arguing that it has become increasingly deferential, selectively activist, rights restrictive, minimalist, evasive, or excessively liberalist while weighing in on timeless and timely conversations about judicial independence, the responsibility of courts in democratic societies, the Court's role in the integration process and the normative critique of its legal reasoning with empirically informed and conceptually rigorous argument.

Finally, the analysis contributes a comprehensive and nuanced understanding of the Court as a legal and political actor by bringing together fou dimensions of judicial decision-making; legal argumentation, law application law-making, and the exercise of legal authority and political power, whicl tend to be studied separately by different disciplines. Because selected case-law (free movement of goods and persons) is legally, politically, and economically central to the European internal market and integration, the findings are valid for other policy areas, and mutatis mutandis for all courts navigating politically fraught terrains.

B. THE STRUCTURE

i. The Premise

The analysis of good judgment assumes that one judgment can uphold several and even conflicting claims and interests. Adjudication is not a zero-sum game with one winner and one loser. This premise refocuses the analysis to the components (elements) of justification; to a set of parameters capturing arguments, case outcomes, doctrinal importance, and methods of interpretation.

Literature typically evaluates the Court's decision-making against the ideal type of adjudication as a zero-sum game, characterised by 1) an independent judge 2) who applies a set of pre-existing rules in 3) an adversarial procedure involving two parties and 4) adopts a binary decision that awards one party the legal right and finds the other in the legal wrong.[1] The idea(l) is consistent with the understanding of law as a rational system even if adopted for dubious reasons and applied by actors with bounded rationality. The insistence upon binary decisions logically follows from the primary function of courts as dispute resolution bodies; the demand for formal equality before the law excludes non-legal, personal considerations as justifying reasons for their decisions; the institutional legitimacy of courts hinges on their political independence and non-partisanship.

Empirically, courts adopt binary or non-binary decisions to settle unresolvable conflicts and protect incommensurate interests, occasionally using interpretation and procedural tools to transform a game with one winner and one loser into a game with two winners and no losers.[2] Good judgment inquires into the mechanics of this transformation against the benchmark of the typical structure of rational justification. The rationale is straightforward: if judges strive for logical arguments and rational justification, the protection of rights, and coherent outcomes (for strategic reasons or because they feel bound by the rules), then good judgment or the non-binary decision which upholds conflicting claims will strain legal logic and the structure of rational justification, departing from the model application of law defined as the reasoning from the meaning of rules and the scope of their application to the concrete decision about the legal

[1] For this conceptualisation see M Shapiro, *Courts: A Comparative and Political Analysis* (Chicago, University of Chicago Press, 1981).

[2] ibid.

claim (the case outcome).[3] The structure of justification will necessarily reflect the conflicting demands imposed by the rules and the practical constraints of the case and its broader circumstances. Broad interpretations will result in narrow outcomes; far-reaching principles will have limited practical implications; precedents will not apply. In other words, the structure of justification will signal good judgment and its varieties, which further analysis will have to identify and examine to confirm. Crucially, good judgment is not legally incorrect or otherwise illegitimate – only atypical to a greater extent than the regular ebb and flow.

The relationship between arguments, protected rights, interests, methods of interpretation, doctrinal contribution, and case outcomes does not necessarily allow for conclusions about the legal correctness of individual judgments to be reached. It is used as an intermediary step for an analysis that seeks to explain the interplay between legal rules with case facts, institutional structures, political conflict, and economic stakes.

Context sensitivity is a continuum, which the conceptualisation of three types of good judgment reflects to a degree. Each type of good judgment accommodates scenarios reflecting different echelons of the Court's sensitivity to the context, ranging from the recognition of high political, social, and cultural stakes of the dispute, to the Court's honouring of the political will of the national or European legislator, and finally, its oversensitivity to the political / electoral mood in the respondent state.

ii. Contribution

The impact of the book is threefold. First, the book presents a novel understanding of the Court, laying the groundwork for further empirically informed theorising. Second, the book's analytical framework supports systematic inquiries in other courts and case-law. Third, the analysis deepens the understanding of free movement of goods and persons which are intrinsic to internal market law.

The book complements and advances the existing empirical research agenda. Edited volumes exploring non-traditional approaches to law and courts are becoming common in European legal studies.[4] A debate about the merits of

[3] B Rudden, 'Consequences' (1979) 24 *The Juridical Review* 193. The implications of a ruling vary. The amendments of national legislation are sometimes negative, like a removal of certain provisions, and sometimes positive – requiring the introduction of new provisions (like interim relief into English law post *Factortame*). For an overview see P Van Cleynenbreugel, 'Procedural Autonomy as Integration-Reinforcement. The Court of Justice of the European Union and National Procedural Choices' in W Werner and L Gruszczynski (eds), *Deference in international courts and tribunals. Standard of review and margin of appreciation* (Oxford, Oxford University Press, 2014).

[4] M Bartl and JC Lawrence (eds), *The Politics of European Legal Research: Behind the Method* (Edward Elgar Publishing, 2022); C Kilpatrick and J Scott (eds), *New Legal Approaches to Studying*

interdisciplinarity and the politics of legal method is unfolding at a very rapid pace. Moreover, European legal studies have increasingly recognised the value of empirical approaches and a growing number of scholars have been actively engaged with and contributed to the empirical legal studies (ELS) movement.[5]

Less effort has gone in the development of a unique empirical legal methodology, meaning that a thin contextual layer and descriptive statistics embellish the legal analysis or that studies apply social science methods by dwarfing the legal argument. The findings rarely infuse the studies of judicial politics and judicial behaviour analysing the same developments and theorising comparable mechanisms. Sharing datasets, protocols, and empirical materials to allow for the reproduction and the building of common resources has so far remained exceptional.

The empirical approach and the aim of the analysis distinguish the book from Bengoetxea's groundbreaking contribution,[6] and other descriptive and prescriptive normative accounts of the Court's reasoning.[7] The findings can also advance and reframe the normative critique of the Court's reasoning as (il)legitimate policymaking. The latter renders an unnecessarily narrow view of the Court, perpetuated by entrenched concepts (judicial activism) and approaches (varieties of critical positivism or latterly, critical legal studies). Reframing the debate can advance a different and more nuanced understanding of the Court as a lawmaker promoting competing interests rather than as a legitimate or illegitimate policymaker.

Three features distinguish the book from older as well as more recent empirical scholarship and contextual approaches, which have most explicitly linked

the Court of Justice: Revisiting Law in Context (Oxford, Oxford University Press, 2021); M Derlén and J Lindholm (eds), *The Court of Justice of the European Union: Multidisciplinary Perspectives*, vol 10 (London, Bloomsbury Publishing, 2018); F Nicola and B Davies (eds), *EU Law Stories* (Cambridge, Cambridge University Press, 2017); MR Madsen, F Nicola and A Vauchez (eds), *Researching the European Court of Justice: Methodological Shifts and Law's Embeddedness* (Cambridge, Cambridge University Press, 2022).

[5] J Frankenreiter and MA Livermore, 'Computational Methods in Legal Analysis' (2020) 16 *Annual Review of Law and Social Science* 39.

[6] J Bengoetxea, *The Legal Reasoning of the European Court of Justice: Towards a European Jurisprudence* (Oxford, Clarendon Press Oxford, 1993).

[7] The existing work studying the legal reasoning of the Court uses the (scholarly constructed) criteria of coherence and consistency as benchmarks for critique and evaluation. Based on the idea of law as a system and following the method of rational reconstruction it can offer a critique of the outcome, departures from precedent, inconsistent application of rules or other faults in reasoning. It is less able to address the mechanics of the process. See M De S.-O.-L'E Lasser, *Judicial Deliberations: A Comparative Analysis of Transparency and Legitimacy* (Oxford, Oxford University Press, 2009); G Conway, *The Limits of Legal Reasoning and the European Court of Justice* (Cambridge, Cambridge University Press, 2012); H Rasmussen, *On Law and Policy in the European Court of Justice: A Comparative Study in Judicial Policymaking* (Leiden, Brill, 1986); E Paunio, *Legal Certainty in Multilingual EU Law: Language, Discourse and Reasoning at the European Court of Justice* (London, Routledge, 2016); S Sankari, *European Court of Justice Legal Reasoning in Context* (Paris, Europa Law Publishing, 2013); M Jacob, *Precedents and Case-Based Reasoning in the European Court of Justice: Unfinished Business* (Cambridge, Cambridge University Press, 2014).

the Court's political success to the ingenious use of legal form, highlighting the ability to placate state governments, speaking a lofty language of common goals, imposing mild remedies, nurturing courteous conversations with national courts, and explaining the rulings outside the courtroom.[8]

First, the analysis focuses on legally relevant characteristics of free movement case-law, linking the context of the Court's decision-making process with legal content, institutional features, and case facts. The analytical framework operationalises the theorising of Helfer and Slaughter, Alter, and other accounts inspired by neofunctionalism,[9] in addition to Weiler's Transformation of Europe.[10] Metaphorically, rather than painting with a broad brush it parses through with a fine-tooth comb. Second, the analysis is comprehensive, surveying all the free movement of persons and goods judgments, regardless of their doctrinal contribution or place in the scholarly narratives. In this sense, the book complements Zglinski's study,[11] considering a much larger sample of judgments through a complementary and conceptually wider prism of conflicting interests.

Third, the book is unique in weaving the theories of judicial behaviour into legal analysis, constructing a bridge between the disciplines separated by assumptions, approaches and vocabulary while pursuing the same aims of understanding courts as (partly or fully) political actors.

The burgeoning methodological debates and the establishment of the European Society for Empirical Legal Studies with the annual conference and a complementary journal make the book especially timely.[12]

C. THE OUTLINE

The argument is structured in three parts. Part I (chapters two to four) develops the analytical framework (concepts and methodology), which can 1) identify and categorise departures from a typical structure of rational justification and

[8] L Helfer and A-M Slaughter, 'Toward a Theory of Effective Supranational Adjudication' (1997) 107 *The Yale Law Journal* 119.

[9] A-M Burley and W Mattli, 'Europe Before the Court: A Political Theory of Legal Integration' (1993) 47 *International Organization* 41.

[10] JHH Weiler, 'The Transformation of Europe' (1991) 100 *The Yale Law Journal* 2403; KJ Alter, *The European Court's Political Power: Selected Essays* (Oxford, Oxford University Press, 2009); MR Madsen, 'The Protracted Institutionalization of the Strasbourg Court: From Legal Diplomacy to Integrationist Jurisprudence' (2011) 2 *The European Court of Human Rights between Law and Politics* 43; A Vauchez, 'The Transnational Politics of Judicialization. Van Gend En Loos and the Making of EU Polity' (2010) 16 *European Law Journal* 1; Helfer and Slaughter (n 8), 273.

[11] J Zglinski, *Europe's Passive Virtues: Deference to National Authorities in EU Free Movement Law* (Oxford, Oxford University Press, 2020).

[12] https://elsacademy.nl/event/2022-international-els-conference/ (page last visited in December 2023).

2) relate them to selected case characteristics. Part II applies the analytical framework to the free movement case-law. Chapters five dealing with the free movement of persons and six dealing with the free movement of goods set the scene for further investigation into the underlying logic and mechanisms of good judgment. Part III (chapter seven) investigates the mechanisms of good judgment, using linear regression to inquire into the relationship between case characteristics, institutional structures, and the broader political and economic circumstances and the three types of good judgment, using legal qualitative analysis to evaluate and theorise the findings. Chapter eight summarises the argument and briefly reflects on whether good judgment is a good idea or not.

i. Chapter Two

The natural starting point for any discussion of judicial decision-making is the prototype of courts and the corresponding idea(l) of judging: A formalised process in which independent judges apply valid pre-existing legal rules to resolve disputes between two parties and render an authoritative decision awarding one party a legal right and the other a legal wrong. Different disciplines have developed complementary approaches highlighting various aspects of this process. The first part of the chapter discusses four perspectives on judging, including those which adopt a normative approach seeking to reproduce the ideal, as well as those which challenge at least one of its components (whether it be legal diplomacy, judicial behaviour or incrementalism). The second part of the chapter outlines and analyses the studies of the Court's decision-making, which explicitly or tacitly incorporate one of the outlined perspectives in a separate research agenda.

ii. Chapter Three

Chapter three elaborates three types of good judgment: 1) non-sanctioning Europeanisation of national policies, which combines the invasive scrutiny of national measures and policies with a state friendly outcome (Type 1); 2) deferential upholding of European rights, which carves out new rights and concepts but leaves their application to the referring court or national administration (Type 2); and 3) bounded undesirable interpretation, which limits the effects of expansive and from the perspective of the respondent Member State, undesirable rulings (Type 3).

In judgments scrutinising but not sanctioning national policies which directly regulate or affect free movement of persons or goods and thus the rights of individual traders and the validity of state measures regulating trade and its related aspects the Court censors national policies against the European benchmark, elaborating a supranational standard. This situation juxtaposes three legally relevant characteristics of case-law or parts of justification: the proportionality reasoning of the Court (proportionality test) as a mode of bringing national policy choices within the Treaty range and thus being subject to common standards; the Court's decision that the national measures or practices are (in)compatible with free movement and (un)justified; and the implications of this outcome on national regulatory choices (autonomy).

A deferential judgment upholding and expanding European rights and principles protects free movement rights without unsettling the power balance between the states and the European Union. The Court suspends the application of a free movement rights-protective or rights-generative interpretation of European law by delegating the decision-making authority to the national courts or administration. This type of good judgment concerns the outcome of the case (i.e. the Court's decision about the legal claim), and the reasoning, which defers a significant aspect of the decision to the referring court beyond the limits of Article 267 of the Treaty on the Functioning of the European Union (TFEU or the Treaty of Lisbon) in preliminary references or other political actors (typically in infringement actions).

A judgment with bounded undesirable interpretation balances the implications of the ruling on the regulatory autonomy of the Member States with the development of European Union law. The three legally relevant characteristics of justification, which reflect the rationale of bounded undesirable interpretation, are the implications for the Member States' autonomy (i.e. does the outcome limit the Member State's power to adopt or apply the adopted policy?), the Court's approach to interpretation and the doctrinal importance of the judgment (its contribution to the acquis).

While it is impossible to create an objective and definite benchmark for context consciousness,[13] which is a continuum of inconspicuous, circumspect, subtle, and barely noticeable conduct, three types of good judgment capture a variety of situations in which the Court departs to a varying degree from the expected justificatory script or model justification / the Court's template of reasoning in free movement case-law[14] without fully breaking with legal logic and rational argumentation. Judgments that uphold conflicting interests are not blatantly contradictory. Deviations appear internally unnecessary but externally mandated. This conceptualisation rationalises the continuum but not in a binary, artificial or over reductionist manner. The findings are reliable and the analysis is still legally informative.

[13] Modern legal theory agrees that judging is not a mechanical activity, as proposed by exegetists, and that rules require interpretation. For a comparative account of statutory interpretation see the classical text by DN MacCormick and RS Summers, *Interpreting Statutes: A Comparative Study* (London, Routledge, 2016).

[14] Restriction (discriminatory measure) – justification – proportionality. See N Nic Shuibhne, *The Coherence of EU Free Movement Law: Constitutional Responsibility and the Court of Justice* (Oxford, Oxford University Press, 2013) 24.

iii. Chapter Four

Chapter four operationalises good judgment, outlining the methodological building blocks. The central building blocks are the characteristics of good judgment which can shed light on the elements of justification and decision-making. They can be divided according to legally relevant characteristics related to justification, like the Court's reasoning, approach to interpretation, and case outcomes, as well as case characteristics, like the information about the applicants, legal issues, the institutional features, and the legal framework of the Court's judgment. The legal characteristics of case-law capture the Court's framing and the use of concepts and tests, the application of principles to concrete situations, the method, the reasoning, and the decisions about the legal claims or correct interpretations of European Union law. Finally, the chapter presents the method of case annotation (hand coding), which supports descriptive statistics, regression, and legal analysis, as a unique legal empirical methodology.

Chapters five and six justify the focus on the free movement of goods and persons.

iv. Chapter Five

The chapter explores three types of good judgment in the free movement of persons case-law against the standard of the Treaty framework and the political context surrounding the legislative process leading to the adoption of the Citizenship Rights Directive. The latter juridified incommensurate political and economic interests of the common market based on the free movement of workers and European citizens, solidarity between the Member States and high level of social protection,[15] and the nationally controlled migration flows, redistributive policies, and public spending. The conflict between these interests has permeated the case-law, straining the law's capacity to adapt to the extra-legal circumstances without compromising its underlying values.

The emblematic cases in which the Court sought to uphold conflicting claims are *Groener*,[16] illustrating the non-sanctioning Europeanisation of national policies (Type 1); *Vaassen-Göbbels*,[17] illustrating the deferential upholding of European rights (Type 2); and *Blaizot*,[18] illustrating the bounded undesirable interpretation (Type 3).

Groener applies European standards to questions of national language policy and identity, but ultimately approves of the Irish language policy. The judgment nonetheless sends a warning to formulate policies which are mindful

[15] Art 3 TFEU.
[16] Case C-379/87, *Groener*, ECLI:EU:C:1989:599.
[17] Case 61/65, *Vaassen-Göbbels*, ECLI:EU:C:1966:39.
[18] Case 24/86, *Blaizot*, ECLI:EU:C:1988:43.

of European Union law, potentially authorising future inroads which may not produce Member State-friendly outcomes. In *Vaassen-Göbbels*, the Court's broad *ratione persone* understanding of social security hinged entirely on the answer to the question of the applicant's entitlement, which the Court stopped short of answering, deferring it to the referring court. Finally, in *Blaizot*, the Court effectively imposed a new obligation on the responding state, expanded the meaning of a European legal concept (vocational training), but limited its temporal application. Only foreign students who had already commenced the proceedings against the Universities could claim the repayment of student fees. These outcomes were legally acceptable but not compelling, being primarily mandated by the non-legal considerations and circumstances of the cases.

Good judgment in free movement of persons cases is uncommon. There are, however, important differences in the frequency by type. Type 1 judgments are the most frequent, and their share has increased significantly (up to 40 per cent) since 1995. Type 2 and Type 3 judgments fluctuated between five and 13 per cent annually up until 2005, whereupon their share increased to 18 per cent and 20 per cent.

v. Chapter Six

The chapter explores three types of good judgment in the free movement of goods case-law in the context of the Treaty provisions, landmark judgment, doctrinal developments, attempts at market harmonisation, and the recurrent question of the bounds of the European Union's regulatory competence. While legal issues and the type of applicant in the free movement of goods disputes differ from the central legal questions in the free movement of persons judgments, the underlying tensions between individual and collective, national and European, applicant and state interest are strikingly alike.

The Court's judgment in *Schmidberger*[19] illustrates the non-sanctioning Europeanisation of national policy choices (Type 1); the judgment in Brasserie *du Pêcheur*[20] illustrates the deferential protection of free movement rights (Type 2); and the judgment in *Newcastle Disease*[21] illustrates the bounded undesirable interpretation (Type 3).

Schmidberger juxtaposed the Treaty duty of the Member State to actively prevent an environmental demonstration blocking the free transit of goods while upholding the protesters' rights of assembly by not preventing the demonstration. The decision allowing Austria to make this choice under

[19] Case C-112/00, *Eugen Schmidberger v Austria*, ECLI:EU:C:2003:333.

[20] Joined cases C-46/93 and C-48/93, *Brasserie du Pêcheur v Germany and Factortame Ltd et al*, ECLI:EU:C:1996:79.

[21] Case C-40/82, *Commission v United Kingdom (Newcastle Disease)*, ECLI:EU:C:1982:285.

European Union law compensated for the prohibition to impose higher tolls or bans under European Union law, a subject of pending infringement action. The Court censured Austrian policy to limit transit without imposing a sanction. In *Brasserie du Pêcheur*, the Court held that a Member State was liable under European Union law for breaches thereof but deferred the application of the principle to the national court under the conditions governing the liability of national law. The plaintiffs subsequently lost their case at the Federal Court of Justice (the Bundesgerichtshof) but the principle of rights protection and State Liability were steadfast. Finally, in *Newcastle Disease*, the Court ruled that the United Kingdom's measures effectively banning the imports of Christmas turkeys from France violated the Treaty. At the same time, it postponed the judgment on the question of the United Kingdom's import licensing system, the legislation which constituted the basis for the Christmas turkey ban. While the outcomes and the reasoning in all above judgments comply with the limits of legally acceptable justification and the acceptable use of procedural tools, further analysis shows they were primarily motivated by external circumstances.

Good judgment in free movement of goods cases is rare. The share of Type 1 judgments fluctuated in the early decades of the common market, until stabilising at 14 per cent to 19 per cent between 1980 and 2000, and then falling steadily. Type 2 good judgments are scarce; their share has been low and stable over time. Type 3 judgments are the most frequent and varied. Their share was especially high in the early 1960s, decreased after the 1970s, increased for shorter periods again around 1995 and 2015 (up to 25 per cent), and significantly decreased in the last five-year period.

Overall, while the share of good judgment in the free movement of persons judgments has gradually increased, and the share of good judgment in the free movement of goods judgments has gradually decreased, the patterns between the free movement of goods and persons have converged; in the past two decades, the share of good judgment in both policy areas has become comparable.

vi. Chapter Seven

Chapter seven assesses the significance of the relationship between three types of good judgment and the available relevant information about the applicants, the legal content of the case, and the institutional features, using simple (linear) regression. Further qualitative analysis of the findings digs deeper into the statistically significant relationships, showing that the Court is sensitive to the high stakes which the dispute presents to the Member States (illustrated by the ruling in *Collins*),[22] the fragility of the national political consensus (illustrated

[22] Case C-138/02, *Brian Francis Collins*, ECLI:EU:C:2004:172.

by *Scotch Whisky Association*),[23] the European political / legislative bargain (illustrated by *X. v Belgium*),[24] and the broader political climate (illustrated by *Commission v United Kingdom (Child Benefits)*).[25] Hence, good judgment is a context-motivated departure from the model justification.

Considering that the Court can tailor its justification to the context without departing from the model law application and typical justification, the chapter explores alternative forms of context-conscious judging, notably the reframing of a dispute, allowing the Court to decide on a less contentious legal problem than the case originally presents (illustrated by the judgment in *Heylens*),[26] the sending of mixed signals by simultaneously issuing more than one judgment with potentially negative implications for the state budget but with opposite case outcomes (the same day rulings in *Lair* and *Brown*),[27] and ruling on explosive issues in cases that present lower than usual stakes in politically more opportune moments (as illustrated by the judgment in *Decker*).[28]

Finally, the chapter argues that the reading of the case-law in terms of the shifting relationships between rights, reasoning, outcomes, and methods of interpretation, viewed through the lens of good judgment, sheds a complete and nuanced understanding of adjudication, legal reasoning and judicial behaviour despite the limitations which the imperfect method and a legally theoretically crude conceptualisation of good judgment.

vii. Chapter Eight

The concluding chapter summarises the argument, appraises the findings, and reflects on the normative implications: is good judgment a good idea?

While the upholding of conflicting claims entails tangible short-term benefits for the Court, its long-term legal cost might be high because courts are at the mercy of their context, as the Court's environment changes once successful legitimisation techniques of rights protection become a liability weaponised by critics. Intervention into the liberalisation of the market for goods and common welfare, previously considered as brave, are remembered as unwarranted meddling into policymaking eroding well-functioning welfare models, and the legitimacy of economic integration.

[23] Case C-333/14, *Scotch Whisky Association*, ECLI:EU:C:2015:845.

[24] Case C-930/19, *X. v Belgium*, ECLI:EU:C:2021:657.

[25] Case C-308/14, *Commission v United Kingdom*, ECLI:EU:C:2016:436.

[26] Case 222/86, *Heylens*, ECLI:EU:C:1987:442.

[27] Case 39/86, *Sylvie Lair*, ECLI:EU:C:1988:322, Case 197/86, *Steven Malcolm Brown*, ECLI:EU:C:1988:323.

[28] Case C-120/95, *Nicolas Decker*, ECLI:EU:C:1998:167.

D. IN SUM …

The book proposes a novel understanding of European adjudication as the positive sum-game in politically or economically adverse circumstances informed by doctrinally meaningful and empirically comprehensive investigation of case-law. The conclusions of the analysis are immediately relevant to the study of judicial reasoning and to the study of judicial behaviour (the interplay between law and extra-legal factors). Social scientists studying the Court have exhaustively explored the mechanisms of context-conscious judging, its drivers, conditions, and implications; legal scholars have poured over legal developments to illustrate the Court's argumentative skill and diplomatic common sense. This book tackles the question of what happens to rights and justification when the Court deploys this sense or yields to non-legal arguments. The exact limits and forms of judicial responsiveness to non-legal circumstances are pertinent to any debate about the mandate and the independence of judicial institutions in democratic societies.

Part I

The Analytical Framework

2

Context-Conscious Judging

SUMMARY

THE NATURAL STARTING point for any discussion of adjudication is the prototype of courts and the corresponding idea(l) of judging: a formalised process in which independent judges apply valid legal rules to resolve disputes between two parties and render an authoritative decision awarding one party a legal right and the other a legal wrong. Different disciplines have developed complementary approaches highlighting various aspects of this process. Section A discusses four perspectives on judging, including those which adopt a normative approach seeking to reproduce the ideal by rationalising or criticising the practice (consequentialism), as well as those which take a non-normative approach that typically challenges at least one of its components (legal diplomacy, judicial behaviour, and incrementalism). Section B examines studies of the Court's decision-making, which directly or indirectly incorporate the premises of the four perspectives to develop parallel research agendas.

A. FOUR PERSPECTIVES ON CONTEXT-CONSCIOUS JUDGING

Legal scholars and social scientists harbour competing views about the law, adjudication, and courts, drawing on an array of theories, models, and methods. Most nonetheless reject the legalist conception of law as an autonomous and complete system of norms. Some see courts primarily as rule-following dispute resolution bodies impervious to power politics; others view them as law-making institutions and political actors actively partaking in the political process. Good sense or context sensitivity emerges as a universally acknowledged feature, underwriting judicial legitimacy, promoting legal values (the rule of law, legal stability, and predictability) and delivering workable outcomes. In other words, giving rise to a legally acceptable or even a desirable mode of casting the rules into a broader societal (political, economic, or social) mould is widely considered 'good judging'.[1]

[1] LR Helfer and A-M Slaughter, 'Toward a Theory of Effective Supranational Adjudication' (1997) 107 *Yale Law Journal* 273, 308.

The four perspectives outlined in the chapter disagree about the primary logic of context-conscious judging, notably the degree to which judges respond to their environment, and the stage of the decision-making process at which they are impelled to do so.[2] In crude terms,

a) The argumentative legal-theoretical position holds that context-conscious judging is primarily principle driven. This type of context consciousness often comes across as prudence which can overcome the rigidity and at times the unfairness of rules with legal sensitivity.
b) The incrementalist framing claims that context-conscious judging is a survival instinct of courts abiding by the logic of bounded rationality.
c) The structural approach considers context-conscious judging as a professional outlook. This type of context-conscious judging does not deny the rationality of the process but suggests that it primarily advances and reproduces the belief in the rational enterprise and neutrality of judging, thereby sustaining the force of law and lawyers.
d) According to the strategic behavioural model, context consciousness is a deliberate strategy of judges juggling the constraints of rules with political demands (among others), and is employed to avoid legislative override, maximise compliance, boost the effectiveness of the law, secure institutional legitimacy, and consolidate political power.

Conceptual differences have methodological implications. Behavioural models seek to untangle the effects of political, institutional, and economic forces in the extra-legal context on judicial choices and outcomes. The analytical argumentative stance reconstructs the content of judgments. Sociologically inspired interpretations focus on the legal actors, whose labour supports the method of rational reconstruction.

Because context consciousness is a feature but not a central theme in these theories, none of them supplies a ready-made analytical framework. However, as the following sub-sections attest, they offer the necessary conceptual and methodological building blocks for developing such a framework.

i. Maximising Legal Values with Sound Legal Arguments

Legal-analytical accounts of judicial decision-making (judicial reasoning) conceptualise context consciousness as prudence. Any context-conscious decision is a legally correct and justifiable decision promoting the values of the area of law in which the case is situated: it is necessarily based on a legally defensible interpretation of rules.

[2] Only the legal approach is primarily normative and motivated by legal values and structural constraints. Others adopt an external or a behavioural perspective wherein values matter but do not determine outcomes, arguing that judges largely react to the non-legal or environmental context.

Consequentialism assumes that judicial decision-making is a rational activity which strives to uphold democratic ideals, most notably the rule of law.[3] In line with this assumption, judges use accepted methods of interpretation to find the meaning of the norms within the constraints of statute, precedent, custom, and legal practice. The need for context-conscious decision-making is evident in so-called hard cases,[4] which allow for more than one interpretation and thus give judges a degree of discretion to choose between them. Consequentialism suggests[5] that rational judges will choose the interpretation with the most desirable consequences.

Consequentialist reasoning has two stages. In the first stage, the judge will interpret the rule and apply it to the facts of the case, reasoning deductively. In the second stage, she will evaluate her conclusions against the principles of consistency and coherence with the relevant body of law. If the arguments derived from the coherence and consistency tests 'leave the case open',[6] she will examine consequences (applying the consequentialist argument). At this stage, her choice will be contextualised against societal demands and the values of the legal system. Context consciousness, which operates at this second stage of the reasoning process, calls for judicial sensibility in evaluating choices against the fundamental values of the legal system.

The problem inherent in legal reasoning is how judges select and evaluate consequences rationally.[7] Judges are badly placed to appraise the effects of their rulings but can form a correct understanding of the societal stakes and see beyond the most immediate facts of a case.

MacCormick distinguishes between the logical implications of a ruling (juridical consequences) and its effects on the incentives and behaviour of legal actors (behavioural consequences).[8] A prudent judge will consider the former, envisaging the range of cases to which her ruling might extend because of the requirement of universalisation which forms the basis of legitimate and valid justification.[9] The reasons which informed the judge's decision should apply to all legally similar cases. A judge considering the latter will take the reasoning from logical implications to prediction, the area of law to which the case belongs dictating the type and range of relevant consequences; family law and environmental law, for example, pursue complementary values. Context consciousness

[3] N MacCormick, *Rhetoric and the Rule of Law: A Theory of Legal Reasoning* (Oxford, Oxford University Press, 2005). For the European Court of Justice see J Bengoetxea, N MacCormick and L Moral Soriano, 'Integration and Integrity in the Legal Reasoning of the European Court of Justice' in G De Búrca and J Weiler (eds), *The European Court of Justice* (Oxford, Academy of European Law, European University Institute; Oxford University Press, 2001).

[4] HLA. Hart, *The Concept of Law*, 3rd edn (Oxford, Oxford University Press, 2012).

[5] The discussion of consequentialism closely follows MacCormick's theory, as set out in MacCormick (n 3).

[6] ibid 104.

[7] ibid 102–103.

[8] MacCormick (n 3); B Rudden, 'Consequences' (1979) 24 *The Juridical Review* 193.

[9] MacCormick (n 3) 91.

will emerge from justification (arguments from coherence, consequentialism, or other valid forms of argumentation), and lend itself to the method of rational reconstruction. Judges will exercise it when the indeterminacy of language will permit several legally valid interpretations. The chances that legal audiences will accept an interpretation are significantly higher if judges proceed with prudence and demonstrate situation-sense.[10]

The consequentialist framework offers a sound method to access and evaluate judicial decision-making by analysing legal arguments. However, it ascribes noble motives to judges, excluding the conceptual possibility of outcomes primarily motivated by non-legal ends and rationalised ex post as legal arguments.

ii. Maximising Power with Strategic Solutions

If Hart's critical positivism, the conceptualisation of hard cases and judicial discretion, was foundational for consequentialism, the realist jurisprudence of Hart's intellectual opponents, most notably Holmes[11] and Llewellyn,[12] inspired the studies of judicial behaviour. The attitudinal and strategic models of judicial behaviour are especially relevant to the discussion of the Court's context-conscious decision-making. The attitudinal model is a reaction to the legalist model of judging or mechanical jurisprudence in which an independent judge applies preexisting rules in an adversary proceeding to issue a binary decision.[13] The strategic model adds complexity and important nuance to the attitudinal model, recognising the relevance of legal rules and political constraints on judges.[14]

Like consequentialists, behaviourists believe that the indeterminacy of rules is the source of judicial discretion in the interpretation and application of law. However, they conclude that indeterminacy liberates judges from the constraints of the law, and that judges leverage this liberty to influence public policy in line with their personal convictions. The attitudinal and strategic models differ with respect to the circumstances that judges must consider.

The attitudinal model supposes that judges will rule freely in line with their political beliefs and preferences. Pritchett, widely considered the pioneer of the field, was a moderate realist who showed that policy preferences were more

[10] Situation sense is a cognitive ability of trained judges and lawyers, which they acquire in the course of their education and experience. KN Llewellyn, *The Common Law Tradition: Deciding Appeals* (Little Brown Company, 1960) 59.

[11] OlW Holmes, 'The Path of the Law' (1897) 10 *Harvard Law Review* 457. 'When we study law we are not studying a mystery but a well-known profession'.

[12] Llewellyn (n 10).

[13] JeA Segal and HJ Spaeth, *The Supreme Court and the Attitudinal Model* (Cambridge Cambridge University Press, 1993).

[14] L Epstein and T Jacobi, 'The Strategic Analysis of Judicial Decisions' (2010) 6 *Annual Review of Law and Social Science* 341.

reliable determinants of judicial choices than legal considerations and structural preferences such as views on federalism and the balance between legislative and judicial authority.[15] His foundational quantitative study[16] examined the link between the voting behaviour of the United States Supreme Court justices and their policy preferences (left – right, conservative – liberal), setting the foundations for an important research agenda.[17] His reflections on the legal considerations and structural or institutional constraints,[18] however, lacked methodological guidance. Political scientists thus focused on the forces[19] shaping judicial decisions rather than their content.

Schubert, often considered the father of the attitudinal model, believed that judges' ideologies accounted for their behaviour on the bench, and – like Holmes – that their behaviour constituted the law.[20] Spaeth and Segal's more well-known study of judicial preferences cemented this view[21] through its claims that the Supreme Court decides disputes in line with ideological attitudes and values of the justices to quote, 'Rehnquist votes the way he does because he is extremely conservative; Marshall voted the way he did because he was extremely liberal'.[22]

A context conscious judge will thus always advance her optimal solution in line with her ideology and preferences within the parameters of rules, precedent, methods of interpretation, and external factors. She will be mindful of circumstances that will maximise her influence and wary of those that could prove harmful.

The strategic model, first proposed by Murphy in The Elements of Judicial Strategy,[23] nuances this view by adding institutional constraints to the models proposed by Schubert and Pritchett. The distinctive feature of the strategic model is the relationship it establishes between the internal decision-making and the external constraints that other political institutions namely the Congress and the President can impose on judges in a system of checks and balances.[24]

[15] L Baum, 'C. Herman Pritchett: Innovator with an Ambiguous Legacy' in N Maveety (ed), *The Pioneers of Judicial Behavior* (Ann Arbor, University of Michigan Press, 2003) 59.

[16] It was the prelude of the so-called attitudinal model. Baum (n 15).

[17] CH Pritchett, 'Divisions of Opinion Among Justices of the U. S. Supreme Court, 1939–1941' (1941) 35 *The American Political Science Review* 890.

[18] L Epstein and J Knight, *The Choices Justices Make* (Washington, Sage, 1998).

[19] L Epstein and NW Waterbury, 'Judicial Behavior', *Oxford Research Encyclopedia of Politics* (Oxford, Oxford University Press, 2020).

[20] GA Schubert, 'The Study of Judicial Decision-Making as an Aspect of Political Behavior' (1958) 52 *American Political Science Review* 1007.

[21] Segal and Spaeth (n 13).

[22] Attitude refers to an enduring interrelated set of beliefs about an object or situation. For social action to occur, at least two interacting attitudes, one concerning the attitude object and the other concerning the attitude situation must occur. The objects are the direct and indirect parties to the suit; the situations are the dominant legal issue in the case. JA Segal and HJ Spaeth, *The Supreme Court and the Attitudinal Model Revisited* (Cambridge, Cambridge University Press, 2002) 91.

[23] WF Murphy, *Elements of Judicial Strategy*, vol 17 (New Orleans, Quid Pro Books, 2016). First published in 1964 by University of Chicago Press.

[24] L Epstein and J Knight, 'Toward a Strategic Revolution in Judicial Politics: A Look Back, A Look Ahead' (2000) 53 *Political Research Quarterly* 625, 629.

Judges do not simply act in line with their policy preferences – they must interact strategically with their peers and other branches of government to maximise the influence of their decisions on public policy. Judicial action is thus understood as a function of personal preferences and expectations about the actions of others:[25] a judge in a collegiate court must convince her colleagues that her legal solution is preferable to alternative solutions to the dispute, and – together with her peers – issue a ruling acceptable to the parties involved, the legislator, and the public. Methodologically, the origins of the strategic model are qualitative given that Murphy proved his points by delving into leading cases and landmark rulings.[26]

The discussion of the model is illustrative of the understanding of context-conscious judging because:

a) It conceptualises context consciousness as a constant in the decision-making process, which impels policy-oriented judges to further their goals by considering and responding to their environment.
b) It assumes that the personal preferences of judges, their political ideology and professional experience, along with structural or institutional considerations shape legal reasoning and case outcomes.
c) It shows that judicial decisions are a product of external and internal constraints imposed on individual judges by their colleagues, the institutions they work in, and the broader political environment. Context-conscious judges can, in Pritchett's words, make private preferences become public law.
d) It works through the rivalry between the qualitatively oriented traditionalists and large-*n* driven behaviouralists of the 1960s and the 1970s, a methodological struggle in the political science community which legal scholars often neglect when arguing about methodology.

Most importantly, the synopsis of the origins and scientific potential of the attitudinal and strategic models shows that behaviourists (with Schubert perhaps being the exception) have never claimed that judicial outcomes were exclusively externally motivated but, as Pritchett and Murphy thought, co-shaped by the concerns of the judges to arrive at a correct interpretation. It also confirms that the same scholarship has not devised a method nor honed the methods proposed by the pioneers to study the law-politics interplay and reveal the legal concerns of judges, thus abandoning a potentially promising line of scientific inquiry permitting a comprehensive understanding of its subject.

Recent literature has questioned the assumption that judges are fully rational actors,[27] suggesting that context consciousness might be a matter of instinct and

[25] Epstein and Knight (n 24).
[26] Epstein and Knight (n 18).
[27] E.g. H Spamann and L Klöhn, 'Justice Is Less Blind, and Less Legalistic, than We Thought: Evidence from an Experiment with Real Judges' (2016) 45 *The Journal of Legal Studies* 255; JZ Liu and X Li, 'Legal Techniques for Rationalizing Biased Judicial Decisions: Evidence from Experiments with Real Judges' (2019) 16 *Journal of Empirical Legal Studies* 630.

poor heuristics rather than reason. This understanding is closer to the legal realist conception of 'judicial hunch'.[28]

iii. Maintaining Authority

The structuralist account of judging emerges as a third alternative, proposing the understanding of law as a juridical or legal field. This field is semi-isolated from the social and the political world, abiding by its own rationality and determination of what is legally acceptable and possible. According to Bourdieu, 'it would not be excessive to say that [law] creates the social world, but only if we remember that it is this world which first creates the law'.[29]

The understanding of law as having the capacity to re-create social reality redirects the focus to the legal agents, operating in objective structures and participating in institutional practices who at the same time co-create and give form to these structures through their practices. It requires a scientific study of group formation and the different geneses of law in the context of varying legal-political and -cultural settings.[30] Judges who resolve conflicts oversee the adaptation of a formal system to reality. Legal scholars rationalise innovations into a coherent system, enabling judges 'to separate their judgments from the overt arbitrariness of a Kadijustiz'.[31]

If the choices and preferences of individual decision makers are shaped by the structures in which they are embedded as members of a particular group, and which they themselves shape, context consciousness can be framed as a professional outlook and an internalisation of accepted forms of language and reasoning formulas. It is qualitatively different from the pursuit of policy goals, consisting of personal biases, instincts, legal intuitions, and deriving from legal values which it furthers as a matter of professional ethics.

Judges will acquire a specific professional outlook during their careers, resorting to accepted tools and a multitude of techniques of judicial adaptation or resilience.[32] They will negotiate the meaning of rules, intuiting when to yield to vital interests of the losing party, especially a powerful state.[33] Legal

[28] JC Hutcheson Jr, 'Judgment Intuitive The Function of the Hunch in Judicial Decision' (1928) 14 *Cornell L. Q.* 274.

[29] P Bourdieu, 'The Force of Law: Toward a Sociology of the Juridical Field' (1986) 38 *Hastings LJ* 805, 839.

[30] Y Dezalay and MR Madsen, 'The Force of Law and Lawyers: Pierre Bourdieu and the Reflexive Sociology of Law' (2012) 8 *Annual Review of Law and Social Science* 433.

[31] Bourdieu (n 29).

[32] MR Madsen, P Cebulak and M Wiebusch, 'Backlash against International Courts: Explaining the Forms and Patterns of Resistance to International Courts' (2018) 14 *International Journal of Law in Context* 197.

[33] MR Madsen, '"Legal Diplomacy" – Law, Politics and the Genesis of Postwar European Human Rights' in S-L Hoffman (ed), *Human Rights in the Twentieth Century. Human Rights in History.* (Cambridge University Press, 2010).

diplomacy involves a tailored use of rhetoric, remedies, and other procedural mechanisms, which enable courts to sidestep or minimise open confrontation with power politics. For instance, international courts learn to balance audacious legal rhetoric with prudent outcomes. They talk in terms of universal principles and yet practice exceptionalism.[34]

Structuralist analyses reveal an interesting rationale of context-conscious judging, determining it as inseparable from the structure and operation of the juridical field. Conceiving of legal outcomes as not necessarily binary and final, but negotiable and multifarious, offers an important methodological opening: courts protect competing interests with legal means, which do not yield binary decisions.

iv. Minimising Conflict by Muddling Through

In comparison to the theories already discussed, incrementalism is not a fully formed account of judicial decision-making but rather a view or a reaction to the assumption of rationality that the other theories share. It describes policymaking and dispute resolution as processes favouring gradual and marginal adjustments gravitating to the status quo.[35] Its most distinctive assumption is that policymakers adhere to the logic of bounded rationality.[36]

Facing the constraints of time, energy, and insufficient information, decisionmakers will at best consider only a handful of alternatives, focusing on the tried-and-tested, politically workable solutions which everyone can accept without necessarily agreeing that they are the best solutions. The incrementalist method attacks the problem by the 'branch', continually building from the current situation instead of dealing with the causes comprehensively at the 'root', and always starting over again from the fundamentals. This 'muddling through',[37] is preferable to the paralysing demands of rationality: the requirement to agree on the goals which a policy should pursue, and gathering complete information to predict the consequences associated with all available alternatives.

[34] JHH Weiler, 'The Transformation of Europe' (1991) *Yale Law Journal* 2403; Helfer and Slaughter (n 1).

[35] Incrementalism is a borrowed term, which acquired a new meaning in the context of adjudication, reasoning, and judicial behaviour. CE Lindblom, 'The Science of "Muddling Through"' (1959) 19 *Public Administration Review* 79.

[36] The expression 'classical' understanding of rationality tries to distinguish the method of rational decision-making from the concept of 'bounded rationality', which guides incremental decision-making. The term stems from Simon's work. It describes rational choice, which considers the limitations of the decision-maker: her knowledge and computational capacity. HA Simon, 'Theories of Bounded Rationality' (1972) 1 *Decision and Organization* 161.

[37] Lindblom (n 35) 80.

When transposed to judicial decision-making,[38] muddling through assumes that judges will instinctively gravitate towards established interpretations rather than considering all rival interpretations, weighing up the pros and cons of all alternatives, or spending time looking for all relevant precedent or assessing the consequences. They will, however, speak the legal language of precedent and *stare decisis*, arguing about legal claims with reference to relevant case-law and statute.

Judging as an endeavour to uncover defensible legal solutions acceptable to all is always context conscious,[39] motivated by practical concerns like avoiding unnecessary work and minimising potential conflict. The incrementalist method has a two-fold advantage: gradual solutions appear prudent, in that they are instantly reversible if proving to be unpopular; and the process of arriving at them can be presented as an exercise in virtue.[40]

Incrementalism supports a conceptualisation of context-conscious decision-making as a prevalent logic of courts, rather than an extra layer of judging which occasionally closes normative gaps. At the same time, it does not impel courts to seek political influence, instead reinforcing the opposite parameter – that courts seek to avoid conflict and the public limelight. It also allows for a framing of context-conscious judging as a process in which judges uphold conflicting claims. Methodologically, incrementalism encourages systematic inquiry into the practical limitations of judging, as well as investigation of judicial tools which may be of use to navigate societal conflicts that play out in the dispute and those in which the dispute is embedded.

B. THE COURT'S REASONING AND POWER

Turning from the studies of judicial decision-making to studies focusing on the Court's reasoning and power, it becomes obvious that the aforementioned perspectives have found limited application in their pure form. It is fairer to say that three branches of legal and political science literature sporadically engaged with the Court's context-conscious decision-making: 1) the constitutionalisation of the Treaties by means of legal interpretation or the constitutionalisation / interpretation literature;[41] 2) the effectiveness of supranational adjudication or

[38] MM Shapiro, *The Supreme Court and Administrative Agencies* (New York, Free Press, 1968).

[39] ibid.

[40] Incremental change is not necessarily a slow change. A series of consequent small steps, taken over a short time, and at a fast pace can quickly result in substantive change. CE Lindblom, 'Still Muddling, Not yet Through' (1979) 39 *Public Administration Review* 517.

[41] The narrative of integration through law has framed the lines of inquiry. The narrative explains the Court's political success and the success of the idea of the European Community (Union) as a community of law. It holds that the oblivious governments with de facto veto power in the Council spared the Court from potentially harmful politicisation. The European Commission and the transnational law associations reinforced the centrality of law in the integration process by pursuing

the effectiveness literature; and 3) the relationship between the European Union and the Member States, notably the Court's political power or the judicial politics literature.

Constitutionalisation / interpretation literature primarily discussed the Court's context-conscious decision-making in terms of the methods of interpretation and their legitimate pursuit the aims of the Treaties and the political will of an ever closer Union[42] or illegitimate / disguised policy making pursuing an integrationist agenda contrary to the political will of the signatories of the Treaty.[43] Without fully engaging in this animated discussion, it is useful to restate that some commentators criticised the use of purposive interpretation in tandem with the Court's authoritative reasoning style as especially problematic.[44] Others, by contrast, hailed it as prudence and a necessity demanded by the broad Treaty provisions and the commitment to an ever-closer Union.[45]

Yet other commentators have underlined the Court's commitment to legal values, and the fulfilment of its institutional responsibility to solve the case at hand and Treaty role as the ultimate interpreter of European Union law (constructive dialogue).[46] According to this version:

> Legal reasoning of the ECJ follows a 'stone-by-stone' approach. This means that, in order to guarantee consensus and as a token of judicial prudence, the argumentative discourse of the ECJ is limited to answering the legal questions that are necessary to solve the case at hand. … the incremental approach followed by the ECJ guarantees a solid and sound evolution of the case-law that allows room for the national courts to engage in a constructive dialogue.[47]

their own interests. Collaborative national courts underwrote the Court's interpretive authority in the preliminary reference procedure. Academics abiding by their professional codex and self-regard, undertook the essential task of rationalisation and legitimisation. The Court reciprocated by gradually, quietly, and surely transforming the European legal and political landscape. For early analysis see E Stein, 'Lawyers, Judges, and the Making of a Transnational Constitution' (1981) 75 *American Journal of International Law* 1.

[42] The Court's interpretations of legal rules beyond the letter of the law are either justifiable by broad Treaty goals, or open-ended Treaty provisions. P Pescatore, *The Law of Integration: Emergence of a New Phenomenon in International Relations, Based on the Experience of the European Communities* (Amsterdam, A W Sijthoff, 1974).

[43] E.g. a blatant or arrogant policy making exercise, or a naïve sacrifice of acquired rights for feeble political gains. For the former see H Rasmussen, *On Law and Policy in the European Court of Justice: A Comparative Study in Judicial Policymaking* (Leiden, Brill, 1986); G Conway, *The Limits of Legal Reasoning and the European Court of Justice* (Cambridge University Press, 2012). For the latter perspective see C O'Brien, 'The ECJ Sacrifices EU Citizenship in Vain: Commission v. United Kingdom' (2017) 54 *Common Market Law Review 209*.

[44] M De S.-O.-L'E Lasser, *Judicial Deliberations: A Comparative Analysis of Transparency and Legitimacy* (Oxford University Press, 2009).

[45] Pescatore (n 42).

[46] N MacCormick *Rhetoric and The Rule of Law: A Theory of Legal Reasoning* (Oxford, Oxford University Press, 2005).

[47] K Lenaerts, 'How the ECJ Thinks: A Study on Judicial Legitimacy' (2013) 36 *Fordham Int'l LJ* 1302, 1369.

This characterisation has not gone unchallenged,[48] with scholars attributing the Court's stone-by-stone approach to practical constraints and flagging up its negative implications,[49] or highlighting its self-serving / strategic aspects:[50]

> [I]n the first case that comes before it, the CJEU will establish the doctrine as a general principle but suggest that it is subject to various qualifications; the CJEU may even find some reason why it should not be applied to the particular facts of the case. The principle, however, is now established. If there are not too many protests, it will be re-affirmed in later cases; the qualifications can then be whittled away, and the full extent of the doctrine revealed.[51]

The effectiveness literature has been the most influential in linking the Court's power, grounded in the effectiveness of supranational adjudication, to the ability of its judges to reconcile legal rules and international politics 'searching always for generalisable principles, even as they search for formulations or procedural mechanisms to render the principles more palatable to the states concerned.'[52] At times, this mandated state-friendly outcomes, while at other times it permitted legal audacity contrary to the political will. The Court's awareness of the audiences and political boundaries was outwardly visible as a series of techniques used to '[edge] principles forward while deciding for those most likely to oppose them in practice'.[53] It was, simply, 'good judging'.[54]

Finally, judicial politics literature emerged most clearly from the theories of economic integration, notably neofunctionalism and intergovernmentalism. Political scientists have focused primarily on the Court's ability to shape policy outcomes and determine the pace and the forms of European integration.[55] Concretely, could the Court transform political processes and impose its will on the legislator represented by the Member States meeting in the Council.

According to the dynamic court view, courts could push their policy agendas unfettered by rules. According to the restrained court view, courts were constrained by a series of factors.[56] Scholars, for example, examined the

[48] JHH Weiler, 'Epilogue: Judging the Judges–Apology and Critique' in M Adams et al (eds), *Judging Europe's judges: The legitimacy of the case law of the European Court of Justice* (London, Bloomsbury, 2013).

[49] D Sarmiento and D Jiménez-Valladolid, 'Half a Case at a Time: Dealing with Judicial Minimalism at the European Court of Justice' in M Claes et al (eds), *Constitutional Conversations in Europe: Actors, Topics and Procedures* (Cambridge, Intersentia, 2012).

[50] TC Hartley, *The Foundations of European Union Law: An Introduction to the Constitutional and Administrative Law of the European Union*, 8th edn (Oxford, Oxford University Press, 2014). The first edn of the book, where Hartley introduced the passage below, is from 1987.

[51] ibid 75.

[52] Helfer and Slaughter (n 1) 314.

[53] ibid 315.

[54] ibid 308.

[55] A-M Burley and W Mattli, 'Europe Before the Court: A Political Theory of Legal Integration' (1993) 47 *International Organization* 41; G de Búrca, 'Rethinking Law in Neofunctionalist Theory' (2005) 12 *Journal of European Public Policy* 310.

[56] Schmidt outlines the main fault-lines of the debate in SK Schmidt, *The European Court of Justice and the Policy Process: The Shadow of Case Law* (Oxford, Oxford University Press, 2018).

constraints imposed during the decision-making process by Member State governments and their power to err towards state-friendly outcomes.[57] They delved into the aftermath of judicial pronouncements to identify how case-law mapped into the legislative process and instruments – the response of politics to law.[58]

The letter literature explicitly or implicitly embraced the premises of the strategic model of judicial decision-making including separation of powers and legislative override. The main insight, relevant to the analysis of context-conscious judging, is that the Court responds to the threat of legislative override by aligning case outcomes with the preference of the median Council member.[59] In spite of the differences in opinion within the discipline,[60] it is safe to argue that politics penetrates legal decision-making, and can be observed and analysed.

Nonetheless, the explanatory power of the legislative override threat is questionable from the legal constitutional perspective. The Court can counteract override by annulling the 'overriding' legislation on the grounds of it being contrary to the Treaty; emasculate / undermine it, by interpreting it according to its own view while ignoring the legislative intent; or avoid it entirely, accepting it as it is, but continuing to apply directly effective Treaty provisions alongside the newly enacted legislation.[61] All three techniques render the restrictive effect of 'overriding' legislation toothless, with minimal cost incurred for the soundness of legal argumentation and, quite possibly, institutional legitimacy. The Court does not need to act context-consciously according to this view but might choose to do so.[62]

See also M Blauberger and SK Schmidt, 'The European Court of Justice and Its Political Impact' (2017) 40 *West European Politics* 907.

[57] J Dederke and D Naurin, 'Friends of the Court? Why EU Governments File Observations before the Court of Justice' (2018) 57 *European Journal of Political Research* 867.

[58] DS Martinsen, *An Ever More Powerful Court? The Political Constraints of Legal Integration in the European Union*, 1st edn (Oxford, Oxford University Press, 2015). See also Blauberger and Schmidt (n 56).

[59] O Larsson and D Naurin, 'Judicial Independence and Political Uncertainty: How the Risk of Override Affects the Court of Justice of the EU' (2016) 70 *International Organization* 377.

[60] For the summary of the debate and the defence of the strategic model (constrained Court) see CJ Carruba, M Gabel and C Hankla, 'Understanding the Role of the European Court of Justice in European Integration' (2012) 106 *American Political Science Review* 214.

[61] G Davies, 'Legislative Control of the European Court of Justice' (2014) 51 *Common Market Law Review* 1579.

[62] For the opposite view (the long shadow of case-law) see Schmidt (n 56).

3

Good Judgment

SUMMARY

CHAPTER THREE INTRODUCES good judgment as a tool to accommodate competing interests and uphold conflicting claims in response to the circumstances of the case or external / non-legal factors. Good judgment diverges from the prototype of judging as dispute resolution which gives rise to binary decisions. Analytically, this conceptualisation delineates the object of inquiry, reducing the spectrum of context-conscious decision-making but preserving its key characteristics and rationale.

Section A conceptualises good judgment in relation to the baseline – the structure of typical justification, differentiating good judgment from other concepts signalling context responsiveness like deference, legal diplomacy, or judicial minimalism, as well as doctrines like proportionality review, margin of appreciation, and the model of restriction-justification reasoning. Section B introduces three types of good judgment: 1) *non-sanctioning Europeanisation of national policies*, which combines the invasive scrutiny of national measures and policies with state-friendly outcomes; 2) *deferential upholding of European rights* that creates new concepts and categories of rights, but leaves their application to the referring court or national administration; and 3) *bounded undesirable interpretation*, which limits the implications of expansive rulings and undesirable interpretations for the respondent Member State. Section D concludes.

A. FROM GOOD JUDGING TO GOOD JUDGMENT

The assumption of context-conscious decision-making is omnipresent in the literature about the Court's legal reasoning and behaviour. Often a peripheral object of inquiry, it remains in need of further conceptual refinement.

The studies highlight competing motivations ('the why') but note similar modes of operation ('the how') of context-conscious judging. Context sensitivity ensures the effectiveness of law, allowing courts to tailor legal solutions to political circumstances without sabotaging their institutional legitimacy. This enhances compliance and secures implementation, an important consideration in international regimes for minimising the risk of political backlash and legislative override.[1] Whether context-conscious outcomes contribute to a body of outwardly coherent case-law and rationalisable legal solutions, however, remains an open legal and empirical question.

Consequentialism assumes that judges consider practical implications when the law allows discretion, primarily to uphold the values of the legal system.[2] Incrementalism argues that context-sensitive judges worry about self-preservation but also accepts that they might still reach the solution that best upholds the values of the legal system. Behavioural accounts address the empirical question left open by consequentialism and incrementalism: which external and internal factors motivate and explain judicial choices and when. Finally, structuralist approaches rarely engage in judicial outcomes and reasoning, but claim that judges as legal professionals engage in the practice of rationalisation to preserve the authority or law and lawyers.[3]

The sections below outline the book's approach to context-conscious judging, which integrates the above insights to first, highlight the requirement of rationality as a benchmark for good judgment drawing from contextualism and rational justification; and second, justify the prism of analysis, that is, good judgment as the upholding of conflicting interests with non-binary outcomes drawing from behavioural and incrementalist perspectives.

i. The Baseline: Model Application of Law and the Structure of Typical Justification

The analysis of good judgment relies on the ideal four-stage model of law application, building on existing approaches: 1) establishing the applicable rule, including its meaning and validity; 2) establishing the facts of the case in relation to the applicable rule; 3) establishing that the rule applies to the facts of the case – meaning that the universal language of an abstract rule extends to the particular facts of the concrete case; and 4) establishing the legal conclusion, which follows from the norm as applied to the concrete facts.[4] The model is an analytical tool which typically supports a critical normative examination of judicial arguments, methods of interpretation, procedural tools, evaluation of evidence, procedural decisions and outcomes in the process of law application.[5] In brief,

[1] E Voeten, 'Populism and Backlashes against International Courts' (2020) 18 *Perspectives on Politics* 407.

[2] N MacCormick, *Rhetoric and the Rule of Law: A Theory of Legal Reasoning* (Oxford, Oxford University Press, 2005).

[3] P Bourdieu, 'The Force of Law: Toward a Sociology of the Juridical Field' (1986) 38 *Hastings L.J.* 805.

[4] J Bengoetxea, *The Legal Reasoning of the European Court of Justice: Towards a European Jurisprudence* (Oxford, Clarendon Press Oxford, 1993) 127.

[5] ibid 128. Even if judges reach a conclusion first and rationalise it ex-post in 'real life' the written / public decision reflects those stages.

it serves as an explicit or unstated benchmark for the analysis, systematisation, and normative critique of justification and legal practice.

In routine or easy cases, law application can follow the logical syllogism or parallel syllogisms, in which the conclusion (stage 4) follows from the major applicable rule established in stage 1, and the minor premise established via facts in stage 2. The reasoning is deductive, proceeding from the premises to the conclusion.[6] Decisions in such cases are legally correct if the minor premise can be clearly subsumed under the tenets of the major premise (stage 3).

The model of law application corresponds to the ideal structure of legal justification – the process or the act of giving legally sound reasons in support of a decision to an audience in a concrete situation. In other words, a judge must prove that the decision is defensible and required by law.[7] Her decision will need to be universalisable – applicable in the same way to similar cases, thereby fulfilling the requirement of formal justice and demonstrating even-handed justice.

A decision in those cases will be legally correct and authoritative if it refers to a previously determined and valid legal source. This will be the case when the decision follows logically from the correctly selected and interpreted premises and the reasoning will therefore be deductive. The parties can disagree about the correct premise, or whether the premise is applicable to the facts of the dispute and case, but the judge will be able to demonstrate its validity with reference to the accepted canons of interpretation and argumentation.

Deductive reasoning will be insufficient in problem cases involving a dispute about the meaning or the choice of a norm – the major premise. In these cases, the Court will have to adapt its justification to show that the conclusion follows from the premises *and* that: 1) the decision is consistent or non-contradictory with the established law; 2) the decision coheres with the established law, meaning that it furthers a general principle or a legal value which fits within the structure of accepted values and principles; and 3) the decision is preferable to other alternatives because it produces desirable normative and even behavioural consequences.[8]

European Union law often raises interpretive doubts which national courts can or must resolve by referring questions of interpretation or validity to the Court pursuant to Article 267 TFEU. The correct interpretation of an already specified provision would free the Court from finding the applicable norm (from stage 1 of law application). However, a correct interpretation of that singled-out norm might require the choice of other provisions to authoritatively clarify and establish its meaning.[9]

[6] MacCormick (n 2). Schauer, by contrast, insists on generalisability, which is a less strict requirement: F Schauer, *Thinking Like a Lawyer* (Harvard, Harvard University Press, 2009).

[7] Bengoetxea (n 4) 141. See also MacCormick (n 2) 99.

[8] Bengoetxea (n 4) 171.

[9] An example of a complex and at the same time simple justification is the case of *the European Commission v Kingdom of Belgium*, Case C-317/14, ECLI:EU:C:2015:63.

Importantly, in the four-stage model of law application and rational justification, the context and circumstances of the case become relevant when decisionmakers arrive at several different yet equally valid interpretations of the applicable provision.[10] The question of context consciousness, however, is most pertinent when courts adopt unorthodox or atypical decisions – when they depart from the logic of rational justification or reinterpret the existing practice before arriving at several different but valid interpretations.[11]

Even if one assumes that judges always apply the law with direct and general circumstances in mind, atypical choices most clearly raise the question about the relationship between law and its societal context. In such situations, the rationalisation and critique can evaluate the choices against the second order criteria, but not explain them.[12]

ii. Non-Binary Decisions: An Illustration

Imagine a situation where person M applies to join a teacher-training programme in Member State B. The vocational training institution of B rejects the application because M is not a national. M challenges the decision before the national administration, bringing their case to the administrative court of State B. The latter refers a question to the Court of Justice: Can B exclude M from vocational training under European Union law?

The national administration of B argues in the affirmative. Teachers are public servants who therefore fall outside of the scope of the application of European Union law. Hence, states may impose the condition of nationality with regards to access to public training. Conversely, M argues that they must have equal access to the labour market of the host Member State under the Treaty, and furthermore upholds that access to the market is conditional on completing vocational training. B may not impose conditions which exclude M from this training on the grounds of foreign nationality, and in so doing exclude them de facto from the national labour market for teachers.

The Court holds that B may not exclude M from the programme nor impose conditions effectively closing its labour market to non-nationals. In Treaty terms, B cannot successfully invoke the so-called public service exception to eschew free movement rules. The idea of equal treatment, the Court reasons, applies broadly and covers the labour market *and* vocational training, the latter being

[10] MacCormick, similarly Dworkin's two conditions (fit and best light), as well as Hart's discretion on the margin (hard cases).

[11] MacCormick (n 2) 149. This commitment not only concerns the so-called legalistic or formalist justification, but is a fundamental assumption on which the model is built. Relaxing the assumption without abandoning the model is impossible.

[12] Bengoetxea (n 4). See also law as a regulative ideal – where the doctrinally constructed legal systems are in part descriptively accurate even though they are not nor should they be perfect descriptions of the legal practice.

a prerequisite to enter that market. Given the Court's broad interpretation, in principle at least, M wins the case. However, B does not by default lose. The Court allows B to condition the access of the applicant and all future applicants on the basis of formal yet reasonable requirements, including but not limited to acceptable educational qualifications, such as a degree obtained in an educational institution of B or an institution recognised by B. Crucially, B may set these requirements unilaterally unless they are disproportionate. It must adapt and rethink, but not abandon, its policy restricting foreign nationals' access to training programmes.[13]

As the example shows, the Court can effectively uphold individual free movement rights without entirely dismantling state policies, expanding the meaning of the rule (its broad interpretation) while at the same time restricting its application in future cases (its narrow application).

Logically, if the applicant has the right to access the labour market under the same conditions as nationals of that Member State under European Union law, then the Member State has a corresponding duty, that is, the duty of equal scope to open its labour market to non-nationals under the same conditions which apply to nationals, the outcome and application therefore being broad. It must do so as a strict requirement of the common European rules. This applies to the applicant in the concrete case and to all future applicants in the same situation.[14] The Court's interpretation of the same provision of the Treaty, on the contrary, allows the Member State to reduce the scope of the right in the stage of application by co-defining the scope of its corresponding duty. It is thus reasonable to argue that the Court is mindful of the potential implications, customising Treaty rules to fit practical constraints,[15] thereby securing implementation while minimising the conflict with the state government, the supposed losing party in the case.

The Court's judgment upholds incommensurate claims about the meaning and the application of free movement law. On the one hand, the broad interpretation of the term 'labour market' gives rights to individuals who wish to enrol in vocational training institutions. On the other hand, the Court's interpretation

[13] Literature argues that it will eventually do so, with Luxembourg in mind. M Blauberger, 'With Luxembourg in Mind … the Remaking of National Policies in the Face of ECJ Jurisprudence' (2012) 19 *Journal of European Public Policy* 109. Azoulai conceptualises the mode of decision-making as the doctrine of totalisation – European Union law expounds by requiring adaptation and a rethinking of the totality of national law regardless of the formal limits of EU jurisdiction. L Azoulai, 'The Retained Powers' Formula in the Case Law of the European Court of Justice: EU Law as Total Law' (2011) 4 *Eur. J. Legal Stud.* 178.

[14] That the decision must be universalisable is a requirement of the rule of law. MacCormick (n 2). The condition that a precedent must 'only' be generalisable is less strict. See Schauer (n 6) p 176.

[15] The situation is different from Alexy's differentiation between rules, which apply in an 'all or nothing' fashion, and principles, which apply more or less (optimisation commands). (Robert Alexy, 'On the Structure of Legal Principles' (2000) 13 *Ratio Juris* 294.) The Court is not engaging in the balancing of two opposing principles but in balancing of the rule / principle and its scope of application.

of the reasonable limits to free movement gives states the right to tailor the application of an individual's right to enrol in vocational training institutions by imposing reasonable conditions. While M themselves might indeed become a teacher in State B, other individuals with similar aspirations in the future might need to overcome more hurdles.

For instance, in the case of M, the Court extends the right to access the labour market of the host Member State by broadening the meaning to include access to vocational training. In practice, however, the state can and is legally permitted to restrict the broad interpretation. A demanding definition of the right of the individual has a moderate application in the concrete case and a still narrower application in future cases. Furthermore, the definition requires an undemanding implementation. There is a further imbalance between the generous interpretation of the right to access the market for teachers under European Union law, and the wider resonance of the implications of this ruling. The erga omnes effect of the Court's ruling signals to Member States that they can enact their own, potentially discriminatory rules rather than implementing common non-discriminatory European rules. Likely, the Court's decisions to uphold conflicting claims, like in M, dissolve tensions in practice.[16]

iii. Conflicting Interests

The concept of good judgment presupposes that courts adopt non-binary decisions which do not pinpoint clear winners and losers in response to the circumstances of the case and non-legal factors. They give one party a legal right without imposing a corresponding duty on the second party, thus upholding conflicting claims.[17]

The analytical framework, described in section i. above, assumes the form of logical syllogism,[18] which logically implies one clear cut conclusion. Even if most cases require multiple syllogisms and various forms of reasoning, the reasoning converges towards a single decision, upholding the values of formal equality and legal certainty. The wins even if Pyrrhic and losses are clear-cut.

To illustrate; following the baseline model of law application and rational justification, an outcome entrenching a new conception of the right to move (the major premise) and granting this right to the applicant in the main proceedings, consequentially grants the same right to all other future applicants in all Member States who find themselves in a legally similar position. It will establish

[16] Different from consequentialism, defined as the awareness of consequences. Consequentialism refers to the process of second order justification, which follows the process of deduction or the first order justification. Good judgment, by contrast, refers to the structure of justification.

[17] Chapter one (Introduction).

[18] Deductive reasoning is an important outward sign that courts apply universally applicable rules to the established facts. MacCormick (n 2) 254.

a corresponding duty for state administrations in all Member States to issue the necessary permits or remove unlawful obstacles to the exercise of said right. This follows from the requirement of universalisation and the principle of equality before the law. A strict proportionality test will more likely find the contested national measure incompatible with free movement rules, given that strict proportionality tests hold the Members States to higher standards than their more lax counterparts.[19] A broad functional method of interpretation of European Union law will likely limit the autonomy of a Member State in a concrete case.[20]

Through the prism of good judgment allowing for non-binary decisions / conclusions however, broad interpretations might lead to narrow outcomes, strict scrutiny to lax standards, the administration of sanctions that may not follow from the findings of violations, and the proclaimed general principles could exclude the dispute at hand. A broad understanding of the right to move might not apply to the circumstances of the case. Rather than proclaiming state policies contrary to European Union law, the Court will limit their application. The justification will not abide by the baseline nor the prototype of courts: respecting the binary decision, the rules of rationality, and the independence of the judge.

Three arguments support the change of perspective.

First, the idea that judicial decisions are non-binary is empirically a more accurate account of judicial decision-making, especially when considering the multiple reasons driving litigants to the Court. Litigants prioritise different aspects of the judicial process, like individual redress, precedent for future litigation, regulatory change or forcing legislative action.[21] While legal counsel – including government lawyers – may take cases to courts to win even if simply because nobody likes to lose all the time, they can also pursue legal change.[22] In the latter case, they won when the Court changes its interpretation regardless of its decision about the legal claim.[23] Ignoring these considerations

[19] The position is neatly illustrated in the German Federal Constitutional Court's disagreement with the Court of Justice in the *PSPP* case. For the analysis see e.g. A Bobic and M Dawson, 'Making Sense of the "Incomprehensible": The PSPP Judgment of the German Federal Constitutional Court' (2020) *Common Market Law Review* 1953.

[20] E.g. H Rasmussen, *On law and policy in the European Court of Justice: a comparative study in judicial policymaking* (Leiden, Brill, 1986).

[21] For legal mobilisation literature, strategic litigation, discussion of courts as agents of social change, see LM Friedman, 'Litigation and society' (1989) 15(1) *Annual review of sociology* 17–29; GN Rosenberg, *The hollow hope: Can courts bring about social change?* (Chicago, University of Chicago Press, 2008); A Sarat, and SA Scheingold, *Cause lawyers and social movements* (Stanford University Press, 2006).

[22] For WTO, see KJ Pelc, 'The Politics of Precedent in International Law: A Social Network Application' (2014) 108 *The American Political Science Review* 547.

[23] The European Parliament's pursuit of standing rules (and Treaty change) through litigation is instructive – even if the cases were 'lost' on the claims they achieved the long-term aim. A good example is the Court judgment in Case 294/83, *Les Verts*, ECLI:EU:C:1986:166.

and the variety of outcomes fails to acknowledge the empirical reality of litigation and judging.[24]

Second, the conception of decisions as non-binary is analytically useful because it supports the analysis of parallel layers of judicial decisions as equally important, some primarily legally mandated, others primarily context motivated. To illustrate, a ruling establishing a new principle of effective judicial control in the European Union's legal order can impose the duty on a Member State to implement judicial review in procedures in which it was previously explicitly excluded for overarching reasons of national security. Simultaneously, it can allow the Member State to consider the public safety derogation and effectively, unilaterally override equal treatment.[25] Such rulings have more than one equally relevant implication or case outcomes. They: 1) further individual protection by requiring judicial review of administrative decisions creating new law; 2) further Europeanisation by bringing decisions within the scope of European Union law and equal treatment shifting the division of competence; and 3) further the Member State's autonomy to apply the principle to future cases according to its own constitutional arrangements allowing autonomous judgment. In line with the Court's decision, the applicant's claim can be rejected in the main proceedings. These go beyond the conflicting 'implications' of the judgments – they are decisions tailored to the parties. They are not examples of diplomacy in the sense of sweetening a bitter pill or negotiating the terms of the ruling, but legal decisions following the Court's interpretation of European Union law which entrench competing interests by upholding conflicting claims (the claim of equal rights protection overriding state security and the claim of state security overriding rights protection). The analysis can support a more nuanced view of judicial law-making, and a methodology that relates to but does not need to abide by the 4-step model of law application.

Third and very relevantly, a non-binary conception of judicial decisions better appreciates the dimensions of the preliminary ruling procedure set out in Article 267 TFEU. Here, the Court can rule on the interpretation of the Treaties and on the validity and interpretation of the acts of the institutions, bodies, or administrative agencies of the European Union. It never rules in the main dispute in the narrow sense, as this task falls to the referring national court. The Court's decision is formally independent from the ruling of the referring court in the main proceedings but functionally and substantially inseparable from it.[26]

In a way, the Court makes two decisions – in the narrow and in the broad sense. The decision in the broad sense is that 'provision x must be interpreted as meaning y', creating a strong presumption that the referring court will grant

[24] M Shapiro, *Courts: A Comparative and Political Analysis* (Chicago, University of Chicago Press, 1981).

[25] An illustrative example is the Court's judgment in Case 222/84, *Johnston*, ECLI:EU:C:1986:206.

[26] Content-wise, European Union law forms part of the national legal framework (featuring as the upper premise) which is thus applicable to the identical fact situation.

remedy (r) to the applicant. The decision in the narrow sense is the decision of the referring court regarding the object of the dispute – aka the claim of the applicant – and is based on interpretation 'y'. The decision in the broad sense will stand as precedent and apply in all Member States regardless of the decision in the narrow sense, that is even if the referring court refuses to observe the Court's answer.

iv. Distinctions

Examining the Court's legal response to context through the prism of conflicting interests accepts that courts do not resolve disputes between two parties by awarding one party a legal right and the other party a corresponding legal wrong; they do not adopt a single legally correct and binary decision. This can challenge the model of law application and a typical structure of rational justification.[27]

Compared to the legal realist premise, which inspired behavioural models, the analysis does not seek to expose a gap between paper rules and real rules, traditionally the legal realist agenda, or judicial bias in law application, which is the critical legal studies agenda. It does not challenge or disprove the model of law application nor question or deny the rationality of justification. Compared to normative approaches, the analysis is agnostic to the question of whether justification must necessarily follow a certain order and meet the criteria of validity and persuasive reasoning.

The perspective of conflicting interests does not primarily seek to evaluate the legal correctness of judicial decisions and the persuasiveness of the reasoning. Unlike doctrinal analysis, it does not aim to describe the valid law, by reconstructing the legal developments, or rationalising the outcomes with reference to the established doctrinal categories. Departures from model law applications are primarily data points / facts. These facts are examined against the case characteristics and external circumstances.

The hypothetical example in section ii. above could be examined within the model framework which uses the established categories of deference, minimalism, and legal diplomacy, or even as an instance of the Court's reasoning template in free movement cases – the so-called restriction-justification model explained below. By way of illustration, in the well-known *Van Duyn* judgment, the Court decided that the Member State (the United Kingdom)

[27] MM Shapiro, *The Supreme Court and Administrative Agencies* (New York, Free Press, 1968). If the normative approaches to law assume rationality to justify the claim of law's relative autonomy (and its legitimacy), behaviourist accounts assume dichotomous decisions to analytically distinguish the winners from the losers in the analysis of the Court's choices, drawing inferences about its autonomy from politics (and other circumstances, including personal, institutional, or economic).

could not invoke the public policy exception to prohibit a national of another Member State from entering the national territory to work but could make an exception in 'particular circumstances.'[28] On the one hand, the Court attested that 'The concept of public policy in the context of the Community and where, in particular, it is used as a justification for derogating from a fundamental principle of Community law, must be interpreted strictly, so that its scope cannot be determined unilaterally by each Member State without being subject to control by the institutions of the Community'.[29] The national court had to examine – as a matter of Community (EU) law – whether the personal conduct of the individual seeking entry justified derogation from the free movement provision.

On the other hand, the Court reasoned that since 'the particular circumstances justifying recourse to the concept of public policy may vary from one country to another and from one period to another, ... it is therefore necessary in this matter to allow the competent national authorities an area of discretion within the limits imposed by the treaty.'[30] Hence, the United Kingdom could invoke its own interpretation of public policy and claim that the work the person in question was seeking, namely a position as a secretary in the Church of Scientology, was related to a socially harmful organisation. It could thus be considered personal conduct contrary to public policy.

The judgment upholds the individuals' interest to claim their European rights in national courts, extending this possibility to directives. The Court considers the interest of the applicants by recognising the requirement to assess their personal conduct rather than their status, in this case membership in a certain church. It makes a long doctrinal and jurisdictional step. It is lenient toward the state in relation to the concrete case and restrictive in relation to future similar cases by no longer allowing the United Kingdom to unilaterally exercise migration control and enforce its own interpretation of public order.

Van Duyn is a good example of an outcome with two winners but also an example of deferential reasoning, which is similar but qualitatively different. The Court uses the state's margin of appreciation as an argument to defer a potentially controversial decision to the national authorities. A degree of deference is inherent in the preliminary ruling procedure under Article 267 TFEU, as the national courts receive the Court's answer on the correct interpretation of European Union law. That said, the protection of conflicting claims is a wider phenomenon in the sense that does not only include deference and does not distinguish between proceedings and considers deference beyond the division of tasks under Article 267 TFEU, extending to cases that do not involve a restrictive state measure, or a Member State entity as a party to the proceedings. It is

[28] Case 41/74, *van Duyn v Home Office*, ECLI:EU:C:1974:133.
[29] *Van Duyn*, para 18.
[30] *Van Duyn*, para 18.

also narrower in the sense that the Court can be deferential without upholding conflicting claims. Importantly, good judgment is not legally mandated but only legally acceptable.

The example also illustrates the typical structure of justification in free movement cases using the 'established template'[31] of three questions: is the disputed measure or action a restriction of free movement rights? If yes, is it justifiable under the Treaty or following the established case-law? If yes, does it pass the proportionality test?

If it concludes that the national measure hinders free movement, the Court typically examines whether the restriction is justified, or delegates this task to the referring court with concrete or general guidelines. This division of labour again requires deference inherent in Article 267 TFEU, and is practically compelling given that the referring courts have full knowledge of the dispute and a better sense of the actual restrictive effects and the national legal context. As with deference, the upholding of conflicting claims is qualitatively different. It is more long-sighted, considering the implications beyond the justification-restriction reasoning and taking into account all cases where the Court does not find restrictions, or cases that concern the correct application of European Union legislations like the classification of products in the Common Customs Code. Restriction justification reasoning implies a binary decision – either the Member State wins or loses. Good judgment allows for two winners, even in cases where the state justifies the restriction or the Court does not find one.

In comparison to the notion of judicial minimalism,[32] the Court does not reserve judgment or interpretation. Judicial minimalism as an explanatory framework focuses on elements that are unsaid, deliberately omitted and therefore absent from the text, making inferences and drawing normative conclusions from them. Good judgment does not dwell on the silence of the Court,[33] treating it as an aspect of the Court's approach or the outcome in the broad sense. Moreover, minimalism, as applied in the European Union context, focuses on the institutional factors leading to judicial silence, such as multilingualism, the absence of dissenting opinions, the collegiate nature of decision-making, the number of judges, or the French legal tradition. Good judgment considers case characteristics, including the characteristics of individual applicants, institutional features, and legal issues, to tease out the effect of external political and legal circumstances on the Court's reasoning and case outcomes.

[31] N Nic Shuibhne, *The Coherence of EU Free Movement Law: Constitutional Responsibility and the Court of Justice* (Oxford, Oxford University Press, 2013) 8.

[32] D Sarmiento and D Jiménez-Valladolid, 'Half a Case at a Time: Dealing with Judicial Minimalism at the European Court of Justice' in M Claes et al (eds), *Constitutional Conversations in Europe: Actors, Topics and Procedures* (Cambridge, Intersentia, 2012).

[33] On silent comparisons and silence generally see M Bobek, *Comparative Reasoning in European Supreme Courts* (Oxford, Oxford University Press, 2013).

B. THREE TYPES OF GOOD JUDGMENT

Literature has considered manifold forms of justification and tools which courts use to navigate politically challenging contexts and institutional constraints without systematising the forms and factors that correlate with their use. This section introduces the varieties of good judgment in the European Union context. The typology is grounded in the literature explaining the Court's political power and the literature analysing the forms of reasoning and legal strategies which facilitated the acceptance of its rulings, some discussed in chapter two. Moreover, these strategies are widely considered as good judging, a skilful, subtle, and prudent navigation between law and politics, which protects rights, upholds the rule of law, and preserves institutional legitimacy.

The below typology is primarily tailored to the characteristics of free movement case-law and doctrinal conversations in the literature on the internal market. However, it is simple to adjust the characteristics and adapt them to the particularities of any policy area.

Free movement of goods and persons disputes juxtapose the interests of the applicants who are natural and legal persons against the collective financial interests, and political interest of the Member States, stereotypically state administrations. Given the interests at play: legal, national, individual, collective, financial, political, and those of the European Union itself and the claims raised in the selected policy areas of free movement of goods and persons including non-discrimination, free movement rights etc., it is possible to formulate and examine at least three distinct types of good judgment: 1) the non-sanctioning Europeanisation of national policies; 2) the deferential upholding of European rights; and 3) the bounded undesirable interpretation.

The first type focuses on the review of national rules and policies – subjecting them to European standards which threaten to dismantle them in the future. The second focuses on the decision of the Court about the legal claim, that is, a concrete negative outcome of the case for the state. Deferring the final decision to the national court or administration can result in a state friendlier or narrower application.[34] The third type focuses on the broader implications of the rulings: when the Court removes obstacles to free movement, it often creates new obligations for the Member States as well as new rights for European citizens, workers and their family members. These affect the state's autonomy to accommodate, integrate and regulate the newly established legal situation. The first and the third type differ in relation to their implications in that Europeanisation restricts autonomy but is policy permissive, whereas the undesirable interpretation is policy restrictive.

The typology relies on the analysis of free movement judgments and scholarly literature inquiring into the contentiousness of free movement. The Court

[34] Case C-281/98, *Angonese*, ECLI:EU:C:2000:296.

could be, for instance more likely to exercise caution when recognising free movement rights if the dispute trespasses on non-harmonised policy areas, historically the right to reside for non-European Union-nationals subject to national visa and immigration rules[35]. It is less prone to go against protectionist interests in sectors that are vital to the national economy, like energy[36] or uphold the principle of non-discrimination where equal treatment would imply considerable financial loss.

To summarise, the Court will more often depart from a typical justification and model law application in response to external (political, economic) circumstances.[37] The Court can also depart from a typical justification for idiosyncratic reasons or protect conflicting interests by abiding to the typical structure of justification. These instances, discussed in chapter seven, require further analysis.

C. CONCLUSION

Good judgment is a term evoking equal parts of legal expertise, prudence, common sense, and political savoir faire in the context of adjudication. The present analysis uses the term to describe a distinct form of context-conscious judging, which upholds conflicting claims to reconcile the law's demands for equality, consistency, coherence, and legal certainty, with societal demands, political circumstances, and economic implications. It does not use the term to claim that good judgment is inherently good / legally correct / morally right, nor that the Court should use it. Good judgment is characterised by a departure from the typical structure of rational justification and model law application in three distinct ways: the Court can censure Member State policies but adopt Member State friendly outcomes; it can limit unfavourable outcomes and interpretations so as to reduce their practical effect; and it can uphold free movement rights while conditioning and deferring key terms of their application to the national courts and administrations. Thereby, the Court ideally ensures individual rights protection, workable solutions, legally correct outcomes, and the effectiveness of its rulings. This conceptualisation of good judgment requires a methodology that can support the analysis of legal reasoning, a prerequisite for understanding the relationship between the law and the broader environment in which judges interpret and apply it.

[35] Case C-291/05, *Eind*, ECLI:EU:C:2007:771.
[36] A judgment in Case C-379/98, *PreussenElektra*, ECLI:EU:C:2001:160.
[37] See also chapter one (Introduction).

4

Operationalising Good Judgment

SUMMARY

CHAPTER FOUR OPERATIONALISES the concept of good judgment, outlining the building blocks and the method. The central building blocks are the parameters of case-law, which can shed light on the relevant parts of justification, case facts, and institutional features. Text annotation, used to systematically record the parameters of case-law, paired with descriptive statistics and legal analysis combines to form a unique legal empirical methodology.

A. THREE STEPS OF THE ANALYSIS

The analysis includes three steps: 1) annotation of different aspects of justification and case characteristics;[1] 2) identification of atypical justification based on case annotation; and 3) quantitative and qualitative analysis of atypical justifications. Annotation combined with legal analysis of judicial reasoning and case outcomes, descriptive statistics of patterns and trends, and regression analysis, is a unique legal empirical methodology[2] for inferring the mechanisms of judging.[3]

The first step of the analysis uses case annotation to record the legal characteristics of the judgments relevant to the analysis of good judgment and collects further information about the case. Annotation maps the recurring characteristics of texts – in this case, the Court's judgments – and the values that they can assume according to detailed coding protocols or codebooks.

[1] The annotation of judgments was completed at the European University Institute in Florence, under the Coding Project (2017–2022) financed by the European University Research Council. Six research assistants (all doctoral students at the Law Department) have hand coded all judgments.

[2] MA Hall and RF Wright, 'Systematic Content Analysis of Judicial Opinions' (2008) 96 *California Law Review* 63. See also O Brook, 'Politics of Coding: On Systematic Content Analysis of Legal Text' in M Bartl, P Cebulak, and J Lawrence (eds), *Behind the Method: The Politics of European Legal Research* (Cheltenham, Edward Elgar, 2022).

[3] Paired with quantitative analysis of text characteristics, it supports valid inferences from texts to the context of their use. K Krippendorff, *Content Analysis: An Introduction to Its Methodology*, 4th edn (Washington, Sage, 2019) 24. Annotation allows inferences from legal texts to their context (in the present inquiry, from the mechanics to the mechanisms of judging).

Those specify the characteristics and the values, for instance, identifying judgments where the Court adopts a broad or a narrow interpretation of a legal provision.

The second step identifies judgments upholding conflicting interests as possible good judgments,[4] based on the predicted interaction of the legal characteristics relevant to the analysis of three types of good judgment, described in the next subsection. The third step of the analysis examines the circumstances in which the Court protects conflicting interests quantitatively and qualitatively to identify whether a particular type of good judgment could be motivated by case characteristics or the general circumstances like the political context or sizeable economic implications.

The remainder of this chapter first describes the legal characteristics of the judgments relevant to the analysis of good judgment and the information about the case, as well as the criteria or rationale warranting their selection and inclusion in the analysis. The chapter then outlines the annotation process in greater detail.

B. THE PARAMETERS OF CASE-LAW

The term parameters of case-law refers to the legal or legally relevant characteristics of free movement cases pertinent to three types of good judgment, and the information about the case: information about the applicant, legal issues, and the institutional features. The former seeks to capture different parts or aspects of justification characteristic of three types of good judgment as defined in chapter three. The latter also called case characteristics refers to the information about the applicants and the legal questions, that is, selected facts of the dispute, and institutional features, which refer to the Court. The distinction is important to the analysis whether good judgment is case or context motivated.

Some legal and case characteristics are universal and relevant to all policy areas, while others are necessarily policy specific. Among the legal characteristics which capture the universal aspects of the Court's decision-making is the approach to interpretation. Concretely, the parameter records the judicial choice to construct the major premise broadly to adopt a broad interpretation of the valid law or governing provision or narrowly, typically by sticking to the wording of the interpreted provision. Among the legal characteristics which are specific to the analysed policy area is the Court's decision to uphold the rights

[4] As mentioned in chapter three, while courts are context conscious, context might only explain certain outcomes. Good judgment could be incidental, arguably owing to the workflow with rounds of partial and inconsistent revisions in the cabinets and pre-publication editing. Judges might respond to case facts instinctively, following an acquired or 'internalised' situation sense.

of economically inactive citizens. This matter arises with respect to the free movement of persons.

The selection of the parameters was based upon four mutually supporting criteria: the selected parameters should ideally reflect 1) the characteristics of justification of good judgments, 2) the political or economic context of free movement case-law and 3) recurring themes / legal questions in the case-law. At the same time, 4) the analysis should be feasible and the findings generalisable.

Regarding the first point, the parameters should speak directly to the justification in three types of good judgment as described below in section i. Regarding the second point, context-conscious judgments are rendered in the political, social, and economic reality in which the Court is embedded. The parameters are sensitive to broader developments and political struggles, like the economic status and the nationality of the applicant(s). Regarding the recurring themes in the case-law and their proximity to the legal reality, the parameters seek to capture the typical claims raised in free movement disputes which tend to pitch the interests of individual citizens and traders against state administrations or reflect conflicting visions of the internal market. Typical claims include unequal treatment regarding access to social security benefits, or more favourable treatment of national products – the so-called protectionist measures.

Finally, regarding feasibility, the parameters balance informativeness with feasibility. The partitioning of the judgments into parameters seeks to reduce case complexity. If the parameters are oversimplified by legal doctrinal standards, this means that they are unable to account for all legally interesting issues addressed in the judgments. This typical objection against any quantitative research is met by a somewhat standard answer that simplification makes social scientific research possible. The distance between the complexities of social life and the thickest of all descriptions will always be greater than the distance between those descriptions and the most abstract quantitative analysis.[5]

i. Legal Characteristics

The legal characteristics of judgments capture different parts of the Court's justification, like proportionality review (the standard of review), the case outcome like the decision about the compatibility of a disputed national measure with European Union law, the decision to allocate the decision-making authority to the referring court or the legislator, the juridical implications of the final decision or the adopted interpretation for the autonomy of the Member States, the approach to interpretation (the law-making initiative) and the doctrinal

[5] G King et al, *Designing Social Inquiry : Scientific Inference in Qualitative Research* (Princeton Princeton University Press, 2021) 48. For the impossibility to capture social life into formal rules see M Galanter, 'The Radiating Effects of Courts' in K Boyum and LM Mather (eds) *Empirical Theories About Courts* (New York, Longman, 1983) 117.

contribution of the judgment to the acquis. The individual legal characteristics do not map into good judgment. Rather, it is possible to infer the latter from their interaction. Three types of good judgment juxtapose two or three parameters.

The Legal Characteristics of Non-Sanctioning Europeanisation of National Policies

The non-sanctioning Europeanisation of national policies examines national regulation through the lens of common European rules and standards, albeit without declaring them incompatible with said rules and standards. Concretely, the Court appraises the disputed national measures against the legitimate aim, necessity, and proportionality in the narrow sense (proportionality review) or assesses whether unequal treatment amounts to the type of unlawful discrimination prohibited by European rules and principles. While the Court upholds the national measures as entirely or mostly compatible with European Union law, its approach threatens or can be read as a signal to dismantle them in the future. Three legally relevant characteristics capture good judgment:

a) Proportionality review / Standard of review
    i) Indicates the level of scrutiny which the Court exercises to assess whether the disputed national measure is contrary to European Union law. A more lax proportionality test includes only the assessment of the suitability of the disputed national measure (legitimate aim). A stricter test includes the suitability test, the necessity test and/or the balancing test – proportionality in the strict sense.
b) Discriminatory national measure
    i) Refers to the Court's consideration of equal treatment and the decision on whether the national measure is discriminatory and the applicant was therefore unequally treated.
c) Decision about the compatibility of the national measure with European Union law
    i) Refers to the Court's decision whether European Union law should be interpreted as precluding or allowing the disputed national measure.

The Legal Characteristics of Deferential Judgments Upholding and Expanding Rights and Principles

A deferential judgment upholding and expanding rights and principles will uphold the claim of the applicant based on European Union law against the interest of the respondent Member State. At the same time, it will grant the Member State genuine as opposed to pro forma deference. The application of a broad outcome of the case – a rights protective interpretation of European law will be qualified or suspended, depending on the potential decision (discretion) of the national court or administrative authority applying national rules. The decision of the national authority might eventually frustrate or curb the enforcement of European rights.

Two legally relevant characteristics – protection of the individual and deference – will reflect the Court's attempt to protect individual rights without unsettling the power balance between the Union and the Member States or setting off a conflict between European and national law:

a) Protection of the individual / applicant / natural or legal person / free movement rights
    i) Refers to the Court's decision about the individual applicant's claim for rights protection or the claim about the protection of free movement rights, typically in the free movement of goods cases
b) Deference / Allocation of decision-making authority
    i) Shows how the Court allocates the decision-making authority. The Court can offer an abstract and general answer to the preliminary questions, leaving the national court wider leeway to decide whether the facts of the case allow or even call for the application of the abstract solution. Alternatively, the Court can defer the examination of facts and the correct interpretation of the rules central to the dispute to the national court. These two instances are important for the conceptualisation of a deferential judgment upholding individual rights.

The Legal Characteristics of Judgments with Bounded Interpretation

Finally, a judgment with bounded interpretation restrictive of national regulatory autonomy directly imposes new obligations on the Member States, removing obstacles to free movement or creating rights, doctrines, and concepts at minimal or limited cost. The Court will try to reduce the implications of its ruling for national regulatory autonomy or limit its effects. The three legally relevant characteristics which reflect the rationale of bounded undesirable interpretation are:

a) Implications for the autonomy of the Member States to regulate free movement and related policy areas such as taxation, healthcare, intellectual property.
    i) Autonomy refers to the implications of the Court's ruling on the regulatory power of the Member State – that is, its freedom to independently adopt legislation conforming with societal values and national interest.
b) Approach to interpretation / the law-making initiative
    i) The law-making initiative refers to the willingness of the Court to interpret European Union law according to its purpose (teleological,

functional, or purposive interpretation), even if its rulings have far-reaching implications or extend the scope of European Union law. The latter means that the interpretation alters the power-balance within the EU or has implications for Member State policies beyond this scope.

c) Doctrinal contribution to the acquis
   i) The legal contribution is reflected in the creation of new free movement or related rights; expansion of those rights to new categories of citizens, undertakings or situations; or the creation of legal principles that increase European rights protection, imposing new obligations on the Member States to facilitate free movement – for instance access, conditions or benefits of free movement, creation of citizenship rights etc.

The parameters doctrinal contribution and the law-making initiative reflect the audacity or the moderation in the law application with precedential effects. The expansion of doctrines or principles does not necessarily entail outcomes that benefit the natural and legal persons that is, the applicants claiming their European rights directly. The Court can interpret the law expansively and limit the autonomy of the Member States without bringing about a positive outcome for the applicant in the main proceedings.[6] New doctrines and principles are not necessarily competence expansive, autonomy usurping, or rights creating.[7]

ii. Case Characteristics

The information about the case includes selected details about the applicants, institutional features, including procedure, and the legal issues discussed in the case.

The Information about the Applicant / Rights-holder

The information about the applicant refers to the characteristics of the parties, notably the parties in the main proceedings. The information is especially

[6] Sometimes the claims of the applicants lack merit. The assumption is that the Court can reject those claims based on the established practice and does not need to develop new doctrines to reject them. On the change in the type of claims and applicants in EU citizenship judgments see G Davies, 'Has the Court Changed, or Have the Cases? The Deservingness of Litigants as an Element in Court of Justice Citizenship Adjudication' (2018) 25 *Journal of European Public Policy* 1442. See, however, Case C-42/17, *M.A.S.*, ECLI:EU:C:2017:936, concerning the requirement of national courts to disapply national law which prevents the application of effective and deterrent criminal penalties in a significant number of cases of serious fraud affecting the financial interests of the European Union.

[7] A classic example, which could imply fewer rights of individuals, would be the Opinion 2/13 on the Accession of the European Union to the ECHR. One might argue that not joining the Convention is per se reducing the scope of supranational protection of individual rights. B De Witte and Š Imamovic, 'Opinion 2/13 on Accession to the ECHR: Defending the EU Legal Order against a Foreign Human Rights Court' (2015) 40 *European Law Review* 683.

important in the free movement of persons, where the Court more often deals with conflicts between individual European citizens claiming their free movement rights and state administrations enforcing potentially discriminatory national rules and standards. Studies hypothesise that the identity of the applicant affects case outcomes.[8]

The information about the case related to the free movement of persons includes more comprehensive information about the individual applicant a natural person, wherever such information is available and relevant to the decision. This can include personal characteristics like gender, economic status like a worker or a student, or family status; typically a link to the European citizen. The information about the case if it concerns the free movement of goods includes basic information about the applicant, natural or legal person, an institution, their nationality meaning the seat of a legal person, or the Member State of origin.

Chapters five and six analysing the case-law describe all parameters in detail.

The Information about the Legal Framework

The information about the legal framework shows how the Court identifies the legal issue as well as the legal questions framing the dispute. Framing can be consequential for the final decision. For instance, if the Court categorises the disputed national measure as tax rather than a charge or levy, the Member State will be free to impose it on goods crossing the border. Additionally, the legal claims of the parties reflect their legal and political or economic interests. For example, by claiming that an applicant is not a worker, the Member State is seeking to avoid the economic consequences of free movement which could include the payment of work-related benefits or study maintenance to the applicant and other citizens in a similar position.

The legally relevant information about the case dealing with the movement of persons includes the rights ensured by the requirement of equal treatment and equal access to benefits and other work or residence related rights. These include determination of whether equal treatment has been respected, the grounds of discrimination, whether the claim is based on the Treaty or legislation, whether the applicant is claiming a benefit and if so, what type of benefit it is, whether the case concerns derived rights, rights of workers, family rights, or residence rights, and/or whether it is a matter of restrictions based on public service or other restrictions to practice a profession.

The examples of information about the case dealing with the free movement of goods are the Court's classification of national measures fiscal barriers or trade restrictions, Common Customs Tariff questions, and the level of harmonisation. While information whether the case concerns mutual recognition, access

[8] Davies (n 6).

to the market, or mandatory requirements, distinctly or indistinctly applicable measures, is interesting, it occurs surprisingly seldomly or not at all.[9]

Institutional Features and Procedure

The information about the institutional features and procedure includes information about the reporting judges and the sitting formation (number of sitting judges and the allocation to the chamber), the language of the case, the referring national court, and the type of procedure. Often, the EU institutions and the Member States are parties to the proceedings or submit observations, meaning that the information about the case indicates the individual institution or the Member State where the case originates or which submitted observations.

C. ANNOTATION

The choice of pairing text annotation with simple descriptive statistics, linear regression, and qualitative analysis of the emerging patterns raises two important points which require appraisal. The first is whether the method is dependable. The second is a narrower point about the reliability of the findings which is related to the role of the researcher.

i. Methodological Choices

Annotation differs from legal analysis and rational reconstruction as well as from expert coding as used in statistical analysis of judicial behaviour.

Unlike rational reconstruction, case annotation classifies only pre-set categories; follows transparent criteria in the selection of cases such as policy area, reporting judge etc.; includes selected judgments regardless of their doctrinal significance; focuses on the legal characteristics to determine their occurrence and their values according to a pre-determined coding protocol.

Annotation is thus reductionist, seeking to reconstruct patterns as they emerge from the classification rather than evaluating the decision of the Court and its reasoning.

In contrast to the analysis of judicial behaviour using expert coding, annotation focuses on the information that supports the study of doctrinal developments, judicial method, and the changing modes of reasoning: legal concepts, arguments and chosen interpretations; considers the whole text of the judgment (facts, law, claims, outcomes, arguments); requires expert legal knowledge of the

[9] See ch six, Table 4 for the overview of the legal issues.

Court's jurisprudence and familiarity with scholarly categories and legal literature; refines the existing information about the case and institutional features from the official sources like Eurlex and Curia, such as the assigned subject matter or type of procedure.

From the legal perspective, a consideration is whether methodology sufficiently accounts for the legal content.[10] This consideration is a variation on a qualitative-quantitative theme omnipresent in legal empirical studies, notably their contribution to legal knowledge. From the empirical point of view, it will be doubtful whether the methodology can stand the test of scientific rigor (by conforming to the rules of inference[11]).

In comparison to legal analysis, annotation is cruder. Its perspective is not chronological and linear. Finally, fragmenting a single judgment according to the selected characteristics, threatens to decontextualise these legal characteristics, losing important nuance. A judgment is presented as a set of highlighted categories, rather than as a source of rights and duties.[12]

Regarding the fear of decontextualisation, scientific research shows that systematic recording and study of smaller constitutive parts of a subject or phenomenon offers greater insight than the study of 'the whole', meaning that fragmentation contributes to gathering fuller and more informative input in the long run.[13] For instance, sampling a person's thoughts, feelings, behaviours, and/or environment on multiple occasions over time presents a more comprehensive and more accurate assessment of their well-being, stress levels, happiness, or job satisfaction than a one-time holistic evaluation at one given point. By analogy, the breaking down of a judicial decision in the text of the judgment into legally relevant characteristics can – when re-contextualised – offer richer and more accurate information about context-conscious judging.

Finally, the methodology is also sufficiently rigorous to present and explain associations between the types of good judgment and the circumstances of their use. As instances of good judgments vary (see chapters five and six), a qualitative study is preferable to explain and contextualise them, offering a fine-grained view on context-conscious judging.

[10] This is the so-called legal relevance claim. See U Šadl and F Tarissan, 'The Relevance of the Network Approach to European Case Law: Reflection and Evidence' in C Kilpatrick and J Scott (eds), *New Legal Approaches to Studying the Court of Justice* (Oxford, Oxford University Press, 2020).

[11] L Epstein and G King, 'The Rules of Inference' (2002) *The University of Chicago Law Review* 1.

[12] This said, systematic analysis of selected legally relevant characteristics offsets the case selection bias, and other, pro-EU bias, of legal doctrine. See R van Gestel and HW Micklitz, 'Revitalizing Doctrinal Legal Research in Europe: What about Methodology?' (2013) *EUI Working Papers*.

[13] D Kahneman et al, 'A Survey Method for Characterizing Daily Life Experience: The Day Reconstruction Method' (2004) 306 *Science* 1776.

ii. A Note on the Role of the Researcher

The role of the researcher (the coder) is key to the reliability of the annotation, and from this perspective the most important division is between descriptive and evaluative or discretionary characteristics and information about the case. The former relies primarily on the wording (the text) of the judgment and available information, the latter requires interpretation of the Court's decision and reasoning. The distinction is not always simple, because annotation is always at least partly discretionary and interpretive.

For instance, the information about the case pertaining to the number of the applicants or their gender relies on the text and appears straightforward and descriptive to ascertain. However, where the Court does not expressly state otherwise, the researcher infers gender from the names of the applicants when possible or the pronouns which the Court uses in the judgment.

Legally relevant characteristics such as deference refer to the Court's decision in the preliminary reference procedure to hand over the final assessment of the legal situation to the referring national court. The Court typically uses a specific formulation to the effect of: 'in a situation such as that at issue in the main proceedings, [the citizenship Treaty articles] must be interpreted as meaning that they do not preclude a Member State from refusing to allow a third-country national to reside in its territory … [if] such a refusal does not deprive those citizens of effective enjoyment of the substance of the rights …, a matter which is to be determined by the referring court.'[14] Other similar formulations can indicate deference. The research assistants must confirm the Court's intention to defer, evaluating the formulations against the Court's final answer to the preliminary questions and the guidance which the Court gives the referring court in its reasoning or justification. More detailed and clearly formulated guidance will not leave any de facto leeway for the referring courts. When annotation requires extensive evaluation by the research assistants, the questions of inter-coder agreement and repeated testing must be raised to ensure the reliability of the findings. Such examples would include the implications of the Court's final decision on the regulatory autonomy of the Member States.

D. CONCLUSION TO PART I

The conceptualisation of good judgment as a paradigmatic form of context-conscious judging, which upholds conflicting claims and protects opposing interests in response to case characteristics and non-legal (political, economic) circumstances, is based on the theoretical insight and the empirical evidence

[14] Case C-86/12, *Alokpa*, ECLI:EU:C:2013:645, where the Court considered the residence permit of a parent who was not a European citizen providing for minor European citizens (children).

presented in chapter two. This provides a starting point to rethink the prototype of courts, adjudication and how the concept of good judgment is formulated. However, the analysis showed that all accounts called for further conceptual work.

Studies have repeatedly proven conflicting claims about the Court's regard for political will:[15]

a) The Court has been sensitive to the preferences and interests of the Member States;
b) The Court has been committed to the integration project and the protection of individual rights;
c) The Court has disregarded the resistance of the Member States.

Moreover, scholars have endorsed competing claims about the nature of the relationship between European law and policy / legislation:

a) Case-law casts a long shadow on policymaking and constrains future policymakers;
b) Member States can reverse judicial pronouncements.

Finally, different approaches imply diverse motivating factors of context-conscious judging and its nature:

a) Courts consider the context to uphold the values of the legal system only when deciding between justifiable rival interpretations / Context-consciousness is prudence, legitimising the legal system;
b) Courts consider the context to sustain their legal authority avoiding conflict and resistance / Context consciousness is a self-preservation or authority-preservation tool;
c) Courts necessarily consider the context and exploit the opportunity to enforce their policy preferences / Context consciousness is a power tool.[16]

[15] Literature demonstrates that courts continuously weigh mutually exclusive goals. When courts authoritatively intervene in societal disputes, their political power increases along with the risk of politicisation. The latter potentially erodes their image of neutrality and non-partisanship, which underwrites the acceptability of their legal pronouncements (and effectiveness). When courts disregard the preferences of the legislators, they risk override, and the loss of power. Resisting political will, expressed as the ability to uphold the law in the face of power, underwrites their legal authority and popular legitimacy, which is intrinsically connected to their a-political and non-partisan decisions.

[16] In practice, these motivations continuously collide, forcing courts into a paradox – the sustainable middle way between two unsustainable extremes. Additionally, institutional factors (collegiality limiting judicial choices) can decisively shape the structure of justification, application of procedural tools or the interpretation of formal sources (statute and precedent). Courts can respond to the particularities of the case (a fact situation). F Schauer, 'Do Cases Make Bad Law' (2006) 73 *University of Chicago Law Review* 883; KN Llewellyn, *The Common Law Tradition: Deciding Appeals* (Boston, Little Brown Company, 1960).

The concept of context consciousness remains open-ended, extending to a continuum of behaviours and forms of reasoning. The connection between individual contextual including institutional factors and the structure of justification apart from the initial recognition that potentially relevant non-legal legal factors at least partly determine legal solutions remains blurry.[17] Unpacking the latter is essential for the understanding of the relationship between law and context.

Good judgment is an analytical tool designed to capture this connection and untangle this relationship.

Against this backdrop, chapter three constructs good judgment as a heuristic tool to identify a mode of decision-making that upholds conflicting claims and protects competing interests in response to particular facts and the broader circumstances of the dispute. The tool supports a refined and informative taxonomy of good judgment particular to the European Union's institutional and constitutional structure:

a) *Non-sanctioning Europeanisation of national policies*, which combines the scrutiny of national measures and policies with state friendly outcomes.
b) *Deferential upholding of European rights* that fashions new rights and concepts but leaves their application to the referring court or national administration.
c) *Bounded undesirable interpretation*, which contains the effects of expansive rulings.

Chapter four sets the methodological parameters of the analysis, which uses case annotation to operationalise the rationale of good judgment as a distinct form of context-conscious judging. Combined with legal analysis of reasoning and case outcomes, descriptive statistics of patterns and trends, and regression analysis, the methodology can accurately identify the instances of good judgment, and establish whether they are motivated by case characteristics, including institutional features, or broader non-legal circumstances.

[17] Consequentialism, by contrast, is under-inclusive, equating context consciousness with discretion and focusing almost exclusively on the structure of justification.

Part II

The Mechanics of Good Judgment

SUMMARY

PART II FOCUSES on the mechanics of good judgment, using the analytical framework developed in Part I to analyse the free movement case-law. Chapters five dealing with the free movement of persons and six dealing with the free movement of goods set the scene for further investigation into the underlying logic and mechanisms of good judgment which will be discussed in more detail in Part III, chapters seven and eight.

The chapters open with a consideration of the current Treaty and legislative framework against the backdrop of legislative history, evaluating the role of the Court's case-law and highlighting the political debate and compromise behind concrete legislative solutions. They then explore the forms of good judgment evidenced in emblematic judgments in the context of these debates. Finally, each chapter concludes with a brief presentation of the patterns, drawing attention to their frequency over time.

5

Persons

A. INTRODUCTION

LEGAL DIVERSITY, PRACTICAL relevance, fundamental position in the single market, and political divisiveness make judgments on the free movement of persons particularly apt for the study of good judgment, including outlier judgments and aggregate developments. The political controversy surrounding migration and the economic considerations behind the payment of social security to migrant workers are amalgamated with case facts and valid rules. They become germane when threatening to override legal rules and established case-law, posing threats to judicial authority.

Free movement of people resonates beyond the internal market and the legal-economic sphere. It directly concerns a diverse group of individuals in terms of age, social status, ethnic background, and nationality. The personal scope of free movement of persons rules includes workers, self-employed persons, economically non-active persons such as students and jobseekers, and dependent family members irrespective of nationality. Substantively, the rights to move and reside, work, study, and enjoy family life extends to receipt of social assistance and intrudes into the regulation of the labour market, employment policy, education, social security, personal income taxation, criminal law, and public order. Free movement and the rights of European citizens intertwine with human rights, the general principles of European Union law like non-discrimination, fundamental Treaty freedoms of establishment and the right to provide and receive services.

The application of free movement rights can trespass on non-harmonised policy areas like personal income taxation of frontier workers.[1] Free movement can unsettle deep-seated societal arrangements[2] and the values underlying fiscal redistribution, work, minimum income and living standards (e.g. concerns over social dumping or welfare tourism).[3] Finally, European free movement

[1] Case C-241/20, *BJ v Belgian State*, ECLI:EU:C:2021:605, concerning Belgian legislation on personal income taxation of cross-border workers.

[2] S Mair, 'Kahn in Luxembourg: A Prolegomena to the Cultural Study of EU Law' (2023) 24 *German Law Journal* 735.

[3] A rich debate has developed over the expulsion of European citizens who repeatedly commit criminal acts in the host Member State. An example of a deferential ruling related to expulsion due to criminal convictions is Case C-348/09 PI, ECLI:EU:C:2012:300.

rights have proved controversial in the context of global/ Union-wide economic (the 2007–2008 financial crisis), political (the 2015 migration crisis), or public health (most recently the COVID 19 pandemic) emergencies.

The European Barometer regularly demonstrates that Europeans consider immigration including intra-European Union mobility as one of the most worrying aspects of integration.[4] The movement of workers and economically inactive citizens has featured in the debates about the suitable level, the pace, and the risks of integration through case-law, highlighting irreconcilable differences between states which are economically stronger and weaker, at the centre and the periphery, the old and the new Member States, and those that institute the welfare state and welfare capitalism. Attempts to overhaul legislation, such as the Posted Workers Directive, have clearly exposed these rifts.[5]

The political resistance to free movement and the related weaponisation of migration have been manifest in courtrooms across Europe – national courts have sought guidance from the Court of Justice on family reunification, residence rights of family members, expulsion, and access of non-nationals to social assistance. On a more concrete level, the political and economic developments have coincided with the gradual tightening of free movement through the vigorous application of rights-curbing legislative rules.[6] Against this background, it is safe to conclude that the external concerns correlate with the judicial arsenal, meaning that the departures from the model justification can be attributed to the political context with more confidence and with strong comparison over time.

As argued in chapter three, three distinct types of good judgment emerge from a reflection on competing legal, national, individual, collective, financial, political and European Union's interests and the typical claims raised in the free movement disputes: the non-sanctioning Europeanisation of national policies; the deferential upholding of European rights; and the bounded undesirable interpretation.

[4] European Union Barometer (summer 2022). Migration is 3rd with unemployment and government debt European Union wide.

[5] P Van Nuffel and S Afanasjeva, 'The Posting of Workers Directive Revised: Enhancing the Protection of Workers in the Cross-Border Provision of Services' (2019) 2018 *European Papers: A Journal on Law and Integration* 1401; DS Martinsen and M Blauberger, 'The Court of Justice of The European Union And The Megapolitics of Posted Workers' (2021) 84 *Law and Contemporary Problems* 29.

[6] Nic Shuibhne illustrates the opposition in the context of European Union citizenship rights, which have become conceptually and practically intertwined with the 'original' free movement rights of workers and self-employed persons. In particular, one can observe a remarkable consistency in the way in which the Court tended to interpret individual rights expansively, while giving a narrow meaning to the duties and the limits of those rights, then reversing this approach. N Nic Shuibhne, 'Limits Rising, Duties Ascending: The Changing Legal Shape of Union Citizenship' (2015) 52 *Common Market Law Review* 889. See also D Thym, 'The Elusive Limits of Solidarity: Residence Rights of and Social Benefits for Economically Inactive Union Citizens' (2015) 52 *Common Market Law Review* 17.

a) The first type focuses on the standard of judicial review of national rules and policies – subjecting them to European standards.
b) The second focuses on the decision of the Court about the legal claim or a concrete negative case outcome for the state following the Court's interpretation of European Union law or its validity.
c) The third focuses on the broader implications of rulings for the regulatory autonomy of the Member State in the policy area under scrutiny or adjacent policy areas, for instance, a decision on access to education can have implications for income taxation.

The remainder of the chapter is structured as follows. Section b) outlines the historical, legal, and political context of the Court's free movement of persons case-law. It first presents the relevant Treaty provisions and legislative acts, pausing at the thorny question of competence division and opposition to the social aspects of the internal market. Then, it walks the reader through the legislative procedure leading to the adoption of the Citizenship Rights Directive as an exemplary legal act reflecting these persistent and unresolvable tensions. Section c) briefly presents the legal themes or legal issues animating six decades of case-law. Section d) elaborates the parameters of case-law against the legal framework and the main themes discussed in sections b) and c), linking the underlying rationale of good judgment with the legal characteristics of the Court's justification and the information about the dispute. Section e) unpacks the justification in three emblematic judgments to demonstrate the mechanics of good judgment, that is, the Court's decision to uphold conflicting interests in response to the broader political circumstances, economic implications, or both: *Groener*,[7] to illustrate the non-sanctioning Europeanisation of national policies; *Vaassen-Göbbels*,[8] to illustrate the deferential upholding of European rights and *Blaizot*,[9] to illustrate the bounded undesirable interpretation. Section f) shows the frequency of all types of good judgment from 1960s to 2020s.

B. THE RULES GOVERNING THE FREE MOVEMENT OF PERSONS AND EUROPEAN CITIZENS

i. Treaty Rights, Legislative Acts, and the Competence to Regulate Free Movement

Articles 45–48 TFEU establish the rights of workers to move and reside freely in the territory of the Member States, accept offers of employment, retire, and enjoy treatment equal to that of national workers in each host Member State.

[7] Case C-379/87, *Groener*, ECLI: EU:C:1989:599.
[8] Case 61/65, *G. Vaassen-Göbbels*, ECLI:EU:C:1966:39.
[9] Case 24/86, *Blaizot*, ECLI:EU:C:1988:43.

The prohibition of all unequal treatment tantamount to discrimination based on a worker's nationality extends to employment, remuneration, and other labour conditions. Article 46 TFEU authorises the Parliament and the Council to adopt measures which ensure close cooperation between national employment services; remove obstructive administrative procedures and practices; or facilitate a balanced supply and demand in the employment market, all with the caveat of avoiding serious threats to the standard of living and level of employment across regions and industries.

Finally, pursuant to Article 48 TFEU, the Parliament and the Council can adopt measures targeting aggregation, eligibility, calculation, and the payment of social benefits to migrant workers including self-employed migrant workers and their dependents. Any Member State can effectively veto any draft legislative act which would affect important aspects of its social security system or its financial balance (the scope, the cost, or the financial structure) by bringing the matter to the European Council. This action suspends the ordinary legislative procedure, and the European Council can either refer the draft back to the Council, take no action, or request that the Commission submit a new proposal.

In addition, Article 49 TFEU prohibits restrictions on the freedom of establishment including setting-up of agencies, branches, or subsidiaries for nationals of a Member State in the territory of another Member State. Freedom of establishment refers to the right to take up and pursue activities as a self-employed person and to set up and manage undertakings under the same conditions laid down for the nationals of the host State. These provisions have remained unchanged since the signature of the Treaty of Rome (1957), bar re-enumeration following Treaty changes.

Pursuant to the Maastricht Treaty adopted in 1992, nationals of Member States are also considered citizens of the European Union who enjoy citizenship rights on the basis of this status (Article 20(1) TFEU). Articles 20(2) and 21 TFEU afford the rights to move and reside freely in Member States, to diplomatic and consular protection, and to vote and stand as candidates in local and European Parliament elections. The Treaties and implementing measures can limit these rights and impose duties. If action by the Union should prove necessary to attain the Treaty objectives and if the Treaties have not provided the necessary powers, the Parliament and the Council may adopt provisions to facilitate the exercise of the right to move and reside and the Council, acting unanimously after consulting the European Parliament, can adopt measures concerning social security or social protection.

Competence wise, the European Union and the Member States can jointly regulate the internal market (free movement of workers), and the European Union can support or coordinate areas that make its functioning relevant to citizens and businesses. This setup has been a topic of inflated dossiers and frustrating negotiations to meet the requirement of unanimity in the Council.

Finally, Article 45(1) of the Charter of Fundamental Rights[10] – proclaimed in 2000 and incorporated into the Treaty of Lisbon in 2009 – repeats that European citizens who are nationals of the European Union's Member States have the 'right to move and reside freely within the territory of the Member States'. The Charter has Treaty rank and therefore constitutes primary law. However, while the provisions fully apply to the institutions, bodies, offices, and agencies of the European Union, they apply to the Member States only when they are implementing Union law, in line with the principle of subsidiarity (Article 51 of the Charter). The Charter (Article 52) does not confer any additional competences to the European Union.

The legislative instruments adopted on the basis of Treaty Articles and later the citizenship provisions are diverse. The key instrument regulating free movement of persons is the Citizenship Rights Directive 38/2004 (the Directive),[11] based on Articles 18 (prohibition of discrimination), 50 (freedom of establishment), and 59 (freedom to provide services) of the TFEU; Articles 46 (free movement of persons), 21 (2) (citizenship of the Union), and 294 (co-decision) TFEU consolidated earlier directives and regulations which governed specific rights for certain groups of persons such as residence rights for students:

> Articles 10 and 11 of the Regulation (EEC) No 1612/68 of the Council of 15 October 1968 on freedom of movement for workers within the Community (Regulation (European Union) No 492/2011 on freedom of movement for workers within the Union repealed it entirely[12])
>
> Council Directive 68/360/EEC of 15 October 1968 on the abolition of restrictions on movement and residence within the Community for workers of Member States and their families
>
> Council Directive 64/221/EEC of 25 February 1964 on the co-ordination of special measures concerning the movement and residence of foreign nationals which are justified on grounds of public policy, public security or public health
>
> Council Directive 72/194/EEC of 18 May 1972 extending to workers exercising the right to remain in the territory of a Member State after having been employed in that State the scope of the Directive of 25 February 1964 on coordination of special measures concerning the movement and residence of foreign nationals which are justified on grounds of public policy, public security or public health

[10] Charter of Fundamental Rights of the European Union, OJ C 326, 26.10.2012, p 391–407.

[11] Dir 2004/38/EC of the European Parliament and of the Council of 29 April 2004 on the right of citizens of the Union and their family members to move and reside freely within the territory of the Member States amending Reg (EEC) No 1612/68 and repealing Dirs 64/221/EEC, 68/360/EEC, 72/194/EEC, 73/148/EEC, 75/34/EEC, 75/35/EEC, 90/364/EEC, 90/365/EEC and 93/96/EEC (Text with EEA relevance); OJ L 158, 30.4.2004, p 77–123.

[12] Reg (European Union) No 492/2011 of the European Parliament and of the Council of 5 April 2011 on freedom of movement for workers within the Union Text with EEA relevance OJ L 141, 27.5.2011, p 1–12.

Council Directive 73/148/EEC of 21 May 1973 on the abolition of restrictions on movement and residence within the Community for nationals of Member States with regard to establishment and the provision of services

Council Directive 75/34/EEC of 17 December 1974 concerning the right of nationals of a Member State to remain in the territory of another Member State after having pursued therein an activity in a self-employed capacity

Council Directive 75/35/EEC of 17 December 1974 extending the scope of Directive No 64/221/EEC on the coordination of special measures concerning the movement and residence of foreign nationals which are justified on grounds of public policy, public security or public health to include nationals of a Member State who exercise the right to remain in the territory of another Member State after having pursued therein an activity in a self-employed capacity

Council Directive 90/364/EEC of 28 June 1990 on the right of residence

Council Directive 90/365/EEC of 28 June 1990 on the right of residence for employees and self-employed persons who have ceased their occupational activity

Council Directive 93/96/EEC of 29 October 1993 on the right of residence for students.

The Citizenship Directive, negotiated and adopted prior to the 'eastern enlargement' in 2004, was intended to facilitate and support the free movement of European citizens, including workers and their family members. It overhauled previous, often fragmented legislation, promising further facilitation and simplification of rules, de-bureaucratisation, and clarity.

The guarantee of social security for migrant workers is not a separate policy of the Union but a prerequisite for free movement of persons and services. As stated by the Court in *Petroni*, free movement of workers and services cannot be achieved if 'as a consequence of the exercise of their right to freedom of movement, workers were to lose advantages in the field of social security guaranteed to them in any event by the laws of a single Member State' (the so-called Petroni principle).[13] Given the limits of European competence to regulate social security, Regulation 883/2004 (the coordination regulation)[14] and Regulation 978/2009 (the implementing regulation) lay down an elaborate structure. Coordination primarily supports free movement by preventing the application of the Member States' social security legislation which could obstruct migrants' access to their social security systems (the territoriality principle). In other words, coordination ideally eliminates any negative consequences for the migrating person arising from disparities in the social security systems of the Member States.

The importance of eliminating the negative consequences for the migrating worker was recognized and formalized in the 1950s. Article 69 of the Treaty of Paris establishing the European Coal and Steel Community (ECSC) provided for free movement of workers, mentioning social security as a factor that must not

[13] Case 24/75 *Teresa and Silvana Petroni*, ECLI:EU:C:1975:129.

[14] Reg (EC) No 883/2004 of the European Parliament and of the Council of 29 April 2004 on the coordination of social security systems; OJ L 166, 30.4.2004, p 1–123.

inhibit labour mobility in the coal and steel industries.[15] However, in June 1955, The Messina Conference placed social security for migrant workers in a wider context, establishing that the common market must include entire economies and hence all industries of the Member States. This prompted the Commission to capitalise on the ongoing or already accomplished work of the European Convention on social security of migrant workers initiated to implement the ECSC. In April 1958, the Commission presented a proposal for a Regulation incorporating the text of the Convention with minimal changes. The Council adopted the proposal as Regulation 3.[16] Meanwhile, the Commission drafted the supporting instruments, which became implementing Regulation 4.[17]

Regulations 3 and 4 came into force simultaneously on 1 January 1959, a decade before the realization of free movement of workers envisaged by the Treaty of Rome. Regulation 3 has been modified fourteen times. Regulation 1408/71,[18] which eventually replaced it, has been modified thirty-nine times. Regulation 883/04, which partly repealed Regulation 1408/71, was modified even before it became applicable.[19]

Regulation 883/2004 was adopted in 2004 after six years of challenging negotiations. The legal basis was provided by Articles 48 (the European Parliament and the Council's competence to adopt the necessary social security measures for workers), 294 TFEU (co-decision procedure), and 352 TFEU (the horizontal legal basis requiring unanimity in the Council).

All legislative instruments have been subject to extensive case-law of the Court, whose interpretations challenged the personal, material, temporal, and territorial scope of their application. The legislators often formalised the case-law and at times reversed it,[20] which signals an interesting dynamic between the legislative and the judicial institutions, as well as of the Court's power to mitigate between law and politics.

The following sub-section uses the legislative history of the Citizenship Rights Directive to contextualise and structure the analysis of the types and

[15] The reconstruction of the legislative history follows the excellent and detailed overview by R Cornelissen, '50 Years of European Social Security Coordination' (2009) 11 *European Journal of Social Security* 9.

[16] Council Reg No 3/1958 on the social security of migrant workers, OJ 30, 16.12.1958, p 561–596, which was replaced by Reg (EEC) No 1408/71 of the Council on the application of social security schemes to employed persons and their families moving within the Community; OJ L 149, 5.7.1971, p 2–50.

[17] Reg No 4/1958 implementing the Reg No 3/1958, OJ 30, 16.12.1958, p 597–664, replaced by Implementing Reg (EEC) No 574/72 of the Council of 21 March 1972 fixing the procedure for implementing Reg (EEC) No 1408/71 on the application of social security schemes to employed persons and their families moving within the Community, OJ L 74, 27.3.1972, p 1–83.

[18] Reg (EEC) No 1408/71 of the Council on the application of social security schemes to employed persons and their families moving within the Community; OJ L 149, 5.7.1971, p 2–50.

[19] Cornelissen (n 15) 11.

[20] Cornelissen mentions Reg 1247/92, which introduced a separate coordination system for the 'special non-contributory benefits' in order to avoid their exportability, which would have resulted from the case-law of the Court bringing such benefits within the scope of the Regulation if they were linked to one of the risks listed in Art 4(1) of Reg 1408/71. ibid 10.

the mechanisms of good judgment in chapter seven. It focuses on the incommensurate interests that the Court has been mitigating, and the political debates to which it has actively contributed. Concretely, the Directive 'juridifies' the opposition between a common market with free movement of persons based on solidarity and high level of social protection[21] and the national control of the labour market, economic policy, migration flows, and public spending. The Member States have expressed these contradictions as reservations towards new rights, reluctance to the enhancement of protection for migrant workers and their family members, stricter conditions of lawful residence, restrictions of the exportability of benefits and the limits of equal protection. Every legislation, including that which is currently in place, has consolidated and formalized these conflicts. External circumstances, like health and financial crises, have added a layer of complexity to the already multifaceted base.

ii. Citizenship Rights Directive: Consolidating Legislative Instruments, Case-Law and Conflict

As aforementioned, the Citizenship Rights Directive (the Directive) operationalises the Treaty provisions[22] under a single framework.[23] Its aim is to give 'a concrete expression to the concept of European citizenship'[24] by consolidating nine directives and two regulations governing free movement rights of different categories of people separately: workers, their family members, retired persons / former workers and students.[25]

[21] Art 3 TFEU.

[22] Along with Arts 12 (prohibition of discrimination), 44 (freedom of establishment), and 52 (freedom to provide services) TFEU. These articles, together with Arts 40 (free movement of persons) and 18(2) (citizenship of the Union), and 251 (co-decision) TFEU served as a legal basis for the adoption of the Dir.

[23] Dir 2004/38/EC of the European Parliament and of the Council of 29 April 2004 on the right of citizens of the Union and their family members to move and reside freely within the territory of the Member States amending Reg (EEC) No 1612/68 and repealing Dirs 64/221/EEC, 68/360/EEC, 72/194/EEC, 73/148/EEC, 75/34/EEC, 75/35/EEC, 90/364/EEC, 90/365/EEC and 93/96/EEC (Text with EEA relevance) OJ L 158, 30.4.2004, p 77–123.

[24] Introduced in the Maastricht Treaty in 1992.

[25] Amending Reg 1612/68 on the freedom of movement for workers, and repealing several directives abolishing restrictions on movement and residence for different groups of migrant citizens and their families: Council Reg (EEC) No 1612/68 of 15 October 1968 on freedom of movement for workers within the Community and to repeal the following acts: Council Dir 68/360/EEC of 15 October 1968 on the abolition of restrictions on movement and residence within the Community for workers of Member States and their families, Council Dir 73/148/EEC of 21 May 1973 on the abolition of restrictions on movement and residence within the Community for nationals of Member States with regard to establishment and the provision of services, Council Dir 90/364/EEC of 28 June 1990 on the right of residence, Council Dir 90/365/EEC of 28 June 1990 on the right of residence for employees and self-employed persons who have ceased their occupational activity and Council Dir 93/96/EEC of 29 October 1993 on the right of residence for students.

The available sources documenting the legislative process reveal three points of contention and compromise: Permanent residence, family members / family life, and expulsion. These contentions have persisted since the adoption of the first legislative acts in 1958, and it is fair to assume that cases touching upon said issues potentially reveal deeper conflicts depending, of course, on the concrete facts.

The Commission's Proposal for 'Real Substance' of European Citizenship

The Commission's initial proposal encapsulates the common European interest of increased, unrestricted mobility and political union between the peoples of Europe. The Commission considered the Directive as 'a major step forward in giving real substance to Union citizenship,' meaning that 'Union citizens should enjoy freedom of movement and residence in the Member States, mutatis mutandis, in conditions similar to those enjoyed by citizens of a Member State moving and changing residence within their own country'.[26]

The main objective of the Citizenship Directive was to facilitate the exercise of rights, minimise administrative formalities, clarify the status of family members, create a new right of permanent residence, and restrict the possibility for Member States to refuse or terminate the right of residence on public policy grounds.[27]

The innovations included: 1) the extension of family reunification rights; 2) the reduction of administrative formalities; 3) the introduction of the right of permanent residence in the host Member State; and 4) an increased protection against expulsion.[28]

As Table 1 below demonstrates, the Commission's proposal invoked the Court's restriction-reducing and integration-promoting judgments in host states in *Watson*,[29] *Royer*,[30] *Echternach and Moritz*,[31] *Diatta*,[32] *Rutili*,[33] *Cowan*[34] and others, addressing the unconditional stay in the host State for up to six months, the abolition of residence cards and administrative formalities, the retention of rights of family members in the event of divorce or departure of the European citizen, and increased protection against expulsion.[35]

[26] Commission's proposal.

[27] ibid.

[28] See the explanatory memorandum to the proposed Dir 2004/38 at https://eur-lex.europa.eu/legal-content/EN/TXT/?uri=COM%3A2001%3A0257%3AFIN.

[29] Case 118/75, *Watson and Belmann*, ECLI:EU:C:1976:106.

[30] Case 48/75 Royer ECLI:EU:C:1976:57.

[31] Joined cases 389/87 and 390/87, *Echternach and Moritz*, ECLI:EU:C:1989:130.

[32] Case 267/83, *Aissatou Diatta v Land Berlin*, ECLI:EU:C:1985:67.

[33] Case 36/75, *Rutili*, ECLI:EU:C:1975:137.

[34] Case 186/87, *Cowan*, ECLI:EU:C:1989:4.

[35] Proposal for a European Parliament and Council Dir on the right of citizens of the Union and their family members to move and reside freely within the territory of the Member States /* COM/2001/0257 final – COD 2001/0111 */ Official Journal 270 E, 25/09/2001 P. 0150–0160.

The Commission's proposal to replace residence cards with a registration form followed the Court's ruling in *Royer*. The Court proclaimed that 'the right of Union citizens to enter the territory of another Member State and to reside there for the purposes specified by the Treaty is a right conferred directly by the Treaty or, in certain cases, by provisions implementing it and, as such, is a right acquired regardless of whether the competent authority in the host Member States has issued a residence card'.[36] By implication, 'the granting of a residence card should be regarded as an act by a Member State acknowledging the status that nationals of another Member State have in their own right by virtue of Community law'. European citizens would thus be granted the possibility to register with the competent authorities with a valid identity card or passport without further formalities.

The judgment in *Echternach* and *Moritz* supported the proposition for Article 12(3), strengthening the residence rights of family members after the departure or death of the European citizen from the host Member State regardless of sufficient resources or permanent residence. In this judgment, the Court held that the children of migrant workers should retain residence if their parents leave the territory of the host Member State for the duration of their secondary or post-secondary level studies. The judgment facilitated the completion of children's education by allowing them to pursue education in the system which they had become accustomed to.

Finally, the Court's judgment in *Adoui and Cornuaille*[37] underpinned the proposal's articles related to the conditions for the expulsion of European citizens, the procedural guarantees, and the duration of the measures.[38] Ms Adoui and Cornuaille, the applicants in the conjoined cases, were French citizens residing in Belgium. They challenged the refusal of the Belgian authority in Liege to issue them residence permits on the grounds of reasons of public policy; concretely, that the applicants were waitresses in a bar considered 'suspect from the point of view of morals' by the Belgian authorities. Among the numerous questions submitted to the Court was whether a Member State could expel and prohibit the citizens of another Member State to enter its territory on grounds of public policy for activities that would not trigger any repressive measures against its own nationals such as, engaging in prostitution. The Court's answer was negative, upholding the reasoning from the earlier *Bouchereau* case.[39] The personal conduct of the individual must present an existing and serious threat which would be equally applicable to nationals and European citizens.

[36] *Royer*, para 31.

[37] Joined cases 115 and 116/81, *Adoui and Cornuaille v Belgian State*, ECLI:EU:C:1982:183.

[38] NNic Shuibhne, 'Derogating from the Free Movement of Persons: When Can EU Citizens Be Deported?' (2006) 8 *Cambridge Yearbook of European Legal Studies* 187.

[39] Case 30/77, *Bouchereau*, ECLI:EU:C:1977:172.

The procedural safeguards, which the Commission relied on in the Directives' proposed Articles 28 to 31, reproduced in Table 1, included the requirement to ensure that the concerned individual understands the decision, that the decision must specify the exact reasons in writing, and offer the opportunity to prepare her defence and enable proper judicial review, repeating the *Rutili* dictum. The proposal also contained the obligation of the national court to review the legality of the contested decision and the facts forming the basis for it, and to reconsider the expulsion order in the case of changed individual circumstances. The Member States could furthermore exclude the concerned individual from their territory pending the hearing while also allowing in-person participation at the hearing. Finally, the Member States could take measures to prevent abuse.

Apart from direct references to individual judgments, the Commission's proposal referred to the Court's case-law writ large on the definition of a family member and the right to family life in the ECHR to strengthen the right of residence of divorced spouses and adult children no longer dependent on the Union citizen regardless of nationality in host Member States. The problem of residence, the Commission argued, was particularly acute for third-country nationals, in whose cases the need to balance family life and human dignity required careful calibration against the fear of the abusive use of rights.[40]

Table 1 Citizenship Rights Directive: Article of the proposal (column 1), the judgment serving as an argument (column 2) and whether the amendment proved contentious in the legislative process

Article of the Proposal / content	Judgment of the Court	Comment
Article 6 During the first six months of their stay, Union citizens may reside within the territory of another Member State simply with their passport or identity card	Case 118/75 *Watson*, paras. 17 and 18	Extension of unconditional stay Council opposed the six months stay, agreeing to a shorter unconditional stay of three months in the final text
Article 8 Abolition of residence cards, obligation to register	Case 48/75 *Royer*, para. 50 (residence card is not an authorisation, but simply a document recording a pre-existing right)	Unproblematic. EP insisted on further simplifications

(continued)

[40] Communication from the Commission to the European Parliament, the Council, the European conomic and social committee and the Committee of the regions; Free movement of European Jnion citizens and their families: Five actions to make a difference, available at https://eur-lex. uropa.eu/LexUriServ/LexUriServ.do?uri=COM:2013:0837:FIN:EN:PDF.

Table 1 *(Continued)*

Article of the Proposal / content	**Judgment of the Court**	**Comment**
Article 12(3) Retention of residence rights of family members after departure / death of European citizen / regardless of sufficient resources or permanent residence	Joined Cases 389/87 and 390/87 *Echternach and Moritz* (children should retain residence if their parent leaves the territory of the host Member State for the duration of the studies / secondary or post-secondary level)	
Article 13(2) Retention of the right of residence of family members in the event of divorce or annulment of marriage (non-nationals)	Case 267/83 *Diatta*, ECR 567, para. 20 (marital relationship cannot be regarded as dissolved if the spouses live separately, even where they intend to divorce at a later date)	The EP supported a broader definition of a family member
Article 19 Territorial scope of the right of residence and the right of permanent residence	Case 36/75 *Roland Rutili v Minister for the Interior* [1975] ECR 1219, para. 50. (Member States can only impose territorial restrictions on the right of residence and right of permanent residence if they also apply to its own nationals)	The Council opposed the time frame of four years as a qualification period. The EP supported the proposal. The final text agreed to a five-year qualification period
Article 21 Equal treatment	Case C-85/96 *María Martínez Sala v Bavaria Freistaat* [1998] ECR I-2691, point 62 (direct link between the principle of non-discrimination and the right of residence), applicable to family members who are not nationals of a Member State but enjoy the right of residence / permanent residence	
Article 22 Residence documents	Case 48/75 *Royer* [1976] ECR 497, para. 50 (inter alia); (The residence card is declaratory, not a precondition for exercising rights.)	

(continued

Table 1 *(Continued)*

Article of the Proposal / content	Judgment of the Court	Comment
Article 23 (1) Identity checks	Case 321/87 *Commission v Belgium* [1989] ECR 997, para. 12 (equal treatment between non-nationals)	
Article 23(2) Identity checks / sanctions	Case C-265/88 *Messner* [1989] ECR 4209, para. 14 Case C-24/97 *Commission v Germany* [1998] (same penalties)	
Article 24 Limits on the right of entry and the right to reside on grounds of public policy, public security or public health	Case 155/79 *Regina v Pieck* [1980] ECR 2171 (Member States may not rely on public policy, public security or public health as general grounds or without case-specific justification in order to restrict the exercise of the right to move and reside freely)	Aim to tighten the definition of the concept of public policy by incorporating established case-law, strengthen procedural safeguards, and provide greater protection against expulsion by taking account of how integrated the Union citizen is in the host country, as well as providing absolute protection for minors with family ties in the host country and for people with permanent residence status.
Article 25 Measures taken on grounds of public policy or public security	Case 30/77 *Bouchereau* [1977] ECR 1999, para. 35 (the threat represented by the individual must be present and serious, and founded on personal conduct). Cases 115 and 116/81 *Adoui and Cornuaille*, point 8 (defines the concept of serious threat and requires equal treatment).	Measures must be based on the personal conduct of the individual. A previous criminal conviction does not justify the automatic adoption of such measures (Directive 64/221/EEC, Article 3(1) and (2)).

(continued)

Table 1 *(Continued)*

Article of the Proposal / content	Judgment of the Court	Comment
Article 28 Notification of decisions refusing entry or expulsion decisions	*Adoui and Cornuaille* [1982] ECR 1665, para. 13 (Member States must make sure that the person concerned understands the decision). *Rutili* [1975] ECR 1219, para. 39 (the decision must specify the exact reasons, so that the person is in a position to prepare their defence, in writing, thus enabling proper judicial review)	Article 7 of Directive 64/221/EEC Article 6 of Directive 64/221/EEC The Member States were almost unanimously opposed to absolute protection against expulsion for Union citizens and the members of their families who have acquired the right of permanent residence in the host Member State. However, they did agree to increased protection for Union citizens who have lived for a number of years in the host Member State. Consequently, the compromise included in the common position takes the form of increased protection depending on the length of residence in the territory of the host Member State.[41]
Article 29 (4) Procedural safeguards (refusal of entry, expulsion)	*Adoui and Cornuaille*, para. 15 (the national court must review the legality of the contested decision and not the facts which form the basis for it.)	

(continued)

[41] Communication from the Commission to the European Parliament pursuant to the second subparagraph of Art 251 (2) of the EC Treaty concerning the common position of the Council on the adoption of a European Parliament and Council Dir on the right of citizens of the Union and their family members to move and reside freely within the territory of the Member States /* SEC/2003/1293 final – COD 2001/0111 */ at https://eur-lex.europa.eu/legal-content/EN/TXT/?uri=CELEX%3A52003SC1293.

Table 1 *(Continued)*

Article of the Proposal / content	**Judgment of the Court**	**Comment**
Article 29(5)	Member States can exclude the individual concerned from their territory pending the hearing, while ensuring the individual's presence in person at the hearing and protecting their fundamental right to a fair trial Case 98/79 (*Pecastaing*, para. 13).	
Article 30 (1) Duration of exclusion orders	*Adoui and Cornuaille*, point 12; Case C-348/96, Donatella Calfa (prohibiting life-long exclusion orders against people who have been expelled on grounds of public policy or public security.)	
Articles 30 (2) and (3)	*Adoui and Cornuaille* (Member States must consider any material changes in the circumstances which justified the first expulsion order). *Adoui and Cornuaille*, para. 12 (avoidance of abuses of the system; no access while new application is being considered).	
Article 31 Expulsion as a penalty or legal consequence	Case 186/87, *Cowan*, para. 19 (States retain competences under criminal law but may not restrict the fundamental freedoms protected under Community law.)[42]	Council strongly opposed absolute protection against expulsion of permanently resident European citizens.

[42] Before ordering the expulsion of a Union citizen or family member, irrespective of nationality, as a penalty or legal consequence in accordance with national legislation, national criminal courts and administrative authorities will now be required to have regard to Community law, principally the provisions of this Dir, and in particular Arts 25, 26, 27 and 30(1).

To summarise, the initial proposal reflects the Commission's interest in greater rights protection and mobility for European citizens, relying on the Court's case-law to entrench or strengthen the rights to move and reside, expanding their scope of application or working out procedural guarantees. On another level, the Commission could strategically incorporate the Court's case-law in the proposal, anticipating future litigation and conflict, increasing the likelihood of the Court's support of its position by pre-empting future interpretation of legislative provisions based on the case-law. Alternatively, the reliance on the Court's case-law could have been sending a reassuring message to the Member States sitting in the Council that they have practically already accepted the legal developments and hence, their codification in the Citizenship Directive would not be adding any new rights to the existing legislation. For the Court, it was symbolic text of the political acceptance of its legal vision of free movement rights.

The Process and the Compromise

The Commission submitted its proposal to the European Parliament in 2001 on the basis of Articles 18, 21, 46, 50, and 52 TFEU following the ordinary (co-decision) legislative procedure (Article 294 TFEU).

The Parliament proposed numerous amendments that were more overtly and ambitiously integrationist and socially progressive than the Commission's proposal, insisting on equal treatment for same-sex couples (broadening the definition of a 'family member' under beneficiaries of the Directive), strengthening the right to family life along with the right to family reunification on humanitarian grounds, and absolute protection against the expulsion of minors and permanently resident European citizens. It strongly recommended further reductions in the administrative formalities burdening migrant citizens and their family members regardless of nationality (unconditional residence for six months, simplified procedure for issuing residence cards on a voluntary basis for the citizens).[43]

The Committee of the Regions endorsed the Proposal, welcoming consolidation, highlighting the narrower interest of streamlining of administrative formalities 'with a view to relieving the bureaucratic pressure on local and regional authorities'.[44] The Social and Economic Committee similarly approved of the simplification, but raised concerns about the scope and the effectiveness of rights protection – a narrower interest of increased social protection within

[43] European Parliament legislative resolution on the proposal for a European Parliament and Council Dir on the right of citizens of the Union and their family members to move and reside freely within the territory of the Member States (COM(2001) 257 – C5-0336/2001–2001/0111(COD)) OJ C 43E, 19.2.2004, p 42–59.

[44] Opinion of the Committee of the Regions on the 'Proposal for a European Parliament and Council Directive on the right of citizens of the Union and their family members to move and reside freely within the territory of the Member States' OJ C 192, 12.8.2002, p 17–19.

its area of competence. Concretely, it held that the Proposal should extend the protection of those enrolled in vocational training to all students admitted to a course of training. Moreover, it held that the wording 'particularly difficult circumstances' in the provision guaranteeing residence rights of family members after the dissolution of their links with the European citizens, should explicitly cover domestic and gender-based violence which it purported, as per the Commission's explanatory memorandum, to cover. Those recommendations came with a series of proposals for further strengthening the rights of disadvantaged groups, like the requirement of sufficient resources depriving the poor of free movement rights.

The Council discussed the Commission's Proposal in section B of the agenda. The latter is reserved for politically sensitive items requiring discussion at the highest political level, items from previous Council meetings, and items without agreement in the Coreper or the working parties.[45]

The discussion of the initial proposal in the Council focused on the registration system in the host State; the concept of a family member; and protection against expulsion.[46] The Council expressed reservations to the proposed period of six months in which the Union's citizens and their families may reside without conditions and with no formality in a Member State other than that of their nationality. It questioned the period of four years of continuous residence, after which time citizens would acquire the right of permanent residence without conditions and with access to social welfare and immunity from expulsion. Finally, the Council debated the idea of broadening and unifying the definition of a family member.

The Commission amended its proposal mitigating between the EP's demands and the Council's concerns. Its communication to the EP reveals that 1) the definition of family members, Article 2(2)(b) has been confined to registered partnership where the legislation of the host Member State regards this situation as equivalent to marriage. The wording excluded de facto long-term relationships, which was offset by the addition of a new provision in Article 3 on the duty of the Member States to facilitate the entry and residence of a partner in such a relationship with the Union citizen having the primary right of residence; 2) that it yielded to the Council's unwillingness to accept the extension of unconditional residence to six months, while also raising the length of residence required to give entitlement to permanent residence from four to five years. 3) Moreover, the Commission accepted the Council's refusal of the proposed absolute protection against the removal of minors and permanent residents, mitigated by the fact that the Council agreed to increased protection of long-term residents.

[45] See Common Position (EC) No 6/2004 of 5 December 2003 at https://eur-lex.europa.eu/legal-content/EN/TXT/?uri=celex%3A52004AG0006.

[46] https://ec.europa.eu/commission/presscorner/detail/en/PRES_02_344.

The Commission insisted that the compromise marked a major step forward in terms of freedom of movement and residence. The European Parliament's Committee on Citizens' Freedoms and Rights, Justice and Home Affairs reluctantly accepted the proposed solutions. The points of contention unsurprisingly remained the rules on permanent residence, the definition of family members, work requirements, and expulsion.[47]

These contentions reflect economic, political, and social concerns of the states dealing with the influx of foreign workers and their family members in relation to social security, employment and social policy, organisation of the labour market and education.

C. FREE MOVEMENT DISPUTES: LEGAL ISSUES

The case-law has not only changed but also diversified. Table 2 offers a cursory glance at the case-law over five-year periods, listing the legal issues that the Court has dealt with.[48] The overview of the legal issues guided the selection of the parameters of good judgment (information about the case). The absolute numbers reflect the legal issues – one judgment can address more than one legal question, typically reflected in the subject matter which the Court assigns to the case. The information in the Table, however, is based on the reading of the judgments and the consideration of the facts of the case with the exception of the information on the expulsion cases, bottom row in Table 2. In this sense, it is independent of the legislative changes and the emergence of new labels, and closer to the legal doctrinal understanding of the free movement law problématique.

As Table 2 demonstrates, questions of equal treatment based on nationality, derived rights (the rights of family members of economically active or inactive persons), and work-related social advantages and benefits are consistently present. The past two decades have also been marked by the increase of cases raising questions of residence rights, recognition of diplomas, expulsion, and tax related questions like tax deductions. By contrast, the first decades' disputes mostly tackled social security matters pertaining to old age, invalidity, and unemployment of migrant workers. Changes in legislation (the adoption of the Citizenship Directive), Treaty changes (the Charter), enlargement, and case-law have likely co-shaped these shifts.

[47] The EP's reservations can be reconstructed from the minority opinions of two Committee members lamenting the EP's timidity and compliance, and habit of giving way to the Council's threats. See Recommendation for second reading on the Council common position with a view to the adoption of a European Parliament and Council Dir on the right of citizens of the Union and their family members to move and reside freely within the territory of the Member States (13263/3/2003 – C5-0014/2004–2001/0111(COD)).

[48] All judgments have been coded by research assistants.

Table 2 Free movement of persons disputes: Overview of legal issues

LEGAL ISSUE / DISPUTE (ALPHABETICAL)	1960	1965	1970	1975	1980	1985	1990	1995	2000	2005	2010	2015	2020	ALL
Access to labour market	0	0	0	1	1	3	2	1	4	6	2	4	1	25
Children or family related benefits	0	0	1	7	10	12	11	14	7	9	15	8	2	96
Derived rights	0	0	7	9	15	28	20	23	18	17	32	22	2	193
Equal treatment (at issue)	0	3	9	15	10	35	35	38	43	42	31	32	9	302
Financial solidarity	0	0	0	0	0	0	0	4	21	21	32	11	0	89
Health related benefits	2	2	5	4	0	4	6	5	10	7	4	1	1	51
Invalidity/incapacity to work	0	0	7	28	17	9	12	12	0	3	4	6	0	98
Old-age related benefits	0	7	9	7	13	7	26	13	12	8	15	18	2	137
Public service exception	0	0	1	1	2	4	3	10	5	6	3	2	0	37
Recognition of diplomas	0	0	0	1	0	2	10	10	14	27	11	6	1	82
Residence rights	0	0	1	6	4	5	10	12	14	17	35	21	5	130
Reunification with family members	0	0	0	0	0	1	0	1	4	5	6	6	0	23
Social assistance	0	0	0	0	0	3	1	4	3	1	1	2	2	17
Student maintenance / grants	0	0	1	1	1	8	5	2	2	5	6	5	1	37
Tax breaks (income)	0	0	0	1	0	3	1	5	6	14	7	13	1	51
Unemployment related benefits	0	0	0	8	4	6	6	6	8	1	1	1	0	41
Work related benefits	2	11	7	11	8	7	17	15	17	19	12	11	0	137
Expulsion (Eurlex data)	0	0	1	2	3	4	4	6	9	17	21	10	0	76

D. THE PARAMETERS OF GOOD JUDGMENT

This section presents and contextualises the parameters of case-law – the legally relevant characteristics and the information about the case – in the free movement of persons judgments, using examples from the annotated judgments. The first subsection describes and illustrates the relevant legal characteristics. The second subsection lists the relevant information about the disputes – the applicants and the legal framework which shape the Court's reasoning and case outcomes. The institutional characteristics are explored in more detail in chapter seven.

i. Non-Sanctioning Europeanisation of National Policies

In a judgment scrutinising but not sanctioning national policies which directly regulate or affect the free movement of persons (like access of non-nationals to certain posts or health and safety at work), the Court de facto scrutinises national policy choices through a European prism, elaborating a supranational standard.

The Court's judgments concerning free movement of goods and persons follow a predictable structure or a typical model of justification. In the first step, the Court examines whether a disputed national measure or practice restricts free movement rights. Upon finding a restriction, it further considers whether a national measure or practice is justified and whether it is proportionate. Although the methodology 'is one of the most predictable and formulaic features of free movement case-law',[49] it is also the most interesting from the perspective of good judgment; the Court can accept a tenuous justification for non-legal reasons, acting under political pressure or avoiding negative economic implications.

A national measure can restrict free movement because it discriminates on grounds of nationality prohibited by Article 18 TEU. Member States can justify such measures on grounds of public policy, public security, or public health (Article 45(3) TFEU, allowing exceptions from equal treatment regarding employment, remuneration and other conditions of work and employment. They can also justify non-discriminatory restrictions, if they pursue legitimate aims and are necessary for attaining them (are proportionate). Literature suggests that the Court often finds a national measure under scrutiny restrictive end obstructing free movement but allows an open-ended list of justifications, meaning that the real scrutiny takes place at the level

[49] N Nic Shuibhne, *The Coherence of EU Free Movement Law: Constitutional Responsibility and the Court of Justice* (Oxford, Oxford University Press, 2013) 24.

of proportionality.[50] Thus, it is sensible to examine the discrimination test and proportionality review – the two significant components of justification – separately and jointly, relative to each other, without pressing them into the mould of template justification.

Proportionality has been described as a legal tool offering judges and lawyers a framework to engage in policy analysis unconstrained by legal authority.[51] In a more lax or two-pronged test, the Court examines whether the State's policy choices are suitable and necessary to achieve the proclaimed aims. In a stricter or three-pronged review the Court also weighs national policy choices against individual European rights. Its judgment about the suitability and necessity of national regulatory choices as well as the intensity of their interference with those rights overrides the regulatory choices of national policymakers. In *Baumbast*,[52] for instance, the Court examined whether a measure justifying the refusal of Mr Baumbast's residence due to a sickness insurance policy which excluded emergency treatment on the territory of the State where he was living disproportionately interfered with his citizenship rights under Article 18(1) EC regulated in Directive 90/364. In *Aladzhov*,[53] the Court examined whether a national measure prohibiting individuals with outstanding tax liability from leaving the national territory was appropriate and necessary to achieve the pursued objective, that is, tax collection.[54]

The Court can engage with the argument of equal treatment referring to the general principle of non-discrimination, often using the vocabulary of distinct, differentiated, different, unequal or identical treatment, Gleichbehandlung, and less favourable position/situation, equality of treatment, and overt or covert. For instance, the Court discussed unequal treatment in *Pusa*[55] with reference to *D'Hoop*:[56] 'in that a citizen of the Union must be granted in all Member States the same treatment in law as that accorded to the nationals of those Member States who find themselves in the same situation, it would be incompatible with the right of freedom of movement were a citizen, in the Member State of which he is a national, to receive treatment less favourable than he would enjoy if he

[50] J Snell, 'General Principles in Free Movement Law: Applicability and Application' in KS Ziegler, PJ Neuvonen, and V Moreno-Lax (eds), *Research Handbook on General Principles in EU Law* (Cheltenham, Edward Elgar Publishing, 2022).

[51] M Kumm, 'Internationale Handelsgesellschaft, Nold and the New Human Rights Paradigm' in MP Maduro and L Azoulai (eds), *The Past and Future of EU Law The Classics of EU Law Revisited on the 50th Anniversary of the Rome Treaty* (London, Bloomsbury Publishing, 2010) 110.

[52] Case C-413/99, *Baumbast and R*, ECLI:EU:C:2002:493.

[53] C-434/10, *Aladzhov*, ECLI:EU:C:2011:750.

[54] Concretely, Mr Aladzhov could not leave the national territory only because a company he was co-managing owed tax to the State, regardless of his personal conduct and threat to a public policy of any kind. The Court held that the measure was incompatible with the Citizenship Dir (Article 27(2)).

[55] Case C-224/02, *Pusa*, ECLI:EU:C:2004:273.

[56] Case C-224/98, *D'Hoop*, ECLI:EU:C:2002:432.

had not availed himself of the opportunities offered by the Treaty in relation to freedom of movement (*D'Hoop*, paragraph 30)'.[57]

In *Commission v. Denmark*, the Court interpreted the prohibition of discrimination (Article 39 EC, now 45 TFEU) with reference to its previous case-law: 'it is settled case-law that Article 39 EC prohibits not only all discrimination, direct or indirect, based on nationality, but also national rules which are applicable irrespective of the nationality of the workers concerned but impede their freedom of movement (*Graf*, paragraph 18, and *Weigel*, paragraphs 50 and 51)'.[58]

Such engagement of the Court with the argument of unequal treatment undoubtedly subject to discussion when delving into the justificatory style is separate from the decision about whether the disputed measure was discriminatory; its decision whether the measure was discriminatory does not lead to the decision that it was incompatible with the rules of free movement, as argued above.

The legal characteristic labelled discrimination refers to the Court's final decision, that is the decision whether the measure unjustifiably treats non-nationals differently from its own nationals. It can overlap with its decision about the compatibility of the national measure with European Union law. The latter category is, however, broader because it extends to non-discriminating and indirectly discriminating measures. An example is the *Sayn-Wittgenstein* judgment,[59] where the Court considered the interference of Austrian rules about the use of nobility titles with individual rights to move freely. The Court assessed the proportionality of the disputed national measure prohibiting the use of such titles with free movement rights of individuals but found it was defensible by European standards using Article 4(2) TEU aka the respect for the national identity clause.

The analytical framework of good judgment is a conceptually more precise and accurate means of examining the interplay of legal arguments in the Court's reasoning and the outcomes that these arguments logically lead to; it is comparable across procedures and disputes, and between the institutions because it broadens the analysis to the consideration of non-legal reasons leading to the same or opposite outcome.

The Court does more than simply engage in a restriction-justification-proportionality analysis.[60] It searches for a solution that reconciles the national constitutional arrangements with sensitive histories such as the Austrian nobility titles, or the Irish language requirements and the common European prism

[57] *Pusa*, para 18.

[58] Case C-464/02, *Commission v Denmark*, ECLI: EU:C:2005:546, para 45.

[59] Case C-208/09, *Sayn-Wittgenstein*, ECLI: EU:C:2010:806.

[60] For the distinction and the argument that the Court is a compulsive reconciler see G Davies 'Free Movement, the Quality of Life and the Myth That the Court Balances Interests' in P Koutrakos, N Nic Shuibhne, and P Syrpis (eds), *Exceptions from EU Free Movement Law: Derogation, Justification and Proportionality* (Oxford, Hart Publishing, 2016).

of free movement. At times, it finds ways to subsume them under the common European arrangement.

An example of interest-reconciliation is *Wencel*,[61] a case concerning the Polish widow of a Polish worker in Germany. Ms Wencel habitually resided between Poland and Germany and was thus entitled to her own old age pension in Poland since 1990 as well as to a survivor's pension in Germany since 2008. The dispute arose when the Polish social security institution demanded that Ms Wencel retroactively repay the pension she had received from Poland for three years. The preliminary reference sought a clarification on the rules of habitual residence and Regulation 1408/71. The Court ruled that Poland could not retroactively withdraw a retirement pension under the European rules (Regulation 1408/71). However, it could reduce the pension paid in Germany by applying its national rules prohibiting the cumulation of benefits. Moreover, the Court held that the reduction of the pension was compatible with Article 45 TFEU if the reduction did not disproportionately disadvantage a person who exercised her free movement rights compared to a person who did not.

The question of double habitual residence was also a consequential decision about overlapping social security benefits – the higher German and the lower Polish. As the Advocate General remarked, the case would allow the Court to clarify its social security case-law and the legal issues which often arose in connection with the accession to the European Union of new Member States and the application to them of transitional provisions.[62]

ii. Individual Protection and Deferral of Authority in Judgments Upholding European Rights and Principles

A deferential judgment upholding and expanding European rights and principles reflects the Court's attempt to protect individual rights without unsettling the power balance between the states and the European Union. The Court will suspend the application of a rights-protective or rights-generative interpretation of European law by delegating the decision-making authority to the national institutions.

The protection of the individual and deference can capture this situation. The former refers to the Court's interpretation directly affecting the claim which a natural person makes in the main proceedings (preliminary reference proceedings) or in a direct action. Outcomes in favour of the individual which go against the respondent Member State are those decisions of the Court which uphold a right based on European law, rights of European

[61] Case C-589/10, *Janina Wencel*, ECLI: EU:C:2013:303.

[62] Opinion of Mr Advocate General Cruz Villalón delivered on 24 May 2012 in Case C-589/10, *Janina Wencel*, ECLI:EU:C:2012:304, para 3.

workers or non-economically active European citizens such as students, their family members, and instances where the Court protects the individual from an expulsion measure.

For instance, in *Lawrie Blum*,[63] the Court decided that a trainee teacher receiving remuneration was a worker within the meaning of the Treaty. This 'categorisation' implied that the applicant, Ms Lawrie Blum, could sit the examination necessary to qualify as a teacher in Germany under the same conditions as German nationals. By contrast, the Court's interpretation of Regulation 883/2004 on the coordination of social security systems in *Schiphorst*[64] allowed the national institutions to refuse the extension of the unemployment benefit export beyond three months as a matter of principle; it did not support Mr Schiphorst's request to extend this period.

Deference is a parameter indicative of the Court's willingness to allocate the decision-making authority. The Court can offer an abstract and general answer to the preliminary questions, leaving the national court substantive leeway to decide whether the facts of the case lend themselves to the suggested interpretation. For instance, in cases concerning the liability of the State for the breaches of European Union law, the Court can let the national court determine whether the breach was sufficiently serious, indicating only general circumstances. Often, the assessment of facts and the correct interpretation of the applicable rules are decisive for the outcome of the case. For example, the Court can decide that the outcome hinges on a particular aspect of national law, which the referring court must interpret, or suggests that the referring court will have to decide whether a measure is appropriate or pursuing a legitimate aim, or whether an Article of the Treaty applies to the dispute. By providing only abstract formulas the Court de facto reneges its interpretive authority.

Deference in the reasoning or in the operative part seeks to establish how the Court allocates the decision-making authority. Deference is not an automatic legal response to politics. National courts often refer unclear or open-ended questions, fail to provide the Court with sufficient background of the dispute, or challenge national legislation through the backdoor of broad Treaty principles.[65] This requires additional analysis of the context, in which the Court decides to defer crucial decision to the referring court.

[63] Case 66/85, *Lawrie-Blum*, ECLI:EU:C:1986:284.

[64] Case C-551/16, *Klein Schiphorst*, ECLI:EU:C:2018:200.

[65] The Court often reformulates the preliminary questions of national courts, who seek answers to the questions of compatibility of national law with European Union law, often using the latter to challenge the former. See HW Micklitz, *The Politics of Judicial Co-Operation in the European Union: Sunday Trading, Equal Treatment and Good Faith* (Cambridge, Cambridge University Press, 2005). Generally on the formulation (and reformulation) of preliminary questions see U Šadl and A Wallerman, '"The Referring Court Asks, in Essence": Is Reformulation of Preliminary Questions by the Court of Justice a Decision Writing Fixture or a Decision-Making Approach?' (2019) 25 *European Law Journal* 416.

iii. Bounded Undesirable Interpretation

A judgment with bounded undesirable interpretation balances the implications of the ruling on the regulatory autonomy of the Member States with the development of European Union law. The three legal characteristics which reflect the rationale of bounded undesirable interpretation are the implications for the Member States' autonomy, the Court's approach to interpretation, and the doctrinal importance of the judgment: its contribution to the acquis.

The legal characteristic labelled as the law-making initiative refers to the willingness of the Court to interpret European Union law expansively. Expansive approach includes comprehensive replies to preliminary questions, at times reformulating them beyond the scope set by the referring court, exhaustive answers and interpretations based on the purpose of the law. Purposive interpretation has become a hallmark of the Court's integrationist approach, at times criticised as competence creep or illegitimate policymaking.[66] Among the typical formulations expanding the scope of free movement, the range of rights and at times European Union's competence in adjacent policy areas are the formulas of the existence and the exercise of competence, the fundamental citizenship status, the effective protection of rights and the full effect of European Union law, a useful answer to the national court, the necessary conditions for the proper functioning of the common market or the protection of individual rights, and a reference to the common constitutional traditions.

By contrast, narrow answers to the preliminary questions, interpretations that contain the scope of application of European Union law, reliance on the wording of the interpreted provisions, a statement that the reasoning or interpretation applies to the circumstances of the case or are valid in the case at hand characterise a restrained approach. Overall, a restrained Court would be more deferential toward the legislator or highlight legislative intent. To illustrate, in *Givane*[67] the Court held 'if the Community legislature had wished that periods of residence further removed from the date of the worker's death could be taken into consideration, it would have been appropriate to include, in the wording of Regulation 1251/70, an express time-limit in that regard as well as conditions relating to the family members of the worker, such as the date of his marriage'.[68]

The legal characteristic of doctrinal contribution relates to the substantive legal aspect of the free movement judgments. It captures the judicial development of the free movement of persons and European citizenship law, often with a ripple effect on adjacent policy areas. Doctrine is a set of rules and principles,

[66] Most famously formulated by H Rasmussen, *On Law and Policy in the European Court of Justice: A Comparative Study in Judicial Policymaking* (Leiden, Brill, 1986).

[67] C-257/00, *Givane*, ECLI: EU:C:2003:8.

[68] *Givane*, para 49.

which determine the scope and the content of rights and duties.[69] The judgments can create tests and principles facilitating free movement rights (equal access to the labour market, conditions of employment or residence, as well as the associated benefits), and expand them to new categories of citizens or situations.

In *Bidar*,[70] the Court ruled that the Treaty prohibition of discrimination (Article 18 TFEU) extended to student subsidized loans and grants. The ruling is remarkable in reversing the established case-law, *Lair*[71] and *Brown*,[72] where the Court held the exact opposite, namely that student loans and maintenance grants fell outside the scope of the Treaty, qualifying as education and social policy. The former fell outside the European Union's competence; in the latter, the Member States retained their competence in areas not covered by specific EEC Treaty provisions.[73]

The Court justified the new development by reading the prohibition of discrimination in Article 18 TFEU with the provisions introduced in the Treaty after its ruling in *Lair* and *Brown*: European citizenship (Articles 20 and 21 TFEU), education, and vocational training. Following *Bidar*, the Member States had to extend the subsidised loans and grants to well-integrated, lawfully resident students from other Member States. Thus, the Court did not unconditionally expand the reach of free movement law (the principle of non-discrimination). Only those students who could establish a real link with the society of the host Member State[74] could access the subsidised loans and grants, for instance by showing that they were educated in or had resided there for a certain period. By contrast, they did not need to show a link with the employment market.

In *Commission v Netherlands*[75] the Court examined a residence requirement which tied the eligibility for exportable higher education grants to a lawful residence in the Netherlands for at least three of the six years prior to enrolment. The residence requirement applied to migrant workers, including frontier workers and members of their families. Following the established case-law discussed extensively in the judgment, the Court concluded that the 'three out of six years' rule was disproportionate, and unnecessary to prevent abuse and unburden the public finances, both recognised as legitimate aims of the legislation. The outcome clarified the case-law on the conditions for eligibility for student grants without adding to the acquis.

[69] This is a simplistic definition. For an exhaustive debate and definition see Aleksander Peczenik, 'A Theory of Legal Doctrine' (2001) 14 *Ratio Juris* 75.

[70] Case C-209/03, *Bidar*, ECLI: EU:C:2005:169.

[71] Case 39/86, *Lair*, ECLI:EU:C:1988:322.

[72] Case 197/86, *Brown*, ECLI: EU:C:1988:323.

[73] *Bidar*, para 38.

[74] A requirement first mentioned in *D'Hoop* where the Court held that the Member States could not refuse tide-over allowances to its citizens seeking their first employment only because they completed their studies (or secondary education) in another Member State. While such general and exclusive condition was unnecessary, the Member States could legitimately impose the requirement of 'a real link between the applicant for that allowance and the geographic employment market concerned' (*D'Hoop*, par. 38).

[75] Case C-542/09, *Commission v Netherlands*, ECLI:EU:C:2012:346.

As the above examples suggest, the analysis sets a high bar to distinguish landmark or legally remarkable free movement of persons and European citizenship judgments from the regular ebb and flow of the jurisprudence. Five categories of judgments will typically be legally significant: 1) judgments reversing the existing case-law like the reversal of *Lair* and *Brown* in *Bidar* discussed above; 2) judgments strengthening or entrenching the existing case-law, especially if the latter stirred debate, for instance *Kücükdeveci*[76] confirming the controversial *Mangold*[77] principle of non-discrimination on grounds of age in horizontal disputes; 3) judgments expanding the scope of application of the existing principles for instance the principle of state liability to courts for failing to refer preliminary questions in free movement of persons disputes like in *Kobler*;[78] 4) judgments introducing autonomous concepts or principles like the concept of a worker[79] or a genuine enjoyment of citizenship rights in *Zambrano*[80]; or 5) judgments assigning constitutional status to Treaty concepts (European citizenship as the fundamental status in *Grzelczyk*).[81] This list is not exhaustive.

Given that the Court typically reverses the case-law tacitly and rarely proclaims new principles or tests explicitly (the latter often being the work of scholars in the civil law tradition), the annotation of judgments relies heavily on the familiarity of the annotators with the policy area and the state of the case-law.

Finally, the legal characteristic implications for the autonomy of the Member States refers to the effect of the Court's ruling on the power of the Member State to independently regulate access and conditions of work, social security, employment, taxation, or healthcare, conforming with societal values and national interest. This includes specific initiatives that the Member State supports, the policies that it pursues, and the means chosen to implement them such as family friendly policies with special family benefits or additional benefits for single working parents and young families; special qualifications for certain jobs; language requirements for civil servants; or stricter immigration controls from non-European Union countries.

Lord Bruce of Donington is an interesting early judgment restricting the regulatory autonomy of the Member State.[82] The dispute concerned the taxation of travel allowances (lump sums) paid to a British member of the European Parliament under the British tax rules. The Court recognized that the Member States were competent to tax the income of the Members of the European Parliament under the national rules. However, the duty of loyal cooperation (then Article 5 EEC) obliged them to support the internal functioning of the

[76] Case C-555/07, *Kücükdeveci*, ECLI:EU:C:2010:21.
[77] Case C-144/04, *Mangold*, ECLI: EU:C:2005:709.
[78] Case C-224/01, *Köbler*, ECLI: EU:C:2003:513.
[79] Case 75/63, *Hoekstra (born Unger)*, ECLI: EU:C:1964:19.
[80] Case C-34/09, *Zambrano*, ECLI: EU:C:2011:124.
[81] Case C-184/99, *Grzelczyk*, ECLI: EU:C:2001:458.
[82] Case 208/80, *Lord Bruce of Donington*, ECLI: EU:C:1981:194.

institutions of the Community and respect the first paragraph of Article 8 of The Protocol on the privileges and immunities of the European Communities, effectively prohibiting inter alia any practices in matters restricting the free movement of Members of the Parliament. To contain this interpretation, the Court allowed the Member States to exceptionally tax the excessive lump sums under the national income tax if they constituted 'disguised remuneration'.[83] However, the Member State had to consider European Union law in matters of taxation of travel allowances.

The Court's interpretation of an annex to Regulation 1408/71 in *Nijhuis*,[84] by contrast, strengthened the national regulatory autonomy. The ruling permits the Netherlands to differentiate between the periods of insurance completed by a worker in another Member State and those completed in the Netherlands under a special scheme for civil servants. In the concrete case, if Mr Nijhuis worked only in the Netherlands, his invalidity benefits would be independent of the length of insurance coverage.[85] The Court held that the situation was unfortunate but unavoidable given the absence of coordination of social security systems between the Member States for civil servants: not a matter of shared competence. The Member States were thus free to introduce their own social security arrangements and impose the conditions for the access to benefits according to their policy preferences.

iv. Relevant Information about Free Movement of Persons Cases

Upholding the claims of individual migrant workers, family members, or other groups of migrants, imposes duties on the Member States, often disturbing or undoing national rules and interfering with national policies.[86] On a more symbolic level, common rules and principles, as well as the intervention of the Court in these matters reconfigures the relationship between the state and the subjects residing on its territory. The controversy over the disruptive influence of the Court on national welfare systems and the suggested alienating effect of European citizenship case-law on the 'bond' between the citizen and her homeland make the Court's rulings in these matters extremely sensitive.[87]

[83] *Lord Bruce of Donington*, para 21.

[84] Case C-360/97, *Nijhuis*, ECLI: EU:C:1999:180.

[85] *Nijhuis*, para 27.

[86] Based on the analysis of the collected judgments in the area of free movement of persons it is possible to conclude that around 85% of judgments concern disputes between individuals and between individuals and state administrations. Literature and case-law seem to corroborate this intuition of opposing interests.

[87] FW Scharpf, 'The European Social Model' (2002) 40 *Journal of Common Market Studies* 645; JHH Weiler, 'To Be a European Citizen-Eros and Civilization' (1997) 4 *Journal of European Public Policy* 495.

The facts of the case – such as the family or economic status of a person (a jobseeker, a worker, a student, retired citizen, or accompanying family member), nationality, or gender of the applicants in the main proceedings or groups of citizens affected by disputed national measures – will intuitively be pertinent in interpreting free movement rules, determining access to benefits, education, or employment, and the right to reside.

Similarly, the information about the legal framework, or the legal provision which the Court is asked to interpret, can influence the Court's reasoning and outcomes. For instance, the Court is freer to interpret vague Treaty articles than concrete legislative provisions, more likely to scrutinise discriminatory than non-discriminatory Member State measures or intangible administrative obstacles, and act as a more legitimate authority in areas where the European Union enjoys shared competence. The information about the legal provision at the heart of the dispute, its legal rank, policy area, and the type of proceedings can prove decisive. In *Wencel*, as discussed above, the relevant information includes nationality, economic activity, the civil status of the applicant (an older retired widow of a former worker), the benefit in question (a retirement pension as well as a survivor's pension), and the legal framework of social security as a policy area where the European Union only exercises a coordinating or supporting regulatory role. The fact that the applicant was a national of the state from which she claimed her benefit might have eased the conflict. Conversely, a ruling indicating that the interpretation would extend to all European citizens in the future required a solution, allowing the Member State to apply its own national rules and make policy choices.

While the information about the applicant sometimes appears important to the Court's decision about the correct interpretation or application of free movement rules and the scope of European citizenship, the institutional characteristics could prove key to the understanding of good judgment. The number of intervening Member States, their positions expressed during the procedure, the participation of the Advocate General in the case, the sitting formation, and the provisions that the Court interprets (the Treaty or the legislation) correlate with doctrinal developments that probe the limits of European competence.[88] The assignment of the case to the first chamber in *Wencel*, for instance, could mean that the case did not raise new legal questions.[89]

[88] U Šadl and S Hermansen, 'The European Court of Justice, an Able and Unwilling Lawmaker: Evidence from 920 Free Movement of Persons Judgments' in M Dawson, E Muir, and B DeWitte (eds), *Revisiting Judicial Politics in the European Union* (Cheltenham, Edward Elgar Publishing, 2024).

[89] Art 60 of the Court's Rules of Procedure states that '[t]he Court shall assign to the Chambers of five and of three Judges any case brought before it in so far as the difficulty or importance of the case or particular circumstances are not such as to require that it should be assigned to the Grand Chamber, unless a Member State or an institution of the European Union participating in the proceedings has requested that the case be assigned to the Grand Chamber, pursuant to the third paragraph of Article 16 of the Statute.' See Rules of Procedure of the Court of Justice OJ L 265 p 1–42.

Furthermore, the legislative history of the interpreted provision can highlight political disagreement and compromise around individual legislative solutions. At times, the Court refers to both. For instance, *Schiphorst* concerned the meaning of Article 64 of Regulation 883/2004, entitled 'Unemployed persons going to another Member State.' The first limb of the Article states that unemployed persons who move to another Member State to seek work can retain their national unemployment benefit for three months. The second limb states that competent services or institutions may extend this period to a maximum of six months. The intervening governments (Dutch, Danish, Swedish, and Norwegian) argued that these extensions were entirely optional. Along with the Advocate General, they supported this reading with the preparatory works from which it was clear first, that the Council rejected the Commission's initial proposal to make the six-month export period compulsory and second, that the Member States only subsequently and reluctantly agreed 'on the form of words which makes up the second limb of Article 64(1)(c) of Regulation 883/2004'.[90]

Commonplace observations, like the date of the judgment, might become relevant in specific circumstances after detailed legal analysis. The Court issued the judgments in *Lair* and *Brown* on the same day, citing *Lair* to support the interpretation of Article 7(2) of Regulation 1612/68 in *Brown*. To briefly recall, *Lair* raised the question of whether former migrant workers who enrolled in university courses in the host Member State could claim student maintenance grants. The Court answered affirmatively, reasoning that those applicants retained their worker status if the previous occupational activity and the studies in question were related.[91]

The Court rejected the argument of the Member States that such interpretation might lead to abuse, and hence ruled out the possibility to unilaterally condition the grant on a period of occupational activity. At the same time, it also recognised that the Treaty did not cover the situations of 'abuse' wherein a worker entered a Member State to enjoy, 'after a very short period of occupational activity, the benefit of the student assistance system in that State.'[92]

In *Brown*, the Court referred to *Lair* concluding that a national of a Member State could not claim a maintenance grant for studies in another Member State as a worker if he acquired that status exclusively to pursue his studies. In this case, the employment relationship, which was the only basis for the rights deriving from Regulation 1612/68, was 'merely ancillary to the studies to be financed by the grant'.[93]

Reading the judgments together highlights the Court's effort to moderate the scope of its interpretations. Both judgments raised the question of maintenance

[90] Case C-551/16, *Schiphorst*, ECLI: EU:C:2018:200, para 38.
[91] *Lair*, para 39.
[92] *Lair*, paras 42 and 43.
[93] *Brown*, para 27.

grants and the national competence to limit the access of foreign nationals to higher education. The Court held that access to vocational training, including university studies in general, fell within the scope of the Treaty and Member States could therefore not treat students from other Member States less favourably than its own nationals.

On the one hand, *Lair* extended the European Union's competence to the area of education and maintenance grants with a broad interpretation of Regulation 1612/68. It stretched the solidarity of the Member States with migrant workers asking for social advantages to pursue university studies without pursuing an economic activity and no longer contributing to the economy of the Member State and the social security system. On the other hand, *Brown* confirmed and contained this broad interpretation, ruling that a person who acquired worker status because he was admitted to university was still defined as a worker and entitled to work related benefits under Regulation 1612/68 but not to a maintenance grant given that his work was merely ancillary.

The Court demonstrated a degree of sensitivity to the Member States' concerns about abuse and fraudulent use of free movement rights, as put forward in the proceedings. If the date was a matter of greater efficiency (the reporting judge, the Advocate General, and government agents were the same in both cases, and the Court held the hearings on the same date), the Court could have easily joined the cases. Of course, this conclusion requires further analysis and reflection.[94]

The following section engages in a detailed legal analysis of three emblematic judgments, demonstrating how the interaction between the parameters of case-law and the external circumstances are interrelated in three types of good judgment. The analysis links the outcomes to the external circumstances, which will be further and more systematically considered in chapter seven.

E. EMBLEMATIC JUDGMENTS: A CLOSE UP

This section defines and analyses three emblematic judgments in which the Court sought to uphold conflicting interests in response to external circumstances of the disputes: 1) the non-sanctioning Europeanisation of national policies (Type 1 / *Groener* type[95]); 2) the deferential upholding of European rights (Type 2 / *Vaassen-Göbbels* type[96]); and 3) bounded undesirable interpretation (Type 3 / *Blaizot* type[97]).

[94] The judgments are discussed in chapter seven as an example of context-conscious judging, alternative to good judgment (without departing from the typical structure of justification).

[95] Case C-379/87, *Groener*, ECLI: EU:C:1989:599.

[96] Case 61/65, *G. Vaassen-Göbbels*, ECLI:EU:C:1966:39.

[97] Case 24/86, *Blaizot*, ECLI:EU:C:1988:43.

As briefly discussed in chapter three and in section d) of this chapter, the first type focuses on the review of national rules and policies – subjecting them to European standards but threatening to dismantle them in the future. The second focuses on the decision of the Court about the legal claim, namely a concrete negative outcome of the case for the state. Deferring the final decision to the national court or administration can result in a state-friendlier or narrower application.[98] The third focuses on the broader implications of the rulings. New obligations for the Member States and new rights for individual applicants imposed by the Court affect the state's autonomy to accommodate (integrate) and regulate the newly established legal situation. The first and the third type differ in relation to their implications. The 'Europeanisation' is autonomy restricting but policy permissive, whereas the undesirable interpretation is policy restrictive.

The examples raise complementary legal issues, stemming from different historical periods, and the modalities of non-legal considerations which permeate the Court's reasoning process and case outcomes. The availability of legal sources, especially the Reports for the Hearing and original Court files, favours judgments where these reports are freely available (before the mid-1990s) and exist (until early 2010s).[99] The Reports reproduce the context of the dispute, its origins, and the arguments of the participants.[100]

i. Non-Sanctioning Europeanisation of National Policies: *Groener*

A non-sanctioning good judgment will subject national rules and policies to common rules and standards without finding issue with them; the Court will conduct a proportionality review or a discrimination test, but conclude that the measures and policies are proportionate, non-discriminatory, or justified. The tension will arise between the Court's ruling (the outcome of the case) and the reach of European Union law (the scope of its application). The state policy threatening reading of the law will yield a state policy permissive outcome.

The Court might rule that the national regulation of the relationships between employers and employees should comply with free movement but

[98] Case C-281/98, *Angonese*, ECLI: EU:C:2000:296.

[99] The Court stopped publishing the reports in the mid-1990s, and seemingly stopped producing them around 2012. Since then, the Court's judgments have become more informative regarding the facts of the case (in the preliminary reference procedure the section related to the dispute in the main proceedings and the arguments of the parties have become progressively longer). The opinions of the Advocates General typically capture the arguments of the parties and the interveners in more depth.

[100] For judgments issued before 1990, the Archives of the European Union hold the full Court files (dossiers). These dossiers typically contain the full texts of the submissions of the parties and the interveners. Both sources offer a less speculative analysis of debates and the broader context of the legal issues discussed.

uphold the national regulation of industrial relations or policies promoting full employment. The judgment sends a warning to formulate a policy mindful of European Union law, potentially creating 'competence' for future inroads which may not produce Member State friendly outcomes.

Groener typifies a non-sanctioning judgment which applies European standards to questions of national language policy and identity but approves of such policy.[101] The national dispute arose between Anita Groener, a Dutch art teacher employed part-time at the College of Marketing and Design in Dublin (the applicant), and The Minister for Education and the City of Dublin Vocational Education. The latter refused to appoint the applicant to a full-time post because she failed the Irish language test.

The test was a formal condition for the appointment imposed by the Irish Vocational Education Act (1930). The applicant claimed that the national rules were de facto discriminatory and unduly restricted free movement. The Irish High Court submitted three questions about the compatibility of the national language requirement with Article 48 of the EEC Treaty as it was at the time and Article 3 of the Regulation 1612/68.[102]

The first question addressed whether the Irish rules had discriminatory effects. The second question requested the interpretation of Article 3 of the Regulation, which allowed differential treatment when the linguistic knowledge was 'required by reason of the nature of the post to be filled'. The third question was whether the language policy fell under the concept of public policy and was thus altogether exempt from free movement rules (Article 48(3) EEC Treaty).

The Court replied only to the second question, ascertaining that the nature of the post mandated and justified the linguistic requirement. Although teachers taught in English, and did not use Irish in daily work, they played an important role in supporting the national language policy. The Court subjected the Irish language rules based on Article 8 of the Irish Constitution to proportionality review and examined whether the Irish rules were discriminatory. It therefore touched upon a sensitive question of Irish identity and language, and the active efforts of the Irish government to promote the former through the latter.[103] The use of national language was not exempted from free movement rules[104] nor the Court's jurisdiction.

The creation of a precedent that the Court could examine matters of language and identity seemed especially 'aggressive' and subjecting those matters to proportionality review seemed daring. However, the Court sought a workable outcome, and upheld the Irish language rule entirely, sidestepping the general

[101] Case C-379/87, *Groener*, ECLI: EU:C:1989:599.

[102] Reg No 1612/68 of the Council on freedom of movement for workers within the Community repealed and replaced by Reg (European Union) No 492/2011 of the European Parliament and of the Council of 5 April 2011 on freedom of movement for workers within the Union.

[103] The judgment mentions the government's efforts to promote the Irish language in para 18.

[104] The (then) Art 48(3) of the Treaty and Art 3 of Reg No 1612/68.

question of discrimination and public policy exceptions. Its ruling rested on the interpretation of secondary law, not of general principle.

The Court's solution is interesting given the fraught political landscape and the procedural history of the case. The Court briefly but conspicuously touches upon the pressing competence issue.[105] The political controversy transpires most clearly from the Report for the Hearing and the Advocate's General Opinion. The Advocate General dwells briefly on the question of competence and the powers of the Member States to determine their so-called linguistic heritage.[106] To bring the posts of teachers who do not use Irish for teaching purposes within the scope of exception to Article 3, he highlights the Community's support for the conservation of Europe's 'cultural richness and the diversity of its linguistic heritage'.[107] Concretely, the Advocate General refers to the European Parliament's declaration of minority languages and the de facto status of the Irish language as a non-widely spoken language in spite of its constitutional status as a national language. He notes that in 1982, the Commission set up the European Office on Minority Languages in Dublin.

Carefully skirting on the margins of the conflict, the Advocate's General Opinion addresses the principled question of public policy with reluctance. Repeating the position of the Commission, the Opinion concludes that in the absence of discrimination under secondary law it was unnecessary to invoke exceptions.

The Report for the Hearing offers additional insight into the background of the case. The applicant commenced the proceedings before the Irish High Court and addressed a petition to the President of the European Parliament. The latter considered the Irish measures contrary to Community law, prompting the Commission to start the infringement proceedings. In reply to the Commission's letter in 1987, the Irish authorities informed the Commission of the applicant's case before the Irish High Court. The Commission thereupon confirmed its preliminary view in a reasoned opinion addressed to Ireland but decided not to pursue the action after receiving a reply from the Irish authorities.

According to the Commission, Ireland convincingly proved the proportionality of its measures and qualifying their necessity. In the Commission's view, the most convincing justification was that the requirement did not apply to part-time employment in order to avoid creating difficulties for educational

[105] The Court acknowledges that 'the EEC Treaty does not prohibit the adoption of a policy for the protection and promotion of a language of a Member State, which is both the national language and the first official language. However, the implementation of such a policy must not encroach upon a fundamental freedom such as that of the free movement of workers. Therefore, the requirements deriving from measures intended to implement such a policy must not in any circumstances be disproportionate in relation to the aim pursued, and the manner in which they are applied must not bring about discrimination against nationals of other Member States.' *Groener*, para 19.

[106] Paras 19–20.

[107] Opinion of the Advocate General, para 17 (in fine).

institutions, that there were provisions on derogations in the absence of fully qualified candidates and that the required level of knowledge was not perfect fluency. The British reporting judge concluded his Report with statistics, which Ireland supplied upon the Court's request. The latter reconfirms the limited practical and the large symbolic dimension of the dispute. In fact, Ms Groener was 'the only national of a Member State other than Ireland who remain[ed] unsuccessful in the special examination' since the entry into force of Circular Letter 28/79.[108]

The Court, as if seeing a satisfactory solution for Ms Groener, specified general guidelines and imposed specific requirements on Ireland. Particularly interesting is the requirement that candidates can retake the examination when they reapply for a given position.[109] Adding such guidelines for the application of Article 3 of Regulation is at odds with the avoidance of a principled answer whether the question of language policy could be exempt from free movement rules based on public policy.[110]

To summarise, the departure from the model justification in *Groener* arises between the application of the proportionality test to the constitutionally protected and politically sensitive issue of Irish identity, on the one hand, and its willingness to uphold the Irish rules entirely on the other. The Europeanisation without sanction slowly grinds down national autonomy but on narrow grounds[111] and on secondary rather than primary law.[112]

ii. Deferential Upholding of European Rights: *Vaassen-Göbbels*

A deferential and rights upholding judgment will support the claim of the applicant based on European Union law against the interest of the respondent Member State, while granting the latter genuine as opposed to pro forma deference. The outcome and the broader implications will not follow the model justification because a broad outcome of the case (a rights protective interpretation of European Union law) will be qualified or suspended, depending on the decision of the national court or administrative authority applying national rules. The decision of the latter can potentially undermine the broad interpretation.

[108] *Groener*, Report for the Hearing, p 3977.

[109] In which she succeeded, and continued her career in Dublin as a lecturer and artist https://anita-groener.com.

[110] Even more so because France, intervening in the dispute, urged the Court to grant said exception.

[111] R Lane and N Nic Shuibhne, 'Case C-281/98, Roman Angonese v. Cassa Di Risparmio Di Bolzano SpA' (2000) 37 *Common Market Law Review* 1237. *Groener* had a delayed effect. *Angonese* concerned a much stricter and disproportionate measure, and the Court limited its ruling to the measure. It was a way to introduce the horizontal effect of non-discrimination.

[112] The Court creates a narrow precedent – tailoring its answer to the Irish case, which would be difficult to apply in France. France intervened in the case, arguing strongly in favour of the exception from free movement on grounds of public policy. Report for the Hearing, p 3971.

The Court can hold that the applicant is a worker if his employment contract satisfies minimum conditions, leaving the appreciation of the terms of the contract to the national court or administration. The latter might find ways to apply national – potentially discriminatory – rules.[113] Deference might accompany rulings in favour of economically inactive citizens who do not contribute to the economy of the host Member State,[114] cases where the individuals in question present a threat to public order or security, or in disputes about the rights of citizens' family members who are third country nationals.

The *Vaassen-Göbbels* judgment is emblematic.[115] The dispute arose between Mrs Vaassen-Göbbels (the applicant), the widow of a non-manual worker employed in the mining sector in the Netherlands, and the Dutch Fund (the defendant) in charge of pensions and social security of these workers. The applicant received a survivor's pension from the defendant and was entitled to benefits from its supplementary and voluntary Sickness Fund – until such time as she decided to move to Germany. Upon the change of residence, the Fund ended her membership. The applicant petitioned the Dutch Arbitration Tribunal of the Fund for non-manual workers employed in the mining industry (the Arbitration Tribunal), which submitted a preliminary reference on the correct interpretation of Regulation 3 of the Council concerning the social security of migrant workers.[116]

The questions raised were whether the rules of the Fund were legislation in the sense of Article 1 and 4 of Regulation 3 and, if so, whether the Fund could tie supplementary and voluntary sickness insurance to residence in the Netherlands?

The Commission insisted that the disputed provisions were legislation, and the Fund could therefore not require residence for their disbursement. Advocate General Gand seemed to harbour certain doubts but concluded – categorically – that the rules of the Fund were enforceable provisions, hence they were legislation within the meaning of Article 1 of Regulation 3. The Fund objected, arguing that it was a private body and that the sickness benefit was not a pension subject to the same rules. Rather, it was a voluntary contribution agreed separately between the Fund and the insured person and the rules governing it could not be legislation within the meaning of Regulation 3.

Regulation 3, to recall, precluded national legislation conditioning any social security benefit on residence. Article 12 was concerned with rights of active workers. Article 22 dealt expressly with the right to sickness insurance benefit of

[113] This scenario is not hypothetical. See C O'Brien, *Unity in Adversity: EU Citizenship, Social Justice and the Cautionary Tale of the UK* (London, Bloomsbury Publishing, 2017).

[114] C-138/02, *Collins*, ECLI:EU:C:2004:172.

[115] Case 61/65, *G. Vaassen-Göbbels*, ECLI:EU:C:1966:39.

[116] Reg 3 of the Council of the EEC concerning social security for migrant workers (OJ 16.12. 1958 p. 561), repealed and replaced by Reg (EEC) No 1408/71, supplemented by Implementing Reg (EEC No 574/72. In 2004, Reg (EC) No 883/2004 of the European Parliament and of the Council on the coordination of social security systems was adopted to replace Reg (EEC) No 1408/71.

a person entitled to a pension, and not with the right to be affiliated to a sickness insurance fund as a family member of a worker, or a non-worker. The residence condition was unacceptable for the social benefits of workers who moved, but could it similarly be deemed unacceptable for their survivors and for voluntary insurance funds?

To bring the applicant within the scope of Regulation 3, the Court interpreted the case according to 'the spirit of Articles 48 to 51 of the Treaty as well as with that of Regulation 3,'[117] which was, 'in addition to protecting the migrant worker stricto sensu, to prevent territorial provisions from being applied against workers or their survivors in matters of social security'.[118]

The unconditional reply to the second question, derived from this broad understanding of the Regulation, would imply that the applicant as well as all future applicants in a similar position fell within its ambit. The case outcome, however, hinged entirely on the reply to the first question: Were the Fund's rules legislation? The Court left this crucial decision to the referring court, who had to examine whether the rules met all conditions for the existence of a so-called 'special scheme' mentioned in the Regulation.

Deference is difficult to attribute to the nature of the preliminary question or the lack of information from the referring court. The Report for the Hearing mentions only that the question was 'badly drafted,' asking the Court to decide whether the applicant was entitled to the benefit, and thus reformulating it as a question of interpretation of European Union law. At the same time, the issue at hand was not legally clear-cut nor trivial in economic and social terms. The Fund raised concerns about the extension of the scope of Regulation 3, arguing that it governed the social security of migrant workers and their family members. It could not cover a deceased worker's widow who had never worked and had, once she obtained a widow's pension, permanently moved to another Member State without any intention to work. Otherwise, the Fund objected, such a person might assume residence in the Member State where she received the best treatment.

The Advocate General addressed the Fund's 'benefit tourism' objection in passing in the final paragraphs of his Opinion. He curtly rejected the logic of the Fund: 'it does not seem that there is any reason for fearing, contrary to what the [Fund] seems to think, that the advantage to be had from greater medical benefits might of itself induce the survivor of a worker to make a change of residence'.[119]

[117] This means that broad interpretation is a necessary element of Type 2 good judgment.
[118] *Vaassen-Göbbels*, p. 275.
[119] H Verschueren, 'Preventing "Benefit Tourism" in the EU: A Narrow or Broad Interpretation of the Possibilities Offered by the ECJ in Dano?' (2015) 52 *Common Market Law Review* 363. The issue of the exportability of benefits and 'benefit tourism' has persisted and gained prominence in later jurisprudence, scholarly literature, and the news. For the latter see https://www.bbc.com/news/uk-politics-30002138 (published on 11 November, 2014, last accessed on 13 November 2023). Perhaps the most blatant judgment bending to the will of a Member State was Case C-308/14,

The debate surpassed the technical questions of social security coordination and conversely raised a deeper controversy about the exportability of social security benefits that the Court might have been eager to avoid. Nonetheless, the Court interpreted the Regulation in favour of the individuals who would have lost their benefits by moving. To reconcile rights with their socio-economic context, the Court opted for good judgment upholding conflicting interests: A judgment protecting individual rights or those who exercises the right to free movement against discriminatory national rules but entirely deferring the terms of rights application to the national administration.[120]

iii. Bounded Undesirable Interpretation: *Blaizot*

A good judgment with bounded undesirable interpretation imposes new obligations on the Member States, removes obstacles to free movement or creates rights, doctrines, and concepts at minimal or limited cost. The Court seeks to minimise the implications of its ruling for national regulatory autonomy or contain its effects.

Blaizot[121] illustrates bounded undesirable interpretation which imposes new obligations on a state, expands the meaning of a European legal concept (vocational training), and limits its temporal application. The case concerned the enrolment fees charged to foreign students by Belgian universities (the so-called *minerval*) and the entitlement of the students to the repayment of those fees. The Court had previously declared fees imposed on vocational training discriminatory and contrary at the time to Article 7 of the EEC Treaty in *Gravier*.[122] The Law on education (the Law), which Belgium adopted in 1985 pursuant to *Gravier*, limited the reimbursement of previously paid enrolment fees to the nationals of Member States who enrolled in vocational training courses and had already brought their actions. The Commission challenged the Belgian Law in a separate infringement action[123] and Belgian courts consequently referred a handful of preliminary questions.[124]

A group of French veterinary medicine students (the applicants) claimed the repayment of fees for the academic year 1985 which had been disbursed to four Belgian universities. The national court in Liege, hearing the case, inquired

Commission v UK, ECLI:EU:C:2016:436. See C O'Brien, 'The ECJ Sacrifices EU Citizenship in Vain: Commission v. United Kingdom' (2017) 54 *Common Market Law Review* 209. The judgment is also discussed in chapter seven.

[120] Case C-456 /12, *O and B*, ECLI:EU:C:2014:135.

[121] Case 24/86, *Blaizot*, ECLI:EU:C:1988:43.

[122] Case 293/83, *Gravier*, ECLI:EU:C:1985:69.

[123] Case 293/85, *Commission v Belgium*, ECLI:EU:C:1988:40. See, however, the injunction order of the President of the Court, issued in the same case, ordering Belgium to suspend the fees upon the written guarantees of the persons concerned to pay the fees in case the Commission's action is dismissed. Case 293/85 R, *Commission v Belgium*, ECLI:EU:C:1985:446.

[124] Case 309/85, *Barra*, ECLI:EU:C:1988:42.

whether vocational training included university courses in veterinary medicine. If it did, the applicants could reclaim the unduly paid fees. The Court held that the reference opened two issues: the question of interpretation whether university studies in veterinary medicine fell within the meaning of the term vocational training, and the question of – retroactive – application.

In *Gravier*, the Court defined vocational training as 'any form of education which prepares for a qualification for a particular profession, trade or employment or which provides the necessary training and skills for such a profession, trade or employment … whatever the age and the level of training of the pupils or students, and even if the training program includes an element of general education'.[125]

The Court did not hesitate to assimilate university courses like veterinary medicine under vocational training. *Obiter*, it went further, stating that the term could apply more generally to university education. It did not seem particularly concerned with the fact that the broad interpretation extended Community competence in Article 128 EEC to education and therefore beyond the limits of the Treaty.[126]

The Court was, nonetheless, willing to uphold the claim conflicting with the implications of this decision. It endorsed the argument of the universities that they 'would be endangered by the removal of the supplementary enrolment fee, which would considerably increase the influx of foreign students to Belgium and thus increase the universities' financial burdens to an intolerable extent',[127] limiting the temporal effects of the judgment.

The justification is interesting for the analysis of good judgment because of its political context. The Court admitted – uncharacteristically – that its judgment raised an entirely new question as to whether university education could constitute vocational training for the purposes of Article 128 of the Treaty. It conceded that the case marked 'a development with regard to the inclusion of university studies in the scope of the term 'vocational training' for the purposes of Community law.'[128] Recalling *Defrenne*,[129] it further explained that practical consequences and repercussions, while important, could not diminish the objectivity of the law and compromise its future application.[130]

The Court anchored the argument to limit the effects of the judgment barring the repayment of the fees in the Commission's framing, attributing the Belgian legislation to the indecisiveness of the former rather than to the well-documented unwillingness of the latter to fully comply with *Gravier*. The Commission evidently considered the imposition of the supplementary

[125] *Gravier*, para 30.
[126] Art 128 EEC, now covered by Art 165 TFEU.
[127] Case 24/86, *Blaizot*, ECLI:EU:C:1988:43.
[128] *Blaizot*, para 31.
[129] Case 43/75, *Defrenne*, ECLI:EU:C:1976:56.
[130] *Blaizot*, para 30.

enrolment fees compatible with Community law until 1985, when – in an informal meeting with the officials of the Belgian Education Ministries – it suddenly changed its position. Two days after the meeting and more than four months after the judgment in *Gravier*, the Commission stated in a meeting of the Education Committee established by the Council that 'it had not yet formed a definite opinion of the conclusions to be drawn from that judgment.'[131] Based on this attitude, the Court reasoned, Belgium could reasonably believe that its legislation complied with Community law.[132] The 'pressing considerations of legal certainty,' outweighed the benefits of the full application of the law.

A judgment protecting conflicting interests and upholding conflicting claims does not mean that the justification is internally incoherent – the Court can and does limit the effects of its judgments.[133] The *Blaizot* judgment is conspicuous because of the protracted and acrimonious struggle between Belgium and the European Union's institutions, transpiring from the Reports for the Hearing and the Opinions of the Advocate General Slynn in *Barra*,[134] *Blaizot*, and *Commission against Belgium*.[135]

These sources highlight the particularity of the Belgian situation. Belgium argued that it was entitled, despite *Gravier*, to charge foreign university students the *minerval* given the large absolute number and a much higher share of foreign students pursuing education in Belgium as compared to any other Member State (4.2 or 4.5 per cent of students in Belgium). Because of *minervai*, the universities could cope with a real influx of predominantly French, German, and Dutch students.[136]

An argument arose during the procedure as to 'the real number of Community students who are in Belgium'. For instance, Belgium claimed that around 800 Luxembourgish students were already exempt from the *minervai*. A debate took place as to the real rate of increase in the number of foreign students in Belgium.[137] It was further argued that Belgium would not face an unprecedented influx of foreign students if the *minervai* were dropped. The applicants submitted that the proportion of foreign students relative to Belgian students had increased negligibly – by 0.5 per cent in 15 years from 1970 to 1984.[138] Finally,

[131] *Blaizot*, para 32.

[132] *Blaizot*, para 33.

[133] D Düsterhaus, 'Eppur Si Muove! The Past, Present, and (Possible) Future of Temporal Limitations in the Preliminary Ruling Procedure' (2017) 36 *Yearbook of European Law* 237.

[134] Case 309/85, *Barra*, ECLI:EU:C:1988:42.

[135] The Advocate's General Opinion in Commission against Belgium suggests that Belgium and the Commission clearly set out on a collision course after the judgment in *Gravier*. 'The Commission was not here seeking to have long-standing legislation repealed, but to obtain the withdrawal of measures implemented since the *Gravier* decision, which on the face of it seemed to the Commission to be deliberately avoiding giving effect to that decision.' Advocate's General Opinion, p 332.

[136] In Belgium 4.25% of all students and 6% of all pupils are from other Member States. Report, p 386.

[137] *Blaizot* (Opinion), p 342.

[138] *Blaizot* (Report for the Hearing), p 385.

the Commission insisted that the real costs of repaying the supplementary enrolment fees were minimal in relation to Belgium's budget.[139]

An issue looming in the background was Belgium's reluctance to bear the implications of *Gravier*. The Court might have feared that Belgium would refuse to implement an even more demanding ruling, reconfiguring its higher education system and imposing a sizeable burden on the state budget. Thus, mindful of the possible negative implications, it upheld conflicting claims, which effectively redrew the limits of European Union competence, and the content of state obligations under the free movement of students at minimal economic and political cost.

Even if the circumstances of *Blaizot* seem extreme and exceptional, one might wonder whether the limiting of the temporal effects could placate Belgium's grievances from *Gravier*[140] and lead to further insistence on the necessity to limit the influx of foreign students.

On the face of it, the Court's decision put a small bandage on a large wound. However, it was not state unfriendly in the broader scheme of things – considering the dismissal of the parallel infringement action on the same day.[141] In the latter, the Court held, formalistically, that Belgium did not have enough time to respond to the Commission's notice and written opinion, hence the action was inadmissible. The judgment in *Blaizot* gave the Commission the necessary green light to develop an educational policy for the Community (the Erasmus programme was launched the year before).[142] It also allowed Belgium to reconfigure its system of university financing.

F. UPHOLDING CONFLICTING INTERESTS: THE LONG TERM 1954–2022

As Table 3 shows, judgments upholding conflicting interests are overall uncommon. There are, however, important differences in the frequency by type. Type 1 or *Groener* type judgments are the most frequent (column Type 1 in Table 3), and their share has increased significantly since 1995 (column Type 1 (share) in Table 3). The *Vaassen-Göbbels* type (Type 2 (share)) and the *Blaizot* type (column Type 3 (share)) had fluctuated between 5 and 13 per cent annually up until 2005, whereupon their share increased to 18 per cent and 20 per cent

[139] *Blaizot* (Report for the Hearing), p 394.

[140] This follows from the Report for the Hearing in Case 293/85, *Commission v Belgium*, as well as the Advocate's General opinion and the Report for the Hearing in this case (p 393).

[141] A similar scenario occurred in relation to the judgment in Case C-73/08, *Bressol et al*, ECLI:EU:C:2010:181. As Garben argues, the decision in *Bressol* is related to the Commission's decision to suspend a second set of infringement proceedings against Belgium facing political pressure to secure the ratification of the Lisbon Treaty. S Garben, 'Case C-73/08, Nicolas Bressol and Others, Céline Chaverot and Others v. Gouvernement de La Communauté Française' (2010) 47 *Common Market Law Review* 1493.

[142] See Report (pp 315, 318) and the Advocate's General Opinion.

(second and third row from the bottom in Table 3, columns Type 2 (share) and Type 3 (share)). Until 1970, the Court dealt with very few free movement of persons disputes. It is thus difficult to draw conclusive arguments from this early period. Types of judgments upholding conflicting interests can moreover overlap – regarding outcome, process, *and* implications. This means that the total share of judgments upholding conflicting interests does not equal the sum of its types.

The patterns in Table 3 appear intuitively sound, and in line with the expectation that judgments upholding conflicting interests should be the exception and not the rule. The relative growth over the past two decades indicates the expansion of context-conscious judging. This period coincides with major political events and developments. The enlargement of the Union in 2004 increased the migration of workers from Eastern Europe, often leading to political tensions within states and in their overall relationship with the Union. Pre-existing contentious issues, like the rights of economically inactive citizens (e.g. students), citizens without the necessary means of subsistence, and those involved in criminal activities, intensified as cases multiplied.

Table 3 Overview of judgments upholding conflicting interests by type. The first column from the left indicates the five-year calendar period (e.g. 1960 means the period from January 1, 1960, to 31 December, 1965, and 2020 the period since January 2020. This explains the low number of cases.). Column 2 provides the information on the number of free movement of persons cases which the Court decided in a given period (e.g. in the period from 2015–2020 the Court decided 123 cases / second row from the bottom). Columns 3–5 (from the left) contain the number of judgments upholding conflicting interests by type: *Non-sanctioning Europeanization of national rules and policies / Groener type, Deferential upholding of European rights against the state / Vaassen-Göbbels type* and *Bounded undesirable interpretation / Blaizot type*. The final three columns from the left indicate the share of free movement of persons judgments upholding conflicting interests in each period by type

Period (5 years)	Number of cases	Type 1	Type 2	Type 3	Type 1 (share)	Type 2 (share)	Type 3 (share)
1960	4	0	1	0	0%	25%	0%
1965	21	0	1	0	0%	5%	0%
1970	35	1	3	1	3%	9%	3%
1975	78	8	3	8	10%	4%	10%
1980	63	4	0	5	6%	0%	8%
1985	83	12	4	11	14%	5%	13%
1990	119	17	5	11	14%	4%	9%
1995	117	12	9	15	10%	8%	13%
2000	120	34	15	11	28%	13%	9%

(continued)

Table 3 *(Continued)*

Period (5 years)	Number of cases	Type 1	Type 2	Type 3	Type 1 (share)	Type 2 (share)	Type 3 (share)
2005	148	46	13	8	31%	9%	5%
2010	139	43	25	25	31%	18%	18%
2015	123	45	24	13	37%	20%	11%
2020	22	9	2	2	41%	9%	9%

Admittedly, other factors and institutional developments – including the extreme increase in and diversity of the Court's membership, the augmented use of the chamber system, the collegiate decision-making style which is prone to last minute compromise, the expansion of jurisdiction, new legislation, and the cacophony of languages – could have contributed to atypical justifications. Moreover, fixed procedural arrangements inherent in Article 267 TFEU (the division of tasks in the preliminary reference procedure)[143] and the formulation of the preliminary questions by the referring courts[144] co-determine the Court's interpretive choices and case outcomes.

Nonetheless, mounting criticism from the political left and right, which is indicative of the faltering support for the integration project and the conflicts between the Member States, is impossible to discount as instrumental to the trend.[145] These factors are subject to a more systematic examination in chapter seven, linking good judgment to case characteristics and institutional features.

[143] G Davies, 'Activism Relocated. The Self-Restraint of the European Court of Justice in Its National Context' (2012) 19 *Journal of European Public Policy* 76.

[144] A Wallerman, 'Can Two Walk Together, except They Be Agreed?: Preliminary References and (the Erosion of) National Procedural Autonomy' (2019) 44 *European Law Review* 159.

[145] O'Brien (n 119).

6

Goods

A. INTRODUCTION

FREE MOVEMENT OF goods is central to the internal market and therefore instrumental to the European success story.[1] The Treaty of Rome signed in 1957 established a customs union, abolishing all quotas and duties between the signatories and introducing a common external tariff on imports from third countries. To date, the customs union remains the 'core of the rules on goods'.[2] Article 30 TFEU also prohibits the imposition of charges with the same effect as customs duties. Articles 34 and 35 TFEU prohibit quantitative restrictions on imports and exports, as well as all other measures with the same effect. Article 36 TFEU allows exceptions from free movement of goods for reasons of public morality, public policy or public security; for the protection of health and life of humans, animals or plants; the protection of national treasures possessing artistic, historic, or archaeological value; or the protection of industrial and commercial property, in so far as they do not arbitrarily discriminate or disguise trade restrictions. These provisions on their own or in combination with other Treaty articles account for a sizeable body of case-law (1538 judgments at last count in 2022).

Six overlapping factors make free movement of goods a particularly well-suited policy area for the analysis of context-conscious judging and good judgment.

First, the symbolic importance of goods for the European Union's legal order. Free movement of goods has acquired an 'iconic' status among legal scholars.[3] The provisions on the free movement of goods and their interpretation by the Court were and continue to be central to the integration through law.[4] The Court's judgments are a natural starting point for the inquiry into

[1] Cited in European Commission, Free Movement of Goods: Guide to the application of Treaty provisions governing free movement of goods (Arts 28–30 EC [Art 34–6 TFEU]) (the 'Commission guide'), SEC(2009) 673, 7. Cited in C Barnard, *The Substantive Law of the EU*, 7th edn (Oxford, Oxford University Press, 2022) 39.

[2] Barnard (n 1) 40.

[3] KA Armstrong, 'Governing Goods: Content and Context' in D Chalmers and A Arnull (eds), *The Oxford Handbook of European Union Law* (Oxford, Oxford University Press, 2021) 508.

[4] S Enchelmaier, 'Free Movement of Goods: Evolution and Intelligent Design in the Foundations of the European Union' in P Craig and G de Búrca (eds), *The Evolution of EU Law* (Oxford, Oxford University Press, 2021) 546.

the European Union as a sui generis legal order, characterised by the judge-made principles of direct effect (established in *Van Gend*[5]) and primacy (established in *Costa v ENEL*[6]). Incidentally, both judgments fall within this specific policy area.

Second, the practical relevance or economic significance of goods. Free movement of goods might be too removed from citizens' daily consumption habits to pique their interest in free trade.[7] Nonetheless, 27 per cent of Europeans mention rising prices, inflation, and the cost of living as three of the most important issues facing the European Union. Over 20 per cent of Europeans are most concerned about the environment and climate change, and the free and sustainable trade in goods has direct bearing on both.

Free movement of goods is economically significant for states and citizens. Economic integration expands the market and decreases the trade-related costs of goods, translating into economic growth, productivity gains, lower prices, more choice, and overall better quality of goods for consumers. Most EU Member States trade more with other Member States than with non-member countries.[8] In 2022, the share of intra-European Union trade varied between 50 per cent to 70 per cent for most Member States.[9] Luxembourg (86.3 per cent), Slovakia (78.5 per cent) and the Czech Republic (76.8 per cent), had the highest shares; Greece (47.3 per cent) and Ireland (37.5 per cent) had the lowest.

Third, individual judgments enjoy a special status in the integration narrative charting the Court's intervention in completion of the internal market. They are inseparable from the neo-functionalist narrative of the 'judicial construction of Europe'[10] and the theorising of the Court's political power as either unleashed or constrained by political actors.[11] The Court's judgments have broken down barriers to trade, in turn shaping and cementing the terms of production, marketing, sales, transportation, and consumption of goods in spite of the political constraints. In parallel, they have defined the relationship between the authority

[5] Case 26/62, *van Gend & Loos*, ECLI:EU:C:1963:1.

[6] Case 6/64, *Costa v ENEL*, ECLI:EU:C:1964:66.

[7] EU Barometer (summer 2022). Migration is 3rd with unemployment and government debt EU wide.

[8] Intra-EU trade (exports and imports) in goods is higher than extra-EU trade (exports and imports) for most Member States. Report by the European Commission https://ec.europa.eu/eurostat/statistics-explained/index.php?title=International_trade_in_goods#EU_trade_increased_strongly_in_2022 (accessed in October 2023).

[9] Report by the European Commission https://ec.europa.eu/eurostat/statistics-explained/index.php?title=International_trade_in_goods#EU_trade_increased_strongly_in_2022 (accessed in October 2023).

[10] A Stone Sweet, *The Judicial Construction of Europe* (Oxford, Oxford University Press, 2004).

[11] For a detailed and excellent overview of the literature on the Court's power see DS Martinsen, *An Ever More Powerful Court?: The Political Constraints of Legal Integration in the European Union* (Oxford, Oxford University Press, 2015). For foundational work see A-M Burley and W Mattli, 'Europe Before the Court: A Political Theory of Legal Integration' (1993) 47 *International Organization* 41; JHH Weiler, 'The Transformation of Europe' (1991) 100 *The Yale Law Journal* 2403.

of European law and the regulatory autonomy of the Member States.[12] By delimiting the scope of Articles 34 and 36 TFEU, the Court 'gradually outlined a blueprint for completing the common market, which the Commission would champion and the Member States would later ratify in diverse ways, not least as part of the Single European Act'.[13] The narrative of political success alone can cast a spell over deliberations in the Kirchberg chambers.[14]

Fourth, free movement of goods provides a window into the Court-mediated power dynamics between the Member States and the European institutions, and between the individual Member States. These relationships are the architype in the law and politics debate. The Court has struck down national measures restricting free movement and sustained the supranational (notably the Commission's) regulatory appetite. Its embrace of the Single Market programme and alliance with the European Commission are legion.[15] However, the Court must have calculated its moves before 'unleashing conferral,'[16] carefully considering the immediate environment and wider implications.[17]

Fifth, the large scope of the policy area involving other legal domains and touching upon societal values. Free movement of goods intrinsically links salient policy areas of the European Union, like consumer protection, common commercial policy, environmental policy, common agricultural policy, competition, and free movement of services or capital. Some domains have not been included in the Treaty of Rome from its inception (intellectual property), others remain outside the Union's reach (national security), or come very close to overstepping core state competences (taxation).

Trade in goods touches upon the societal values underlying the right to conduct a business; to the protections of cultural heritage, public health, morality, healthy competition, and animal welfare; the protection of traditional production methods and artefacts; as well as to media pluralism and free speech. They emerge in vastly different political, economic, and institutional circumstances.

Among the best-known examples are the political crisis triggered by Hallstein's (the Commission's) financing plan for the common agricultural policy which stalled the momentum of an originally ambitious harmonisation

[12] KJ Alter and S Meunier-Aitsahalia, 'Judicial Politics in the European Community: European Integration and the Pathbreaking Cassis de Dijon Decision' (1994) 26 *Comparative Political Studies* 535.

[13] Stone Sweet (n 10) 109.

[14] A Vauchez, 'Keeping the Dream Alive: The European Court of Justice and the Transnational Fabric of Integrationist Jurisprudence' (2012) 4 *European Political Science Review* 51.

[15] On the latter see KJ Alter, *The European Court's Political Power: Selected Essays* (Oxford University Press, 2009); Weiler (n 11); E Stein, 'Lawyers, Judges, and the Making of a Transnational Constitution' (1981) 75 *American jJournal of International Law* 1.

[16] S Weatherill, *The Internal Market as a Legal Concept* (Oxford, Oxford University Press, 2016).

[17] See for instance the argument of majoritarian activism in LM Poiares Pessoa Maduro, *We the Court: The European Court of Justice and the European Economic Constitution* (Oxford, Hart Publishing, 1998).

programme. Another example is the geographical redesigning of the markets in goods after seven rounds of Member State accessions and one secession, tapping into geopolitical concerns. The Court has weathered economic recessions and revivals caused by energy crises, financial meltdowns, technological advances,[18] as well as natural and health emergencies (such as the mad cow and the foot and mouth disease outbreaks). Finally, shifts in supranational regulatory ambition and methods of market regulation from early attempts of unification to the principle of minimum standards,[19] the open method of coordination, or smart regulation required a shift in judicial action.[20]

There is a caveat to the last point. It might be difficult to discern the most consequential relationships from a multitude of factors. Directing the gaze towards handpicked parameters and a general systematic approach might be too crude. Combining systematic and detailed legal analysis with the criteria of the selection of the relevant parameters (the reading of judgments and literature) seeks to minimise this potential risk.

Sixth, and finally, representativeness and external validity. Free movement of goods judgments support the study of outlier judgments, trends, and exceptional vs recurring circumstances. Regarding representativeness; even if the judgments based on the Treaty provisions on goods have become scarcer over the past decade,[21] the framework and the principles they have created apply across the board, cross-cutting policy areas.[22] Practically, the free movement of goods has created a large body of case-law, representing 15 per cent of judgments issued by the Court since 1960, ranging from path-breaking cases to routine clarifications of the Common Customs Tariff.

In conclusion, the characteristics of the free movement of goods discussed above suggest that the analysis of these judgments can support an empirically accurate and nuanced account of the relationship between the external context and the departures from the model justification, formulated as three distinct types of good judgment: The non-sanctioning Europeanisation of national policies; the deferential upholding of free movement rights; and the bounded undesirable interpretation.[23] To recall, these emerge from the accounts of judicial decision-making discussed in chapter two, and the reading of case-law through the lens of competing interests (European Union, legal, national, individual, collective, financial, political) to identify typical claims raised in individual disputes.

[18] Reg (EU) 2022/2025 on contestable and fair markets in the digital sector and amending Directives (EU) 2019/1937 and (EU) 2020/1828 (Digital Markets Act), OJ L 265, 12.10.2022, p. 1–66.

[19] A Vauchez, 'When Scholarship Matters: Theory-Building and Theory Effects in the EU Polity Context' [2020] *iCourts Working Paper Series, No. 200, IMAGINE Paper no. 7, 2020* 1.

[20] F Mancini, 'The Making of a Constitution for Europe' (1989) 26 *Common Market Law Review* 595.

[21] ICON 2023.

[22] Art 34 TFEU has generated especially lively academic discussions. See R Schütze, "Re-Constituting" the Internal Market: Towards a Common Law of International Trade?' (2020) 39 *Yearbook of European Law* 250.

[23] Ch three.

Because free movement of goods case-law raises a different set of legal questions than the free movement of persons case-law, the same parameters or types of good judgment might vary in importance and relevance, not only because one citizen's right to purchase the brand of washing powder of their choice and the other to supply it is trivial compared to the rights to social security, privacy, and family life.[24] An additional advantage in selecting goods and persons is that they are at once quite similar and yet distinct; together, they provide insight into the range of factors that compel the Court's legal response to context. General considerations underpinning the selection of the parameters and types of good judgment, however, remain unchanged:

a) The non-sanctioning Europeanisation of national policies, which subjects national rules and policies to European standards. The analysis focuses on the standard of judicial review (proportionality review).
b) The deferential upholding of European rights unpacks the relationship between the Court's legal decision about the applicant's claim for rights protection or a concrete negative outcome for the state and the choice to delegate the terms of its application to the national court.
c) The bounded undesirable interpretation, which considers the broader implications of individual interpretations or interpretive choices for the regulatory autonomy of the Member State in the free movement of goods or adjacent policy areas. For instance, a decision that a national system of sanitary inspections restricts the imports of poultry has implications for the regulation of human and animal health.

This chapter could never do justice to the intimidatingly complex scholarship nor present a fair and nuanced picture of the case-law. It focuses on a limited set of recurring and relevant parameters which permeate these debates and case-law and embody conflicting visions of European integration and illuminate the relationship between the Court's reasoning, the legal solutions it reaches and their immediate political and economic implications.

The remainder of the chapter is structured as follows. Section b) outlines the existing legal framework governing the free movement of goods in two subsections. It first presents the relevant Treaty provisions and ensuing legislation, painted in broad strokes, to illustrate the magnitude of regulation and the recurrent question of the bounds of the European Union's regulatory competence and the Court's power. Then, it engages with substantive legal questions and judge-made concepts through individual judgments animating academic debates and jurisprudence. The discussion includes the conception of goods, the nature of measures restricting trade, the application of mandatory requirements, the

[24] That said, free movement of goods can be linked to fundamental rights such as media pluralism (*Familiapress*) and free press / speech when restrictions are placed on the importation or exportation of books, magazines or video cassettes. P Oliver et al, *Oliver on Free Movement of Goods in the European Union* (Oxford, Hart Publishing, 2010) 13.

scope of Article 36 TFEU and the limits of Article 30 TFEU. The examples illustrate how abstract concepts and general discontent with free movement and a common market for goods emerge from concrete disputes.

Section c) is a cursory portrait of the legal questions and issues in the case-law from the 1960s to the 2020s. Section d) outlines the parameters of good judgment in the free movement of goods case-law, linking the logic of good judgment with the legal framework governing free movement of goods. Section e) illustrates how the parameters interact in three types of good judgment via three emblematic judgments: *Schmidberger*, to illustrate the non-sanctioning Europeanisation of national policy choices; *Brasserie*, to illustrate the deferential protection of free movement rights; and *Newcastle Disease*, to illustrate the bounded undesirable interpretation.[25] Section f) summarises the argument and reflects on the long-term trends.

B. THE LEGAL FRAMEWORK OF FREE MOVEMENT OF GOODS

i. The Ambiguous Heart of the System

The Treaty on the European Union (TEU) envisages the internal market in Article 3. Article 26 TFEU defines it as an area without internal frontiers in which the free movement of goods, persons, services, and capital is ensured. The free movement of goods is often considered the most fundamental of the four freedoms.[26]

By omitting any indication of the proper balance between the manifold objectives listed in Article 3 TEU,[27] the hierarchy of regulatory priorities and the precise methods of achieving them,[28] the Treaties have effectively introduced a constitutional ambiguity at the heart of the internal market.[29] This has left the

[25] Case C-112/00, *Eugen Schmidberger*, ECLI:EU:C:2003:333, Case 40/82, Commission v United Kingdom (Newcastle Disease), ECLI:EU:C:1982:285 and Joined cases C-46/93 and C-48/93, Brasserie du Pêcheur and Factortame, ECLI:EU:C:1996:79.

[26] E Spaventa, 'The Classic Freedom? The Free Movement of Goods: Old Doctrines, New Cases and Contemporary Reflections' in S Garben and I Govaere (eds), *The Internal Market 2.0* (Oxford Hart Publishing, 2021); Armstrong (n 3); R Schütze, *European Union Law* (Oxford, Oxford University Press, 2021).

[27] Art 3 TEU lists the objectives of the internal market: sustainable development of Europe based on balanced economic growth and price stability and a competitive social market economy with full employment and social progress, and a high level of environmental protection. The Union will promote scientific and technological advances, social justice, equality between women and men, solidarity between generations and protection of the rights of the child, combat social exclusion and discrimination. Finally, it shall promote economic, social, and territorial cohesion, and solidarity among Member States while ensuring rich cultural and linguistic diversity, safeguarding Europe's cultural heritage. The final (6th) para of Art 3 concludes that 'The Union shall pursue its objectives by appropriate means commensurate with the competences which are conferred upon it in the Treaties.' Art 3(3) of the Treaty on European Union (TEU).

[28] N Nic Shuibhne, *The Coherence of EU Free Movement Law: Constitutional Responsibility and the Court of Justice* (Oxford, Oxford University Press, 2013) 44.

[29] Weatherill (n 16).

European institutions, especially the Court of Justice, with the freedom, authority, and legitimacy to make key regulatory choices within the broadly framed Treaty provisions.

The TFEU regulates the customs union and the free movement of goods in Title II of Part Three, Articles 28 to 37. Among these, Articles 30 and 34 TFEU take centre stage in case-law and scholarship. Article 30 TFEU prohibits all customs duties on imports and exports as well as any other charges with the same effect. Customs duties are charges levied on imported or exported goods, making imported goods more expensive than the competing domestic products. Export duties are an indirect subsidy for domestic manufacturers of primary goods, encouraging exports of products with a higher value added and thereby making domestic products more competitive on the global market.

The most famous case in which the Court considered the prohibition of customs duties on imports is *Van Gend*.[30] At stake was Article 12 EEC or the standstill clause, a precursor to the current Article 30 TFEU, which obliges Member States to 'refrain from introducing between themselves any new customs duties on imports or exports or any charges having equivalent effect, and from increasing those which they already apply in their trade with each other'. The Court decided that the importer (a private party) could refuse the payment of a higher import duty imposed unilaterally by the home state, enforcing the prohibition of Article 12 EEC directly in national courts.

Article 30 TFEU, which prohibits customs duties and chargers with equivalent effect, invites interpretive choices. The Court defined 'any pecuniary charge, whatever its designation and mode of application, which is imposed unilaterally on goods by reason of the fact that they cross a frontier and which is not a customs duty in the strict sense' as a charge having equivalent effect within the meaning of Article 12 and the succeeding/pursuant Articles of the Treaty.'[31] However, a charge is not a charge having equivalent effect to a customs duty if it relates 'to the general system of internal taxation applied systematically in accordance with the same criteria and at the same stage of marketing to domestic and imported products alike,' and is paid for 'a service actually rendered to the importer or the exporter and is of an amount commensurate with that service'.[32]

Typically, these borderline situations trigger the application of Article 110 TFEU, which prohibits the Member States from imposing, 'directly or indirectly, on the products of other Member States any internal taxation of any kind in excess of that imposed directly or indirectly on similar domestic products. The Member States may not impose on the products of other Member States any internal taxation that would afford indirect protection to other products'.

[30] Case 26/62, *Van Gend en Loos* ECLI:EU:C:1963:1.
[31] Case 39/82, *Donner*, ECLI:EU:C:1983:3, para 7.
[32] ibid., para 7.

The boundary between prohibited charges in Article 30 and permitted non-discriminatory taxes in Article 110 TFEU is porous and ambiguous, meaning that the Court's conceptualisation of the charges is the decisive point in a concrete dispute – if the Court finds that the charge is a tax, the Member State can impose it if similar foreign and domestic products are treated alike. Hence, claimants will insist on the application of Article 30 TFEU, increasing the chances that the Court will find the national measure incompatible with free movement of goods, while the respondent Member State will insist on the application of Article 110 TFEU, increasing the chances that the Court will find the national measure compatible with free movement. The underlying conflict in such disputes is not only legal, but concerns a deeper question of sovereignty, which is constitutional-political.

Articles 34 and 35 TFEU prohibit quantitative restrictions on imports and exports, as well as all measures with the same effect. They have never been amended and have simply been renumbered pursuant to Treaty changes. Quantitative restrictions are non-pecuniary burdens imposed on the import or export of goods, like specific numerical limits on the quantity or value of goods that can be imported or exported during a given period.[33]

The Court first defined quantitative restrictions in *Geddo* as 'measures which amount to a total or partial restraint of, according to the circumstances, imports, exports or goods in transit'.[34] In *Dassonville*, the Court defined measures having an effect equivalent to quantitative restrictions as 'all trading rules enacted by Member States which are capable of hindering, directly or indirectly, actually or potentially, intra-Community trade'.[35] The Member States could continue to maintain reasonable national measures guaranteeing the authenticity of a product's designation of origin for consumers to prevent unfair practices in so far as they did not hinder intra-Community trade and were accessible to all Community nationals.[36] However, the Member States could not impose national restrictive measures which arbitrarily discriminated against foreign products or presented a disguised restriction under any circumstances.[37]

In substance, the sentence cited from *Dassonville* echoes the final sentence of Article 36 TFEU, which allows derogations from the free movement of goods grounded in public morality, public security, or the protection of industrial and commercial property if they do not arbitrarily discriminate or disguise trade

[33] For the basic definitions see the Commission's Glossary of terms https://trade.ec.europa.eu/access-to-markets/en/glossary.

[34] Case 2/73, *Geddo v Ente Nazionale Risi*, ECLI:EU:C:1973:89, para 7.

[35] Case 8/74, *Dassonville*, ECLI:EU:C:1974:82, para 5.

[36] *Dassonville*, paras 6 and 7.

[37] *Dassonville* concerned a national provision prohibiting the import of goods bearing a designation of origin where such goods are not accompanied by an official document issued by the government of the exporting country certifying their right to such designation. Only direct importers could obtain such certificate with ease.

restrictions. The list of derogations is finite, mirroring Article XX of the GATT, and reflecting the values that the signatories considered important in the 1950s.[38]

The Court effectively expanded this list via interpretation of Article 34 TFEU, in line with the changing times. The judgment in *Cassis de Dijon* introduced the so-called mandatory requirements, stating that:

> Obstacles to movement within the Community resulting from disparities between the national laws relating to the marketing of the products in question must be accepted in so far as those provisions may be recognized as being necessary in order to satisfy mandatory requirements relating in particular to the effectiveness of fiscal supervision, the protection of public health, the fairness of commercial transactions and the defense of the consumer.[39]

The dispute arose because of a designated product requirement rule: a French-produced Cassis could not be sold or marketed as a liquor in Germany because it did not meet the minimum German alcohol content of 25 per cent, although it met the minimum alcohol content of liquors in France set to 15–20 per cent. The German rule was neither contrary to European Union law nor incompatible with free movement because the European legislator did not yet regulate the alcohol content of liquors.[40]

The Court saw 'no valid reason why, provided that they have been lawfully produced and marketed in one of the Member States, alcoholic beverages should not be introduced into any other Member State',[41] and Germany therefore had to recognise French standards of production as equivalent to its own standards of production (the presumption of equivalence).

The implications of the judgment were wide-ranging and at times conflicting. Practically, the presumption of equivalence possibility stimulated cross-border trade by removing regulatory obstacles, increasing the choice of products for consumers, widening the market for traders, and disadvantaging domestic producers of competing products.

As a precedent in terms of juridical consequences, the judgment expanded the reach of free movement to a potentially unlimited set of national measures while also making sure that the Member States could invoke an equivalent unlimited set of justifications if they could demonstrate that those measures were reasonable; the list was non-exhaustive. In subsequent cases, the Court considered the justifications if the measures applied indistinctly to foreign and domestic products, meaning that they did not directly or indirectly discriminate against foreign goods.

Institutionally, Cassis changed the Commission's harmonisation approach. Following the judgment, the Commission issued a communication which argued

[38] Barnard (n 1) 146.

[39] Case 120/78, *Cassis de Dijon*, ECLI:EU:C:1979:42, para 8.

[40] The situation has changed dramatically. See e.g. contributions in A Albors-Llorens, C Barnard and B Leucht, *Cassis de Dijon: 40 Years On* (London, Bloomsbury Publishing, 2021).

[41] *Cassis*, para 14.

that much harmonising legislation became unnecessary due to the presumption of equivalence.[42]

In terms of legal authority or jurisdictionally, the judgment placed additional weight on justification at the Court's discretion. The presumption of lawfulness put the Member State on the defensive, forcing it to justify its regulatory choices in the Court's jargon of mandatory requirements (the effectiveness of fiscal supervision, the protection of public health, the fairness of commercial transactions etc.), and demonstrate that regulation pursued legitimate aims with the necessary and least restrictive means (proportionality).

An early doctrinally clear position was that the Member States could rely on mandatory requirements only when the measures were indistinctly applicable based on *Cassis*. To justify distinctly applicable measures, Member States could only invoke express Treaty derogations (based on Article 36 TFEU). Over time, and under the circumstances of individual cases, the Court increasingly acknowledged that mandatory requirements could similarly justify distinctly applicable measures, muddling the distinction between judge-made and Treaty imposed derogations from free movement, as well as between national measures that differentiated between domestic and foreign goods and those that did not.[43] More recently, the Court accepted justifications under Article 36 TFEU and mandatory requirements in cases of measures that interfered with market access.[44]

Finally, the horizontal clauses of Articles 114 and 115 TFEU authorise 'the approximation of the provisions laid down by law, regulation or administrative action in Member States which have as their object the establishment and functioning of the internal market'. In addition, Article 352 TFEU allows Union regulatory intervention when necessary to attain one of the objectives set out in the Treaties without and beyond the explicitly conferred powers. The Council can adopt the necessary measures acting unanimously on a proposal from the Commission and after obtaining the consent of the European Parliament. Importantly, the adopted measures may not harmonise or approximate Member States' laws or regulations where the Treaties exclude harmonisation.

Articles 114 TFEU and 352 TFEU have served as a legal basis for innumerable legislative instruments. Free movement of goods is extensively regulated and the legislation related to the customs union and the free movement of goods currently in force comprises 1255 legal acts; over 4800 further legal acts are no longer in force.[45] Strikingly, most instruments concern the application of

[42] Communication from the Commission regarding the *Cassis de Dijon* judgment, 1980 OJ C256/2.

[43] The literature disagrees on this point, leaning towards the opinion that mandatory requirements also apply to distinctly applicable measures. See for instance Oliver et al (n 24).

[44] Case C-110/05, *Commission v Italy (Italian Trailers)*, ECLI:EU:C:2009:66.

[45] Statistics available at https://eur-lex.europa.eu/browse/directories/legislation.html?displayProfile=allRelAllConsDocProfile&classification=in-force (last accessed in October 2023).

the Common Customs Tariff. The closely related common agricultural policy regulating inter alia agricultural goods counts 3725 legal instruments, and fisheries another 725. Finally, the Union adopted 1172 instruments approximating the national laws in the internal market, with 189 governing motor vehicles, 500 governing foodstuffs, 47 governing dangerous substances ... and so on.[46]

Regulation has both upsides and downsides. On the upside, goods become cheaper and more readily available; the selection diversifies and their quality increases. The downsides, however, range from mundane to severe. A good example of the former is the regulation of bendy cucumbers (innocuous bar a small group of frustrated producers and traders[47]), which the public cited for decades as an exemplary symbol of the European Union's absurd and unnecessary regulation. The common organisation of agricultural markets, allowing for the excess production of agricultural goods, has been more serious. Butter mountains and wine lakes have displayed the distorting effects of centralised market regulation which is unresponsive to actual market demand.[48] Today, one could argue that path-dependent heavy regulation of agriculture and the organisation of common agricultural policy stands in the way of green transition, causing irreparable harm on a global scale.[49] Over time even mild frustrations and harmless downsides accumulate and increase political resistance to free movement and the upholding of a common market for goods. Regulation of goods upends traditions, aspirations, and values (even those that appear doubtful or idiosyncratic at first sight),[50] such as the traditional Italian production of pasta,[51] the English Sunday,[52] or the Danish recycling system.[53] These conventions persist even when customers continue buying pasta made of pricier durum wheat, become accustomed to extended opening hours, and internalise the new rules on bottle deposits.

ii. Rights at Stake and Interests at Play in the Case-Law

The Court resolves real life disputes with abstract concepts, principles, and standards, (re)drawing the limits of national regulatory autonomy and the reach

[46] The statistics are available at https://eur-lex.europa.eu/browse/directories/legislation.html?root_default=CC_1_CODED%3D02&displayProfile=allRelAllConsDocProfile&classification=in-force#arrow_02 (last accessed in November 2023).

[47] European Commission (Press Release, 30 June 2009), 'The Return of the Bendy Cucumber: "Wonky" Fruit and Vegetables Back on Sale from 1st July'.

[48] LJ Reinhorn, 'Butter Mountains and Wine Lakes' (2007) 94 *Economics Letters* 197.

[49] G Pe'er et al, 'Action Needed for the EU Common Agricultural Policy to Address Sustainability Challenges' (2020) 2 *People and Nature* 305.

[50] F De Witte, 'Sex, Drugs & EU Law: The Recognition of Moral and Ethical Diversity in EU Law' (2013) 50 *Common Market Law Review* 1545. See also S Mair, 'Kahn in Luxembourg: A Prolegomena to the Cultural Study of EU Law' (2023) 24 *German Law Journal* 735.

[51] Case 407/85, 3 *Glocken*, ECLI:EU:C:1988:401.

[52] A Arnull, 'What Shall We Do on Sunday?' (1991) 16 *European Law Review* 112.

[53] Case 302/86, *Commission v Denmark*, ECLI:EU:C:1988:421.

of free movement, the relationship between the public and the private sphere which interact through the market, as well as the relationship between European courts and legislators. Often, it appeals to the common constitutional traditions of the Member States, and to European values, aims, and the common commitment to an ever-closer Union among the peoples of Europe. Typically, it stresses the importance of the proper functioning of the internal market, reminding the audiences of its sizeable and well-documented economic benefits.

A judgment on a correct interpretation of a Treaty Article and related legislation has both immediate economic and more long-term non-economic (political, symbolic) implications. It either promotes the idea of free markets and a market driven economy, or conversely lends itself to the opposite idea of state coordinated markets and market interventionism. *Cassis* promotes the Union's economic and political interest for market integration by contravening national standards that present barriers to free movement of goods in the internal market. As democratically elected national legislators have adopted these standards, *Cassis* and other similar judgments supersede the authority of those governments to govern. Because the Court's judgments cannot replace national standards with new common standards – the latter being the domain of the Union legislator – its interpretation of Treaty provisions and its weighing of legal arguments has a (de)regulatory effect. De-regulation plays into a specific ideology of neoliberalism, and while the Court might not share said ideology (the philosophy of the market), it effectively contributes to its realisation.[54] Hence, the interpretation of Treaty provisions and the weighing of legal arguments is symbolically important in determining what kind of Europe there will be for which kind of citizens.[55]

The economic benefits of trade gloss over the social, cultural, and political differences between the Member States, and divergence in their moral standards, values, religious beliefs, or political ideology. The analysis of case-law clearly shows that these differences continue to exist and resurface in disputes. The Court has repeatedly managed the conflict between common and national economic interests of rival Member States[56] which emerge from the rules and practices shielding the home market from out-of-state competition (the national protectionist instincts). In every case thus far, the concern was identical for each protected product – Italian wine, Spanish strawberries, French turkeys, or Belgian tomatoes.

[54] E.g. MA Wilkinson, *Authoritarian Liberalism and the Transformation of Modern Europe* (Oxford, Oxford University Press, 2021).

[55] A Somek, *Individualism: An Essay on the Authority of the European Union* (Oxford, Oxford University Press, 2008).

[56] On the role of the Court as a mediator of the conflicts between the Member States see W Phelan, *Great Judgments of the European Court of Justice Rethinking the Landmark Decisions of the Foundational Period* (Cambridge, Cambridge University Press, 2019).

The parameters of jurisprudence, detailed in section d) below, capture the concepts, principles, and standards which reflect the Court's approach to interpretation, its conception of free movement of goods, and the object of litigation (the main legal issues over time, see section c) below). Crucially, the combinations of parameters capture key parts of justification, the reasoning, approach to interpretation, and case outcomes relevant to the study of three types of good judgment.

C. FREE MOVEMENT JUDGMENTS: AN OVERVIEW OF LEGAL QUESTIONS

Table 4 describes the legal issues arising in relation to the Treaty provisions on free movement of goods and the often-overlooked customs union. It does so by listing the legal issues that the Court has addressed since the 1960s. Scholarship agrees that the Court chiselled the foundations of free movement of goods in the 1970s, nuancing the understanding of the regulatory barriers and potential justifications through the mandatory requirements doctrine during the 1980s, and trying to define the boundaries of free movement throughout the 1990s.[57] In each period, numerous tests and doctrines emerged and developed, some particular to the free movement of goods (the principle of mutual recognition) and others of general application which were imported from other fields (the proportionality test). The Table focuses exclusively on the free movement of goods, omitting the latter.

As is clear from the Table, questions pertaining to the Common Customs Tariff, Articles 30, 34, and 35 TFEU have been generating the steadiest jurisprudence. The Court has often dealt with disputes arising due to alleged discriminatory treatment of goods based on their origin. Issues concerning the level of harmonisation and the intensity of the regulation of free trade peaked after 1980, following the Court's judgments in *Dassonville* and *Cassis de Dijon*, and coinciding with the adoption of the Single European Act in 1987. While these judgments primarily had a liberalising, de-regulatory effect, the Single European Act has spearheaded legislation approximating the Member States' laws (regulation). The harmonisation label in the Table captures both under one heading (in one row) given that the Court has often been asked about the significance of harmonising measures and their impact on national regulatory autonomy, either in relation to European rules or in the lack thereof – a 'two sides of the same coin' phenomenon. The four rows in Table 4 under the label harmonisation reflect the possible scenarios.

[57] Spaventa (n 27).

Table 4 Free movement of goods judgments: Overview of legal issues. The first column from the left identifies the legal issues discussed in the judgments, for instance questions about the common customs tariff (row number 6) or the level of harmonisation (the four bottom rows). The columns starting from the second column from the left indicate the number of judgments in which the selected legal issue occurred. The total number of issues does not correspond to the total number of judgments because one judgment can address more than one legal issue

Object of dispute / legal issue	1960	1965	1970	1975	1980	1985	1990	1995	2000	2005	2010	2015	2020	Total
Article 30 TFEU (fiscal barriers, charges of equivalent effect)	2	7	4	8	17	17	20	20	19	28	28	29		199
Article 110 TFEU (internal taxation measures)	1	3	3	3	8	2	2	5	5	6	7	6		51
Article 34 TFEU & 35 TFEU (measures of equivalent effect on imports / exports)	2		6	26	32	52	39	20	37	31	23	18	3	289
Selling arrangement / falling outside A 34 TFEU							3	4	1			1		9
Restrictive measures: New tariffs, import quotas	2		4	10	8	13	12	10	15	12	3	4	3	96
Common customs tariff		1	14	21	34	25	31	21	18	42	42	49	12	310
Distinctly applicable national measure		1	2	4	6	10	2	3	4	2	1	1		36
Indistinctly applicable national measure	1		1	3	9	7	7	1	8	7	3	1		48
Discrimination on grounds of the origin of the goods	1	2	4	17	18	20	16	7	11	10	3	3		112

(continued)

Table 4 *(Continued)*

Free movement of goods provisions	10	12	42	83	155	177	173	139	147	178	150	134	22	1,422
Reference to another freedom	1		2		1	2	3	6	3		1	1		20
Reference to two or more freedoms					1		1			1				3
Reference to ECSC	1				1	1								3
Reference to provisions on agriculture	2	2	8	11	6	6		1	2	1		1		40
Reference to the Treaty provisions / competition law			2	6	2	3	10	2	4	1		1		31
Reference to the Treaty provisions / State Aid				4	2	1	7	1	3	1				19
The Court establishes that the policy area is not yet harmonized				9	23	21	21	12	15	13	8	4		126
The Court does not discuss the level of harmonization				4	9	12	10	13	16	12	11	5	6	98
The Court acknowledges minimum harmonization				3	8	7	13	4	14	9	8	7		73
The Court acknowledges exhaustive harmonization			5	2	3	8	5	6	9	9	6	4	2	59

The Table also suggests how legal scholarship and legal practice can create parallel legal universes – the questions that preoccupy scholars are principled conceptual questions of selling arrangements, access tests, and acceptable justification of distinctly applicable measures, the convergence of four freedoms, and the limits of where the Court redraws the lines of competences and changes accepted interpretations and categorisations. The Court has rarely pronounced itself on selling arrangements or actively considered the relationship between more than two freedoms. One of the most debated principles in European Union law, the principle of mutual recognition, is almost absent from the case-law in its doctrinal form. While brought for consideration by the parties to the disputes from time to time, the Court has actively engaged with the concept in only eighteen judgments (1.4 per cent of the sample).[58]

D. THE PARAMETERS OF GOOD JUDGMENT

This section considers the parameters of free movement of goods case-law, defined as legal characteristics and information about the case. The first subsection describes the former, illustrating them with examples from the annotated judgments. As chapter five (free movement of persons) already introduced and described the same characteristics, the section is concise, highlighting the distinct features of the free movement of goods where appropriate. The second subsection lists the relevant information about the disputes – the applicants and the legal issues pertinent to the Court's decision-making – and details underlying reasoning and case outcomes. Chapter seven explores the institutional characteristics more closely, comparing judgments on the free movement of goods with those on the free movement of persons.

i. Non-Sanctioning Europeanisation of National Policies

In a judgment scrutinising but not sanctioning national policies which directly regulate or affect the free movement of goods, the Court de facto examines national regulatory choices through a European prism, elaborating or applying a supranational and often judge-made standard of review.

This situation juxtaposes three legally relevant characteristics of case-law: the proportionality reasoning of the Court (proportionality test) as a mode of bringing national policy choices within the Treaty range and thus being subject to common standards; the Court's decision that the national measures or practices are (in)compatible with free movement and (un)justified; and the

[58] Data on file with the author.

implications of this outcome on national regulatory choices (autonomy of the Member State).

As mentioned in chapter five, the free movement judgments follow a predictable structure. To recapitulate, the Court first examines whether a disputed national measure or practice restricts free movement. Upon finding a restriction, it considers whether a national measure or practice is justifiable and proportionate – does it pursue a legitimate aim and is it necessary to achieve this aim? This highly standardised methodology is designed to allow for creative application tailored to the specificities of concrete cases. It has also allowed the Court to extend the reach of free movement judge-made rules and principles while finding unique solutions to address different national measures and administrative practices when declaring them incompatible with said rules and principles.[59]

A decisive factor in the Court's review of national measures and practices obstructing or banning trade in goods is the assessment of the nature of the restrictions they impose and whether they discriminate between domestic and foreign products. In *Torfaen*,[60] the referring court asked whether national rules prohibiting retailers from opening their premises on Sundays were incompatible with Article 34 TFEU (then Article 30 EEC), which prohibits measures having an effect equivalent to quantitative restrictions. The Court first established that the rules were indistinctly applicable to domestic and foreign products; hence, they were compatible with free movement if the obstacles they created were necessary to achieve legitimate aims with the least restrictive means.[61]

To clarify, the requirement of justification arises only when a national measure restricts and therefore creates a barrier to inter-state trade. When this is the case, Member States must defend their regulatory autonomy within the scope of Article 36 TFEU or mandatory requirements, and against a European standard set to evaluate their proportionality. The Court can examine whether the Member States have pursued a legitimate aim and chosen the least restrictive means if it recognises the justificatory ground as acceptable. Occasionally, the Court comes close to adjudicating the relevance or 'appropriateness' of moral choices and values. In *Henn and Darby*, the Court examined the English rules imposing criminal sanctions on the importers of obscene material (pornography) from Denmark. It held that the measures certainly restricted trade, but did so on acceptable grounds in line with European Union law.[62]

Overall, the literature suggests that the Court has extended the reach of free movement by exercising caution (good judgment) in the assessment of social and economic policy choices. When finding objection with those choices, for instance, the Court has limited its rationalisation to the particular way in which

[59] For the argument see LR Helfer and A-M Slaughter, 'Toward a Theory of Effective Supranational Adjudication' (1997) 107 *Yale Law Journal* 273.

[60] C-145/88, *Torfaen*, ECLI:EU:C:1989:593.

[61] *Torfaen*, para 12.

[62] Case 34/79, *Henn and Darby*, ECLI:EU:C:1979:295.

the states have implemented the choice. *Commission v Austria*[63] is a typical example of this practice: the Court accepted the need for national measures prohibiting heavy traffic on a major highway to reduce the nitrogen dioxide emissions but held that the traffic ban imposed was disproportionate. Interestingly, the Court did not condemn Austria because the measure was disproportionate, but because Austria had not carefully examined the possibility for alternative, less restrictive means before adopting such 'a radical measure' which cut off 'a vital communication link between certain Member States' to certain types of traffic. Moreover, the transitional period of two months between the enactment and the entry into force of the traffic ban did not allow the parties affected to adapt to the new circumstances.[64]

Because national rules and practices will rarely be beyond the reach of free movement law – trade in goods touches on all aspects of social life across Member States – understanding the Court's methodology of justification,[65] the circumstances in which it accepts the justification put forward by the Member State, and how it qualifies measures and policy choices as being lawful under the common rules becomes crucial to the understanding of good judgment and thus the Court as a context-conscious lawmaker.

ii. Deferral of Authority in Judgments Upholding Free Movement Rights and Principles

A type of good judgment characterised by the deferential upholding and expanding of European rights and principles juxtaposes the Court's recognition of free movement rights (the decision about the applicant's claim) with its decision that the national courts or legislators are better suited to fix the terms of its application to the facts of the cases. The Court can suspend the concrete application or determination of the terms of the application of European Union law by delegating the decision-making authority to the national institutions.

The parameter protection of free movement rights reflects the Court's position regarding the applicant's free movement claims. In free movement of goods cases (as shown in section c) of this chapter), domestic or foreign traders will typically challenge restrictive national rules hindering or prohibiting imports or occasionally claim restitution for damages arising due to the unlawful restrictions of free movement.[66] The Court can either uphold or reject these claims

[63] Case C-320/03, *Commission v Austria*, ECLI:EU:C:2005:684.

[64] F Jacobs, 'The Role of the European Court Of Justice in the Protection of the Environment' (2006) 18 *Journal of Environmental Law* 185.

[65] Weatherill (n 16) 99.

[66] Historically, this has proven to be a typical case, also feeding into the theorising of European market integration / the neo-functionalist account. See for instance Stone Sweet (n 10); A Stone

put forward by a private individual (a physical or a legal person), and / or defer the decision on whether the measure is unduly restrictive, disproportionate, or impossible to justify in the concrete circumstances to the referring court. Deference is discussed in chapters five and seven.[67]

iii. Bounded Undesirable Interpretation

A judgment with bounded undesirable interpretation balances the actual implications of the ruling for the regulatory autonomy of the Member States with the legal development of European Union's law and legal system: its precedential effect or juridical consequences. The three legally relevant characteristics which reflect the rationale of bounded undesirable interpretation are the implications for the Member States' autonomy, the Court's interpretive choice and the judgment's contribution to the acquis.

The Court's interpretation extends or restricts the reach of the internal market, thereby determining how entrenched European concepts and standards will be. In *GB-Inno-BM*,[68] the Court proclaimed that free movement of goods concerns not only traders but also individuals; particularly in frontier areas, it requires that consumers resident in one Member State may travel freely to the territory of another Member State to shop under the same conditions as the local population. According to the Court, this freedom for consumers was compromised if they did not have access to advertising available in the country where they were intending to make purchases. Hence, the national measure prohibiting the distribution of such advertising was examined under the Treaty free movement of goods rules.

In the (in)famous *Buy Irish* case,[69] the Court extended the reach of free movement to non-binding measures promoting national products as measures attributable to the State, holding that they could be measures of equivalent effect. Finally, in *Bluhme*,[70] the Court rejected the *de minimis* defence, arguing that Article 34 TFEU prohibited a restriction on apiculture for certain species of bees on the tiny Danish island of Læsø. These judgments positioned the Court as the final authority on a potentially unlimited set of national measures irrespective of their temporal or spatial scope, economic importance, and political considerations.

Sweet and TL Brunell, 'The European Court and the National Courts: A Statistical Analysis of Preliminary References, 1961–95' (1998) 5 *Journal of European Public Policy* 66.

[67] Ch five, pp 46 and 192.

[68] Case C-362/88, *GB-INNO-BM*, ECLI:EU:C:1990:102.

[69] Case 249/81, *Commission v Ireland*, ECLI:EU:C:1982:402, para 28. For a discussion see J Hojnik, 'Free Movement of Goods in a Labyrinth: Can Buy Irish Survive the Crises?' (2012) 49 *Common Market Law Review* 291.

[70] Case C-67/97, *Bluhme*, ECLI:EU:C:1998:584.

Far-reaching definitions of key concepts and judgments elaborating the individual elements of these definitions can set non-negligible limitations on national regulatory autonomy. From the national point of view, such interpretations seem undesirable beyond the facts of the disputes: for instance, in the *Beer Purity* infringement action,[71] Greece enacted the same rules on beer production as Germany (a party to the case) and all other EU Members States regulated the production of beer in one way or another. Finally, unpredictability in the Court's interpretation can create expectations that the losing state should prepare for further litigation and possibly further inroads into its regulatory autonomy.[72]

The Court can also contain or delimit the implications of its interpretive choices for the responding Member State. *Scotch Whiskey*,[73] a case about the lawfulness under the Treaty of the Scottish Alcohol (Minimum Pricing) Act imposing a minimum price per unit of alcohol, offers a good example. While the Court clearly held that the Act obstructed trade within the meaning of Article 34 TFEU, it focused primarily on justification under Article 36 TFEU and the question of proportionality. Given the sensitive aim of the Act – to combat well-documented and alarming rates of consumption of cheap strong alcohol in Scotland – the Court adopted a more nuanced approach towards public-health considerations at the intersection with free movement of goods. Its ruling was that the national authorities could select the most effective measure to achieve specific public-health goals even if less restrictive measures could achieve its broader and more general health objectives. In short, the Court 'subtly moderated free movement and other common-market principles in favour of national autonomy'.[74]

iv. Relevant Information about Free Movement of Goods Cases

Disputes about the scope and the substance of free movement create opposition between traders' and state administrations' and regulators' interests. Upholding traders' claims imposes duties on Member States to enable free movement (imports, exports, or transit of goods) in contravention of national administrative practices, technical standards, safety requirements and so on. Infringement actions brought by the Commission have the same potential effect. The Commission often stands between two or more Member States,

[71] Case 178/84, *Commission v Germany (Beer Purity)*, ECLI:EU:C:1987:126.

[72] Under the assumption that the Court's judgments will spur new litigation. See e.g. R Daniel Kelemen, *Eurolegalism: The Transformation of Law and Regulation in the European Union* (Harvard, Harvard University Press, 2011).

[73] Case C-333/14, *Scotch Whisky Association*, ECLI:EU:C:2015:845. The case is also discussed in ch seven.

[74] A Albors-Llorens, 'The Alcohol (Minimum Pricing) (Scotland) Act 2012 and the Collision between Single-Market Objectives and Public-Interest Requirements' (2017) 76 *The Cambridge Law Journal* 25, 28.

using its institutional role to de-bilaterilise conflicts and thus turning them into infringements of European Union law by one Member State.[75] This effective Europeanisation of disputes and their transformation from horizontal to vertical contestations is often visible at the level of interventions – Member State governments typically intervene in support of either the Commission or the responding government. Hence, the participation of the Member States in the proceeding can be relevant in the analysis of good judgment.

Private persons, such as importers, can be natural or legal persons (undertakings), the latter often being better placed to bring 'high-profile' cases of principle to the Court or to litigate an issue repeatedly.[76] One example is the litigation which hammered out an entire sub-area of free movement law: 'As far as the place of industrial property within 'the free movement of goods' concept is concerned, those various *Centrafarm* rulings of the Court, between them, cover most of the ground'.[77] The Commission is a typical specialised repeat player with a strong influence on the Court.

Similarly, the information about the legal framework or legal provision which the Court is asked to interpret will influence the Court's reasoning and outcomes. Elements of a case, such as the range of justifications put forward by the Member States and the number supported or rejected by the Court, reflect an underlying or broader interest at stake (whether genuine or faux/hypothetical), and the significance of this for the Member States. The classification of the restriction as trade restriction, as a charge, or taxation, can be decisive.[78] Similarly, information about the date of the judgment can be indicative of the economic and political context in which the Court operates. Events like the empty chair, oil, or financial crises often increase governments' interventions into the economy, giving rise to unlawful protectionism. They also increase the political pressure on the Court to turn a blind eye to protectionist measures that would clearly be unlawful in normal circumstances.

E. EMBLEMATIC JUDGMENTS

i. Non-Sanctioning Europeanisation of National Policies: *Schmidberger*

The non-sanctioning Europeanisation of national policies is a type of good judgment which 1) subjects national policies and the ensuing rules adopted and

[75] See, in particular, the analysis of the Newcastle Disease in the following section. The point is made strongly by Phelan (n 56).

[76] On repeat players in European litigation see for instance H-W Micklitz, *The Politics of Judicial Co-Operation in the EU: Sunday Trading, Equal Treatment and Good Faith* (Cambridge, Cambridge University Press, 2005).

[77] M Van Empel, 'Centrafarm Revisited: A Few Comments on Cases 102/77 and 3/78' (1979) 16 *Common Market Law Review* 251, 251.

[78] See discussion about the delimitation between fiscal barriers and taxation.

administered at the local level to common European norms interpreted, applied and possibly constructed by the Court, 2) without declaring them objectionable or contrary to European Union law. The analysis focuses on the standard of judicial review (proportionality review) as a common methodology of the Court, often signalling a subtle imposition of a common standard designed to 'approximate' local divergencies without offending local sensitivities or aggravating brewing disagreement.

An important illustration of this type of good judgment is *Schmidberger*,[79] which juxtaposed the common interest of free transit of goods with local concerns relating to the associated environmental degradation. This conflict found a legal expression in the Treaty duty of the Member State (in this case, Austria) to act to prevent road closure during an environmental demonstration while upholding the protesters' rights of assembly and free expression by not preventing the demonstration.

Scholars have treated *Schmidberger* as a straightforward case,[80] providing a beautifully simple opportunity for the Court to address difficult principled questions.[81] The straightforwardness, however, follows only after a complete de-contextualisation of the legal questions and their separation from the underlying dispute.

As argued in more detail below, the Court decided *Schmidberger* when it was clear that Austria could not reduce traffic through the Inn valley by imposing higher tolls which disproportionately affected non-national traders, nor could it unilaterally restrict heavy traffic to protect the Inn Valley from suffering serious and concerning environmental degradation.[82] The Court's judgment offered a 'political' concession to resolve the issue, deciding that Austria could protect the environment indirectly by protecting the political rights of environmental activists, which were also recognised as common European values. Politically, Austria gained ground to press for a political compromise and the national and international levels while incidentally, indirectly, and at least partially containing its domestic political conflict arising from the frustration of the local population, disappointment of environmentalists, and the waning patience of haulers. This outcome could only be legally envisaged because the concerns it addressed could be considered as meeting the European common standard (i.e. they could be Europeanised). This message could, moreover, easily be conveyed through legal argumentation as an unsanctionable, 'state-friendly balancing' of conflicting interests and values.

[79] Case C-112/00, *Eugen Schmidberger v Austria*, ECLI:EU:C:2003:333.

[80] C Brown, 'Case C-112/00, Eugen Schmidberger, Internationale Transporte Und Planzüge v. Austria' (2003) 40 *Common Market Law Review* 1499, 1510.

[81] Weatherill (n 16) 137.

[82] Case C-205/98, *Commission v Austria (Toll rates)*, ECLI:EU:C:2000:493.

The Dispute

The Austrian authorities (the government of Innsbruck province) permitted Transitforum Austria Tirol, a group for the protection of the biosphere in the Alpine region, to demonstrate on the Brenner motorway. The protest blocked all traffic on the motorway between the Europabrücke service area[83] and the Schönberg toll station from 11am on Friday 12 June, 2000, until 3pm on Saturday 13 June, 2000. The timing of the closure was significant. Given the Austrian rules regulating road transit, heavy goods traffic stood still for almost four days (from Thursday, a public holiday, until Sunday evening), thus far exceeding the 30-hour window during which the demonstration was permitted.[84]

For Schmidberger, a German international transport company carrying timber from Germany to Italy and steel from Italy to Germany, the Brenner motorway served as a main transit route.

Schmidberger brought an action for damages against Austria because its lorries could not use the Brenner motorway for four consecutive days due to the protest. It argued that the regional authorities should have prohibited the demonstration, preventing the road closure which amounted to a full-blown restriction of the free movement of goods and which the protesters' right to freedom of expression and freedom of assembly was not deemed to justify. Austria was therefore liable for a breach of European Union law.

Austria objected, arguing that the local authorities only approved the demonstration after a detailed examination of the facts, disseminating the information about the closure of the motorway across Austria, Germany, and Italy well in advance to minimise disruption. The demonstration did not cause substantial traffic jams or other incidents, and the restriction of free movement was considered 'neither permanent nor serious'.[85] Finally, Austria submitted that it prioritised constitutionally protected freedoms of expression and assembly, given their fundamental and inviolable character in a democratic society.

The first instance court dismissed Schmidberger's action due to lack of proof that the lorries needed to use the Brenner motorway during the protest or an impossibility for routes using this road to be changed. The second instance court, seized by appeal, considered it necessary to determine whether Austria was obliged to keep the major transit route open by the TFEU's free movement of goods rules and the principle of sincere cooperation (Article 4(3) TEU). It also questioned whether this obligation should or could take precedence over the fundamental rights of freedom of expression and the freedom of assembly

[83] The location was symbolic – the European Bridge was a symbol of community and prosperity.

[84] Austria bans heavy goods traffic from 3pm to 12am on Saturdays, from midnight to 10pm on Sundays and public holidays and, for vehicles exceeding certain noise limits, from 10pm to 5am every night.

[85] Para 17.

guaranteed by Articles 10 and 11 of the European Convention for the Protection of Human Rights (ECHR). If it did, the appeal court inquired, could Austria then be liable for the breach of those rules and principles instead?

The Advocate General considered that the (in)action of the Austrian authorities could fall under Article 34 TFEU and seq. read in conjunction with the principle of sincere cooperation. Austria could be liable for not preventing the action of private individuals which caused a considerable restriction to free movement.[86] However, the decision to allow the protest was justifiable via the competing rights of the protesters to free expression and assembly, and made further permissible because of the particular circumstances of the protest. Among those exonerating circumstances, the Advocate General highlighted that the demonstration was a peaceful, non-threatening, isolated exercise of fundamental rights which was announced in advance. He added that the authorities tried to mitigate the obstruction by disseminating information about and ensuring the accessibility of alternative transit routes, making the case substantively different from the *Spanish Strawberries* case.[87] In the latter, the Court found France in breach of the Treaty for not preventing repeated violent incidents linked to French farmers protesting primarily against imports of strawberries from Spain. Although *Schmidberger* based its action on the *Strawberries* case, the Advocate General made a concerted distinction between the two cases. Finally, the Advocate General weighed in on the principle of State liability, engaging at length with the national rules on the burden of proof and evidence.

The Judgment

The Court reached the same conclusion as the Advocate General. It framed the conflicting interests in the case through the free movement of goods lens. Echoing the Advocate General's Opinion, the Court restated the central importance of the internal market, the fundamental nature of the free movement of goods for its proper functioning, and sincere cooperation.[88] It concluded that free movement was restricted, and this action was potentially contrary to Article 34 TFEU because the road closure effectively stopped all traffic of goods for more than thirty hours.

This logically raises the question of potential justification. The reasoning is built on two pillars: the European Union's commitment to fundamental rights protection (from restating the role of common constitutional traditions and related case-law, to the Preamble of the Single European Act), and the precedent establishing that the State bears the responsibility for the action of private

[86] The Advocate General did not think that the restriction to trade was negligible and could under any circumstance be treated as *de minimis*.

[87] Case C-265/95, *Commission v France (Spanish Strawberries)*, ECLI:EU:C:1997:595.

[88] *Schmidberger*, para 51.

individuals restricting free movement (the *Spanish Strawberries* case).[89] Like the Advocate General, the Court had to engage with the *Spanish Strawberries* case. The first pillar implied that the States's reliance on human rights protected under its constitution was valid justification for the restriction of free movement of goods, not a self-evident matter at the time.[90] It was a conscious choice on the part of the Court to 'pan-Europeanise' the conflict, deescalating the dispute from being a conflict between national constitutions and European Union law (two-level conflict) to a less explosive conflict of European Union values and protected interests (single-level conflict). In substance, the conflicting interests remained identical.

This emerges from paragraphs 76 and 77 of the judgment. The Court acknowledges that 'the national authorities relied on the need to respect fundamental rights guaranteed by both the ECHR and the Constitution of the Member State concerned in deciding to allow a restriction to be imposed on one of the fundamental freedoms enshrined in the Treaty'. However, the Court proceeds by stating that the case 'thus raises the question of the need to reconcile the requirements of the protection of fundamental rights in the Community with those arising from a fundamental freedom enshrined in the Treaty … , where the former are relied upon as justification for a restriction of the latter'.[91]

The Court effectively reassessed whether the national authorities struck the right balance between the relevant aspects of free movement and human rights as a matter of European Union law. The Court's recognition of the State's 'wide margin of discretion' led to a favourable outcome for the State but did not shield national choices from the Court's interference in the future in areas where Member States enjoyed full competence under the Treaty (e.g. protection of public security and health, fundamental rights protection when acting outside European Union law).

The Lost Highway

In *Schmidberger*, the Court searched for good judgment – a legally sound as well as politically and economically workable solution 1) showing Austria, the European Commission and the intervening Member States that European Union law did not tolerate unilateral measures to appease domestic protests and dissatisfaction, and 2) showing Austria that it would tolerate its handling of domestic protests and the dissatisfaction of domestic stakeholders. The following aspects of its reasoning, when contextualised, are interesting from the perspective of good judgment.

[89] Case C-265/95, *Commission v France (Spanish Strawberries)*, ECLI:EU:C:1997:595.

[90] Para 74. 'Thus, since both the Community and its Member States are required to respect fundamental rights, the protection of those rights is a legitimate interest which, in principle, justifies a restriction of the obligations imposed by Community law, even under a fundamental freedom guaranteed by the Treaty such as the free movement of goods.'

[91] Paras 76 and 77.

Once again, the Court's typical methodology of restriction-justification (proportionality) reasoning leads to atypical justification. In most instances, the Court finds that national measures restricting fee movement of goods fall foul of European rules and standards in judgments where it conducts a proportionality test (63 per cent).[92] This type of good judgment (non-sanctioning Europeanization) is rare, representing only 14 per cent of all judgments decided in the free movement of goods in the period between 2000 and 2005 when the Court decided the first Austrian case on road tolls (2000), *Schmidberger* (2003), and the second Austrian case on the sectoral ban (2005).

Moreover, the Advocate General and the Court downplayed the duration of the restriction scheduled for 30 hours but effectively stopping heavy traffic – its main target – for four days and over-benignly framed the protest as an isolated peaceful event.[93] Impacted by nitric oxide emissions, noise and road congestion, in as early as the 1980s, vocal and politically powerful local interests began pressuring the Austrian government to act decisively to regulate commercial traffic.[94] Traffic obstructions were common and included highway sit-ins, religious services held on the motorway, a rifle parade, and occasional roadblocks. Attended by hundreds of people, the protests became part of the collective memory of Tyrol.[95]

The Advocate General and the Court did not mention that *Schmidberger* was the first case to have raised the issue of human rights as a justification for the restriction of free movement, hence its precedential potential and the signalling of the high stakes commonly involved in such landmark cases.[96] Furthermore, the Court never questioned or engaged with the Austrian argument (or threat) when assessing the absence of alternatives, namely that all the alternative solutions would have caused a 'more serious disruption to intra-Community trade and public order, such as unauthorised demonstrations, confrontation between supporters and opponents of the group organising the demonstration or acts of violence on the part of the demonstrators who considered that the exercise of their fundamental rights had been infringed'.[97] This alternative was dangerously reminiscent of the French situation – an aching memory to recollect.

[92] Data on file with the author.

[93] AG Opinion, para 117 and para 108 mentioning also the likely-deliberate choice of the date for the protest.

[94] See for instance R Heinisch, 'Austria: Confronting Controversy' in E Zeff (ed), *The European Union and the Member States. Cooperation, Coordination, and Compromise* (Boulder, Lynne Rienner Publisher, 2001) 267–284), available at https://www.demokratiezentrum.org/wp-content/uploads/2022/10/heinisch_controversy.pdf (accessed in November 2023). In contrast, these local interests never raised issue with non-commercial traffic bringing tourists to the region via the Brenner motorway.

[95] R Aschwanden et al, 'Moving Mountains: The Protection of the Alps' in A-K Wöbse and P Kupper (eds), *Greening Europe* (Berlin, De Gruyter, 2022) 231.

[96] See e.g. F Schauer, 'Precedent' (1987) 39 *Stanford Law Review* 571. For the European Union context, see Helfer and Slaughter (n 59); S Dothan, *Reputation and Judicial Tactics: A Theory of National and International Courts* (Cambridge, Cambridge University Press, 2014).

[97] *Schmidberger*, para 92.

Most importantly in the context of the analysis of good judgment, the exercise of silence and the designation of interpretive choices appear calculated considering the circumstances of the dispute. Holding Austria responsible for the economic consequences of the environmental protest was legally justifiable but politically unthinkable.

The Court acknowledged that the Brenner motorway was a major transit route and primary land link without revealing that it has been a constant source of diplomatic conflict and frustration between Italy, Germany, and Austria. Rather, it focused exclusively on the normative conflict between economic and political rights in the Union and European values.

The public debate about Austria joining the EU in the 1980s brought the Brenner motorway to Brussels and eventually to Luxembourg. Transit became one of the three key topics shaping Austria's accession negotiations. Regional politicians in Tyrol were trying to contain the protests on the one hand, whilst using them as leverage in their negotiations with policymakers in Vienna and Brussels on the other.[98]

In this political and historical context, the Advocate's General sermon on human rights and State liability appears distracting – true, the national Court inquired about the aspects of State liability but the answers were irrelevant unless the Court found Austria in serious breach of European Union law, concretely Article 34 TFEU. The Advocate General concluded that this was not the case, highlighting inter alia the isolated nature of the protest and the great pains the Austrian authorities had gone to to mitigate the consequences for the transit of heavy goods and non-commercial traffic. The Court's deep scrutiny of the circumstances of the case focused on the Austrian legislation, and the discussion dedicated to the moot question of admissibility was unnecessarily longwinded; clearly, the dispute was all but hypothetical. Together these two issues take up 50 out of 96 paragraphs. The Court never mentions the position of any intervening government (which included the Dutch, French, Italian, German, Greek, and Finnish governments, with the latter only submitting its observations at the hearing) or the Commission.[99] In all, the proceedings lasted more than three years and four months.

The Court received the preliminary reference in *Schmidberger* in March 2000. This came one month after the Advocate General had delivered his Opinion in an infringement case against Austria,[100] in which he held that Austria had

[98] The historical context of the environmental protests along the transit routes in the Alpine region are outlined in M Buck and KJ Schmidt, 'Special Section: Technical Infrastructures, Transnational Protest Movements and the Use of Counter-Expertise' (2022) 30 *NTM Zeitschrift für Geschichte der Wissenschaften, Technik und Medizin* 271.

[99] The Advocate General refers to the Greek government's position on primacy of European Union law and the duty of the Austrian authorities, supported by the Commission (para 53).

[100] Case C-205/98, *Commission v Austria*, ECLI:EU:C:2000:493.

failed to comply with the Council Directive[101] by adopting two decisions which raised tolls for certain vehicles travelling on the full itinerary of the motorway in effect from 1 July 1995, to 1 February 1996. In September 2000, the Court delivered the judgment in the infringement case, holding that – as suggested by the Advocate General – the measures indirectly discriminated against foreign haulers contrary to Article 7(b) of the Directive, and added a further layer of discrimination on the basis of the origin or destination of the vehicle contrary to that same provision.

A month after the Court delivered the judgment in *Schmidberger* in June 2003, the Commission lodged an infringement action against Austria for its sectoral traffic ban (a case which Austria lost in 2005 because of a fundamental refusal to consider the alternative solutions proposed by the Commission and fellow Member States).[102] This is illustrated in Table 5.

Table 5 Schmidberger and Commission v Austria: A timeline of litigation concerning the Inn Valley

Date	Decision
1 February 2000	*Schmidberger* (Request for the preliminary ruling)
26 September 2000	Case C-205/98, *Commission v Austria* (judgment)
11 July 2002	*Schmidberger* (AG Opinion)
27 May 2003	C-320/03, *Commission v Austria* (Regulation by the Landeshauptmann (First Minister) of the Tyrol limiting transport on the A 12 motorway in the Inn valley)[103]
12 June 2003	*Schmidberger* (judgment)
24 July 2003	C-320/03, *Commission v Austria* (the Commission lodges the infringement action)
30 July 2003	C-320/03, *Commission v Austria* (first Order / interim measure of the President of the Court of Justice ordering Austria to suspend operation of the traffic ban until the order terminating the interim measure). Second order on October 2, 2003, and the third order issued on April 30, 2004, extending the interim measure until the final judgment.

A conflict that required sensitivity toward social and political freedoms was a political and economic conflict that took the form of individual freedoms and the right to ensure free transit of goods in the *Schmidberger* case. Like the

[101] Council Dir 93/89/EEC of 25 October 1993 on the application by Member States of taxes on certain vehicles used for the carriage of goods by road and tolls and charges for the use of certain infrastructures.

[102] C-320/03, *Commission v Austria*, ECLI:EU:C:2005:684.

[103] The regulation prohibits a category of lorries (over 7.5 tonnes) carrying certain goods (e.g. waste) from using a 46km section of the A12 motorway for an indeterminate period since 1 August 2003.

Newcastle Disease case, discussed in detail below, *Schmidberger* tapped into a conflict implicating multiple Member States, notably Italy and Germany which relied on the passage through the Tyrolean valley and the use of the Brenner motorway for the transit of goods. A legally straightforward solution could only be formalistic.

The Aftermath

The Brenner motorway continues to present a major problem for the European institutions and key stakeholders: locals want fewer trucks but ideally the same number of tourists; truckers and national politicians want uninterrupted cargo traffic; Italy wants to take Austria to Court; and the IRU wants to find an overall solution.[104] In response to all these demands, the European Union has invested 8 billion euros in the construction of a 64-kilometre Brenner Pass Tunnel, a project repeatedly delayed.[105]

ii. Deferential Judgment Upholding Free Movement Rights: *Brasserie du Pêcheur*

A deferential judgment upholding European rights and principles reflects the Court's commitment to protect free movement while deferring the terms of application and the ultimate decision-making authority to national institutions, typically the referring court or administration.

From the justificatory perspective, this type of good judgment concerns the relationship between two aspects of justification: The outcome of the case or the Court's decision about the applicant's claim), and its choice of interpretive methods and doctrinal position. It examines how the Court reframes a negative outcome with considerable implications for the state budget by 'suspending' or conditioning its effect.

A case in point is *Brasserie du Pêcheur*, which the Court decided jointly with *Factortame*.[106] As explained below, the division of labour inherent in Article 267 TFEU and the limits of European competence in procedural law (the duty of

[104] IRU is the world road transport organisation representing the bus, coach, truck and taxi industries. IRU, 'Speed up Brenner Negotiations, IRU Says to European Commission President' <https://www.iru.org/news-resources/newsroom/speed-brenner-negotiations-iru-says-european-commission-president>. (last accessed in November 2023).

[105] H Cokelaere, 'How a Fight over an Alpine Pass Turned into an EU-Wide Political Headache' *POLITICO* (7 September 2023). Available at https://www.politico.eu/article/eu-fight-over-alpine-pass-turned-into-wide-political-headache-mobility-trade-trucks/ (last accessed in November 2023).

[106] Joined cases C-46/93 and C-48/93, *Brasserie du Pêcheur v Germany* and *The Queen v Secretary of State for Transport*, ex parte: *Factortame Ltd et al*, ECLI:EU:C:1996:79. While the Cour joined the cases for the purposes of the procedure and the final judgment, the dispute in *Factortam* primarily concerned the freedom of establishment. Hence, it is not discussed in the chapter togethe with the free movement of goods (beer) that gave rise to the *Beer Purity* and *Brasserie* judgments.

national courts to protect European rights effectively and without discrimination, and the principles of effectiveness and equivalence) do not fully account for the margin of discretion which the judgment gave the Bundesgerichtshof in the application of the principle.[107] The plaintiffs predictably lost their case before Bundesgerichtshof.

The Soap

> '… two of the longest running judicial soap operas in the Community's history have been brought together in this ruling.'[108]

The origins of *Brasserie* are Articles 9 and 10 of the German Biersteuergesetz (the Law on beer duty, adopted in 1952) which is better known as the Reinheitsgebot or the purity requirement. This Law required that only fermented beverages made from malted barley, hops, yeast, and water could be marketed and sold as 'Bier'. In the *Beer Purity* case (*Commission v Germany*,[109] decided in 1987), the Court held that the purity requirement unduly restricted trade and ruled that Germany failed to fulfil its obligations under Article 34 TFEU by prohibiting the marketing of beers lawfully manufactured and marketed in another Member State if they did not comply with Articles 9 and 10 of the Biersteuergesetz.

Brasserie du Pêcheur was an Alsace-based French brewery whose product did not meet the German beer standards. The brewery's only German importer refused to renew its distribution contract due to the persistent checks conducted by the German authorities at retailers' premises.[110] The Brasserie was forced to discontinue all exports to Germany in 1981 at enormous financial loss. After the Court's judgment in Beer Purity in 1987, the company tried to partly recuperate its loss by claiming damages from the German State. Two lower courts rejected the claim because German legislation and legal practice (the case-law of the Federal Court of Justice or the Bundesgerichtshof) provided no legal basis.[111] The Bundesgerichtshof, hearing the case at the final (revision) stage,

[107] On the argument that the Court of Justice uses procedural autonomy as prudential avoidance, see D Halberstam, 'Understanding National Remedies and the Principle of National Procedural Autonomy: A Constitutional Approach' (2021) 23 *Cambridge Yearbook of European Legal Studies* 128. Halberstam argues that deference to the national rules on procedure and remedies often stem from the Court's prudential interpretation of European Union's legislation as intended to permit national rules to govern national proceedings. On the question of delimiting rights from remedies and procedures see W Van Gerven, 'Of Rights, Remedies and Procedures' (2000) 37 *Common Market Law Review* 501.

[108] P Oliver, 'Cases C-46/93 and C-48/93, Brasserie Du Pêcheur v. Germany, and The Queen v. Secretary of State for Transport Ex Parte Factortame, [1996] ECR I-1029; Case C-392/93, The Queen v. Her Majesty's Tre' (1997) 34 *Common Market Law Review* 635.

[109] Case 178/84, *Commission v Germany*, ECLI:EU:C:1987:126.

[110] Opinion of the Advocate General Tesauro in Joined cases C-46/93 and C-48/93, *Brasserie du Pêcheur v Germany* and *The Queen v Secretary of State for Transport*, ex parte: *Factortame Ltd et al*, ECLI:EU:C:1995:407, p. 1068.

[111] Under the German Civil Code and the Basic Law, the State could incur liability if the party claiming damages was a beneficiary of the breached obligation (the so-called third party). The

stayed the proceedings to clarify whether the principle, as first established in the contentious *Francovich* judgment,[112] also extended to the acts of the national legislature, notably the Parliament. If national legislators incurred liability for breaches of European Union law, did the national law govern the conditions for liability – and if so, then to what extent?

The Judgment

As argued below, the Court walked a thin line of rights protection and deference. The former aspect entails negative consequences stemming from European Union law for Germany and all other Member States, especially Greece, which had an equivalent purity requirement in place, five of which intervened in the procedure with the Commission.[113] The latter allows the Member States to mitigate, minimise, or eliminate those negative consequences by 'domesticating' the protection of individual rights through the application of national procedural rules, established doctrines, and liability standards.[114]

Regarding the basis for liability; Germany, the United Kingdom, and all intervening governments objected to the extension of the principle to Member State legislators, arguing that direct effect offered acceptable protection of individual rights and sufficiently guaranteed the effectiveness of European Union law. Liability, they argued, could only compensate for the lack of direct effect, as was the case in *Francovich*. The Court rejected the reasoning, stating that the right to reparation was 'the necessary corollary of the direct effect of the Community provision whose breach caused the damage sustained'.[115] National rules could not affect the Community rights of individuals to obtain redress in the national courts for damage caused by such a breach.[116]

The magnitude of legal innovation is exceptional even for the Court which is known for this quality. The Court constructed the basis for liability on a contentious precedent set in vastly different circumstances: in *Francovich*, the national administration was responsible for the breach, and the unimplemented Directive

German Law on beer duty did not, however, address third parties and only referenced the public generally.

[112] Joined cases C-6/90 and C-9/90, *Francovich et al*, ECLI:EU:C:1991:428.

[113] Meaning that seven out of 12 governments who were members of the European Union in 1992, when the Court received the preliminary reference in *Brasserie*, submitted written observations. This is an unusually high number of interventions, as an average case typically receives one to two interventions (one of them usually coming from the Commission). Data at https://www.iuropa.pol.gu.se/ (accessed in November 2023). See also S Arne Brekke et al, 'The CJEU Database Platform: Decisions and Decision-Makers' (2023) 11 *Journal of Law and Courts* 389.

[114] Studies have demonstrated that the applicants rarely succeed with their 'Francovich' claims at the national level (the victory of *Francovich* was Pyrrhic). See T Lock, 'Is Private Enforcement of EU Law through State Liability a Myth? An Assessment 20 Years after Francovich' (2012) 49 *Common Market Law Review* 1675.

[115] *Brasserie*, paras 20–22.

[116] *Brasserie*, para 35.

conferring rights did not have direct effect.[117] In these circumstances, the Court held that liability was the last and only remedy for individuals to claim their rights, and thus the only gateway to European Union law's effectiveness.

Equally important and novel from the legal substantive perspective were the conditions for liability, elaborated by analogy to Article 340 TFEU governing the non-contractual liability of European institutions, Article 4 TEU (the principle of sincere cooperation),[118] and the general principles common to the Member States.[119] After *Brasserie*, the legislator would be liable for damages resulting from the infringement of European Union law, and the individuals who suffered damages entitled to reparation before the national courts if: 1) the rule of law infringed confers rights on individuals; 2) the breach is sufficiently serious; and 3) there is a direct causal link between the breach of the obligation resting on the State and the damage sustained by the injured parties.[120]

Deference in *Brasserie* goes beyond the division of labour encapsulated in Article 267 TFEU, which requires the national courts to present the facts and raise questions of interpretation and validity of European Union law and the Court of Justice to deliver a binding interpretation or an authoritative verdict on validity. As is well-known, the Court does not observe this division of labour consistently, using different tools such as reading down statutes[121] to avoid difficult questions of principle.[122] Moreover, deference in *Brasserie* differs from the deference inherent in the principle of national procedural autonomy which is limited, on the one hand, by the judge-made principles of effectiveness and equivalence (the *Rewe / Comet* established line of cases)[123] but loosened, on the other, by the no-new-remedies jurisprudence (*Rewe Kiel*).[124] Conditions of liability go beyond procedural rules governing substantive assessment and embedding policy choices.[125]

[117] *Francovich*, para 27.

[118] *Brasserie*, para 39.

[119] *Brasserie*, para 85 (with reference to *Mulder*, Joined cases C-104/89 and C-37/90, *Mulder and others and Heinemann v Council and the Commission*, ECLI:EU:C:1992:217).

[120] *Brasserie*, para 51.

[121] Halberstam (n 107).

[122] U Šadl and A Wallerman, '"The Referring Court Asks, in Essence": Is Reformulation of Preliminary Questions by the Court of Justice a Decision Writing Fixture or a Decision-Making Approach?' (2019) 25 *European Law Journal* 416. See also D Sarmiento and D Jiménez-Valladolid, 'Half a Case at a Time: Dealing with Judicial Minimalism at the European Court of Justice' in M Claes et al (eds), *Constitutional Conversations in Europe: Actors, Topics and Procedures* (Cambridge, Intersentia, 2012).

[123] Case 33/76, *Rewe-Zentralfinanz eG and Rewe-Zentral AG v Landwirtschaftskammer für das Saarland*, ECLI:EU:C:1976:188 and Case 45/76, *Comet BV v Produktschap voor Siergewassen*, ECLI:EU:C:1976:191. The judgments were issued on the same date just before the Christmas break (16 December 1976).

[124] Case 158/80, *Rewe-Handelsgesellschaft Nord mbH and Rewe-Markt Steffen v Hauptzollamt Kiel*, ECLI:EU:C:1981:163.

[125] On the latter aspect, see G Calabresi and A Douglas Melamed, 'Property Rules, Liability Rules, and Inalienability: One View of the Cathedral' (1972) 85 *Harvard Law Review* 1089.

Beer and Beyond

From the perspective of the deferential upholding of free movement rights, three sets of factors are crucial. First, the sanctity of the object of the dispute, the Beer Purity law and German beer production itself. Second, the legal choices of the Court setting a high bar for liability, mentioning a wide discretion of state legislatures, bypassing the question of competence allocation and supremacy, and differentiating between the rules on denomination and additives. Third, the procedural choices: the Court joined *Brasserie* with *Factortame* and rejected the German request to limit the temporal effects of the judgment.[126]

These circumstances, discussed below, imply that in broaching a doubly sensitive subject for the second time in a case pitting ancient laws as a source of national pride and state protectionism and the opportunity of building a far reaching legal principle on contentious precedent (*Francovich*) against one another, the Court strengthened the protection of free movement rights by extending the remedy for breaches of rights that individuals derived from European Union law whilst continuing to condition their application on the national rules of tort and civil procedure. In these circumstances the Court did not see the limitation of temporal effects as necessary.[127]

The beer purity requirement (and the disputed law) draws its mythical status from history, tradition, and culture. German political, economic, and social history is inextricably linked to its brewing history; the world looks to Germany for brewing techniques, equipment, trained brewing personnel, beer styles and ingredients, nomenclature, glassware and, of course, beer.[128] The law adopted in 1516 is the world's oldest surviving food law and is revered in Germany.[129] When adopted, the law might have had other motivations, like protecting Bavarian brewers from international competition and preventing peasants from turning valuable wheat into liquid bread.[130] Following the Court's judgment in 1987, the Reinheitsgebot was formally modified but maintained the rules for German brewers. German consumers continued to drink local German beer produced in accordance with the ancient laws, and imports accounted for less than 10 per cent of the market. Liberalisation attracted foreign companies to begin brewing their beer in Germany adhering to the purity requirement with minor

[126] Germany cited immeasurable financial repercussions. See *Brasserie*, Report for the Hearing, pp I-1064.

[127] *Brasserie*, para 98: 'Substantive and procedural conditions laid down by national law on reparation of damage are able to take account of the requirements of the principle of legal certainty'.

[128] HD Dornbusch, *Prost!: The Story of German Beer* (Boulder, Brewers Publications, 1998).

[129] A Curry, 'Germany Celebrates a Half Millennium of Beer' *National Geographic* (2016) <https://www.nationalgeographic.com/travel/article/germany-celebrates-500-years-of-german-beer-reinheitsgebot-purity-law>.

[130] F van Tongeren, 'Standards and International Trade Integration: A Historical Review of the German "Reinheitsgebot"' in JFM Swinnen (ed), *The Economics of Beer* (Oxford, Oxford University Press, 2011).

permissible tweaks.[131] In 2013, the German Brewers Association attempted to add the Reinheitsgebot to UNESCO's Intangible World Heritage List alongside Spanish Flamenco, the French gourmet meal, and Indian yoga.[132]

Four interpretive choices illustrate how non-legal factors permeated the reasoning and outcome. The first is the analogy to the non-contractual liability of the European Union's institutions pursuant to Article 340 TFEU, which set the bar for liability as high as it could legally be.[133] The intervening Member States and Germany insisted on the analogy as the only appropriate standard, with full knowledge that the Court has traditionally been deferential towards the European institutions, insisting that the legislature should not be hampered by the threat of liability. This stance is formulated as wide discretion and the criterion of grave and manifest disregard of the limits when exercising institutional powers.[134]

The Court agreed, and made a second interpretive choice, additionally and explicitly underlining that the national legislators in *Brasserie* and *Factortame* enjoyed wide discretion. In paragraph 48, it stated that:

> In the case which gave rise to the reference in Case C-46/93, the German legislature had legislated in the field of foodstuffs, specifically beer. In the absence of Community harmonization, the national legislature had a wide discretion in that sphere in laying down rules on the quality of beer put on the market.[135]

This interpretive choice is at odds with the practice following the *Cassis de Dijon* judgment, which clearly minimised state discretion. The Court elegantly solved the logical contradiction by returning to the distinction between the rules on denomination and the prohibition of additives, a third consequential interpretive choice[136] which effectively rendered the breach excusable. The Bundesgerichtshof anchored the dismissal of Brasserie's claim for damages in this distinction, finding that the breach was excusable and thus not sufficiently serious.[137] The *Beer Purity* ruling thus provided for a legally sophisticated exonerating ground, accepting an ex-post justification based on fictitious health

[131] Tongeren (n 130) 60.

[132] The application was unsuccessful but not entirely dismissed.

[133] According to the case-law, to which the Court refers in the judgment, 'the Community cannot incur liability unless the institution concerned has manifestly and gravely disregarded the limits on the exercise of its powers (Joined Cases 83/76, 94/76, 4/77, 15/77 and 40/77 *HNL et al v Council and Commission* [1978] ECR 1209, paras 5 and 6).' *Brasserie*, para 45.

[134] *Brasserie*, Report for the Hearing, I – 1058. See also Advocate's General Opinion, para 73 (the non-contractual liability of the Member State builds on the concept of a manifest and serious breach; also, the intervening governments insisted 'on fault as the element necessary to 'characterise' (as serious) the breach of the provision or, in any case, as an indispensable, inherent ingredient of liability'.).

[135] *Brasserie*, para 48.

[136] *Brasserie*, para 59.

[137] BGH, Urt. vom 24.10.1996 – III ZR 127/91.

protection arguments.[138] German courts have since dismissed most claims for damages raised by individuals against the state.[139]

The fourth interpretive choice was the Court's decision to keep the entire political weight of the case implicit – brushing aside the fundamental question of competence allocation. The German government submitted that a general right to reparation for individuals could only be established through legislation and that for such a right to be recognised by judicial decision would be incompatible with the allocation of powers between the Community institutions and the Member States, and with the institutional balance established by the Treaty.[140] The Commission considered that infringements of the national legislators constituted a failure 'to observe the principle of the supremacy of Community law'[141] and hence the 'entitlement to compensation should not be made subject to restrictions which have been developed in national law in order to safeguard legislative autonomy and which have no bearing on Community law'.[142] The Court replied succinctly to Germany's argument, asserting that 'the existence and extent of State liability for damage ensuing as a result of a breach of obligations incumbent on the State by virtue of Community law are questions of Treaty interpretation which fall within the jurisdiction of the Court'.[143] It did not engage with the Commission's argument.

Procedurally, the order to join *Brasserie* and *Factortame* as two of the most complex and long lasting litigations which deal with establishment and goods is not obvious. The Court's procedural routines are inconsistent but often strategic.[144] Packing all difficult questions into one judgment might have been preferable to dealing with them separately. The soap opera of *Brasserie* also falls within the period of excessive procedural delays, speaking for the joining of cases as a matter of procedural efficiency and reinforcing the principle of timely justice.

Finally, the Court rejected the German request to limit the temporal effects of the judgment:

> It must be borne in mind that, were the national court to find that the conditions for liability of the Federal Republic of Germany are satisfied in this case, the State would

[138] '… having regard to the relevant case-law, the criteria available to the national legislature to determine whether the prohibition of the use of additives was contrary to Community law were significantly less conclusive' (*Brasserie*, par. 59). See also N Reich, 'Francovich Enforcement Analysed and Illustrated by German (and English) Law' in A Jakab and D Kochenov (eds), *The Enforcement of EU Law and Values: Ensuring Member States' Compliance* (Oxford, Oxford University Press, 2017) 115.

[139] According to Lock, only 22 per cent of actions for damages against Germany are successful. T Lock, 'Is Private Enforcement of EU Law through State Liability a Myth? An Assessment 20 Years after Francovich' (2012) 49 *Common Market Law Review* 1675, 1685.

[140] *Brasserie*, para 24.

[141] *Brasserie*, Report for the Hearing, pp I-1057.

[142] ibid.

[143] *Brasserie*, para 25.

[144] U Šadl et al, 'Law and Orders: The Orders of the European Court of Justice as a Window in th Judicial Process and Institutional Transformations' (2022) 1 *European Law Open* 549.

> have to make good the consequences of the damage caused within the framework of its domestic law on liability. Substantive and procedural conditions laid down by national law on reparation of damage are able to take account of the requirements of the principle of legal certainty.[145]

This passage effectively means that given the deference accorded to the national court and national standard, the ball was literally out of the Court's court.

An Afterthought

Brasserie deals with the implications of unlawful Member State action under the general principles of European Union law rather than the lawfulness of Member State action under the free movement of goods Treaty provisions. In some ways, it is a typical free movement of goods judgment, and in others it is not. It is, however, a typical European rights protective judgment in an economically important and culturally sensitive domain supporting the free movement of goods and the individuals' right to hold states accountable for Treaty violations. Goods epitomise the extreme lengths to which the Court is willing to go to ensure the proper functioning of the internal market; in *Brasserie*, creating new principles and new remedies outside the European Union's competence.

iii. Bounded Undesirable Interpretation: *The Newcastle Disease*

In a judgment with bounded undesirable interpretation, the Court is trying to minimise the broader undesirable implications of its decision for the national regulatory autonomy. In other words, the Court removes obstacles to free movement or creates rights, doctrines, and concepts at limited policy cost for the responding Member State.

The judgment in *Commission v United Kingdom* also known as the *Newcastle Disease* or the *Christmas Turkeys* case is illustrative.[146] The Court ruled that the United Kingdom's measures effectively banning most imports of poultry and a range of poultry products were measures with equivalent effect to quantitative restrictions, prohibited by Article 34 TFEU. At the same time, the Court postponed the judgment on the question of the United Kingdom's import licensing system, the legislation which constituted the basis for the ban, and the import ban to Northern Ireland. It ordered the United Kingdom 'to take all the necessary measures to comply with this judgment,' noting 'the Commission's statement that it intends to contact the British authorities in order to permit, without delay, the re-establishment of trade which has been interrupted by the 1981 measures while at the same time safeguarding animal health in conformity with the Treaty'.[147]

[145] *Brasserie*, para 98.
[146] Case C-40/82, *Commission v United Kingdom (Newcastle Disease)*, ECLI:EU:C:1982:285.
[147] *Newcastle Disease*, para 46.

The Dispute

The dispute in *Newcastle Disease* originated in the provisions of the United Kingdom's Animal Health Act from 1981 and the Importation of Animal Products and Poultry Products Order from 1980, as amended by the Importation of Animal Products and Poultry Products Order from 1981.[148] These acts and measures were adopted in an attempt to change the national animal health protection policy, from vaccination to the slaughtering of infected animals. They implied a complete ban of imports on poultry and eggs from the Member States that continued to follow the 'old' vaccination policy – in practice, all Member States except for Denmark and Ireland. The United Kingdom maintained that the measures were necessary to protect animal health; without vaccinations which could hide the presence of the disease, the British flock would be susceptible to infection from imported eggs and poultry.

The United Kingdom government informed the Commission of the change on 27 August 1981, only a few days prior to the date when the measures took effect (1 September 1981). Meanwhile, the Commission received complaints from French producers, claiming that the British restrictions were causing them severe financial loss.[149]

The veterinary reports submitted by the Commission demonstrated that the United Kingdom decided to adopt the contested legislation to prevent the disease, which was practically eradicated.[150] Moreover, the statistics produced by EUROSTAT for 1980 showed that the United Kingdom imported considerable quantities of poultry meat and poultry products from other Member States, and that the imports of whole turkeys from France rose significantly. By contrast, the imports from Denmark fell considerably.[151]

The Commission initiated an infringement procedure, arguing that the British measures were contrary to Article 34 TFEU, and could not be justified under Article 36 TFEU, which permitted derogations inter alia on grounds of animal health protection; they were discriminatory, disproportionate, and arbitrary. France, intervening in support of the Commission, claimed that the import ban was blatantly 'a means of arbitrary discrimination and a disguised restriction on imports of poultry products from other Member States, in particular from France'.[152]

[148] The Animal Health Act 1981 and the Importation of Animal Products and Poultry Products Order 1980 (Statutory Instrument 1980, No 14), as amended by the Importation of Animal Products and Poultry Products (Amendment) Order 1981 (Statutory Instrument 1981, No 1238).

[149] Report for the Hearing, p 2805.

[150] The facts of the case have been reconstructed from the Report for the Hearing. The disease first appeared in Europe in 1926 in Newcastle, resurfacing during the 1960s as well as from 1969 to 1972.

[151] Report for the Hearing, p 2799.

[152] Judgment, para 6.

The Advocate General considered the legal aspects of the dispute 'simple'.[153] He harboured no doubt that a measure which categorically denied seven Member States, adhering to their system of preventive vaccination, any possibility of exporting fresh or frozen poultry meat to Great Britain and at the same time subjecting them to special licensing for any importation of egg products, was equivalent to a quantitative restriction on imports. Moreover, and equally simple to articulate, a measure of that kind would only be compatible with Community law if it fell within the scope of the derogation provided for in Article 36 TFEU. The Advocate General concluded that the contested measures were incompatible with Article 36 TFEU, 'inter alia because they concealed their true protectionist nature'.[154]

Among the circumstances leading to the conclusion that the measures were 'simulated,' the Advocate General cited:

a) the protests and threats of boycott by British breeders between February and July 1981 and their pressure on the Government authorities to ensure that French imports were in some way hindered;
b) the approaches made by the United Kingdom authorities requesting the Commission to reduce French exports, basing their argument on the aid given by the French Government to poultry breeders (cf. interview with the United Kingdom Minister of Agriculture, Mr Walker, reported in the article 'Warning on French poultry', in which it was suggested that traders should not rely upon imports of turkeys from France for Christmas);
c) the failure of those approaches, since the Commission considered the French support measures to be compatible with Community rules (cf. reply given by the Commission on 29 January 1982 to Written Question No 896/81 by Mr Welsh, Official Journal C 53 of 1 March 1981, p. 2);
d) the extremely brief period between the issue and the entry into force of the measures of 27 August 1981 – with the objective consequence that it became impossible to order and secure the arrival of French turkeys for Christmas sales; and
e) the subsequent total refusal to consider alternatives with regard to measures restricting imports.[155]

The First Judgment

The Court carefully examined the facts of the case, laying out the context in which the United Kingdom adopted and amended its restrictive measures,

[153] Opinion of the Advocate General Capotorti, delivered on 7 July 1982 in Case 40/82, *Commission v United Kingdom*, ECLI:EU:C:1982:261, para 2.
[154] Opinion, para. 10.
[155] Opinion p 2846.

noting a protracted conflict between the United Kingdom and France preceding the Commission's action. The Court quickly established that the prohibition of imports from 1981 ('the 1981 measures') was contrary to Article 34 TFEU: 'the legal machinery used by the United Kingdom in introducing the 1981 measures' prevented most imports.

It then considered whether the United Kingdom could justify the 1981 measures on the grounds of animal health protection. First, it noted that 'matters of animal health remained within the exclusive competence of the Member States as long as no Community harmonisation has taken place'. The Unted Kingdom could thus freely change its policy from vaccination to non-vaccination and compulsory slaughter except if said policy change was a disguised restriction on intra-Community trade.

Recalling the facts, the Court concluded that 'the real aim of the 1981 measures was to block, for commercial and economic reasons, imports of poultry products from other Member States, in particular from France'. In other words, the disputed measures were a disguised restriction because of their protectionist aim. Finally, the Court examined the possibility of there being less stringent measures, referring to the Danish policy of health certificates and administrative cooperation with the exporting states. Despite the United Kingdom's assertion that its poultry market was unlike Denmark's, the Court upheld that those less restrictive measures would have been possible, safe, and sufficient to guarantee animal safety without obstructing trade.

Two aspects make the Court's reasoning especially interesting from the perspective of good judgment.

First, and more subtly, the Court engaged with the economic-political context but went about it carefully and with a measured tone, laying out of the facts and the arguments put forward by the United Kingdom's government and Ireland which intervened in the proceedings on the United Kingdom's behalf. The detail of engagement with the facts is remarkable given the Court's usual abstract treatment of facts and context, as well as the obvious protectionist aim of the measures.

It is plausible that the Court deliberately treated the situation as unique rather than for what it really was, another 'shoddy attempt …' of another Member State 'to defend protectionist rules dressed up in the implausible garb of public health'.[156] Moreover, the Court was eager to communicate that it set a very high bar for the Commission to prove the 'abuse' of Article 36 TFEU in this area under Member State competence (protection of animal health), implying that it would only exceptionally consider peering behind the veil of Member State competence to protect human and animal health on its territory.

The Court delved into the suddenness of the policy change, notably its suspect timing and questionable context. Regarding the timing, the United Kingdom, under the pressure from its poultry producers, hastily introduced a policy effectively banning imports to the United Kingdom when the contracts

[156] Weatherill (n 16) 109.

with the French poultry suppliers were being negotiated. The measures would 'prevent the imports of Christmas turkeys from France into Great Britain for the 1981 season and that these imports had constituted a very substantial part of the total imports of turkeys in the preceding years'.[157] The Court also recalled that the United Kingdom replaced the policy of non-vaccination and compulsory slaughter with a policy of vaccination in 1964, after the thorough consideration of an elaborate report delivered by a committee of experts as well as various studies and discussions among veterinary experts. It made no similar effort in 1981 when deciding to reintroduce the pre-1964 policy. Hence, the Court concluded, the measures did not form part of a seriously considered health policy.[158]

Regarding the political context, the government of the United Kingdom openly admitted to being 'gravely concerned by the continuing increase in the importation of turkeys from France, and in particular by the degree of subsidisation available to French producers and whether it was lawful'.[159] The Commission previously accepted that the French subsidies were permissible under the Treaty. The British measures could thus also be seen as retaliation against the French government. This argument appears more than plausible given that France was unsuccessfully trying to retain its poultry outlets on the British market. Among other concessions, it introduced a policy like the United Kingdom's, prohibiting the use of vaccines and instituting a policy of compulsory slaughter in the event of an outbreak of disease. Nonetheless, the British authorities refused to admit French poultry products to their territory, claiming that France had not restricted poultry imports from non-member countries, notably from Spain and Eastern European countries, where the vaccine was still in use.[160]

Hence, the United Kingdom and the Court knew that the policy – even if short-lived – would have the desired political and economic effect. For the United Kingdom, subsequent litigation with the French turkey producers was less costly than antagonising its own farmers – historically, conservative voters – during an economic crisis and a politically turbulent year of high inflation, a summer of race riots, and rising unemployment threatening the policies and the trust in the newly elected Thatcher government.[161]

For the Court, careful engagement with the facts and the arguments of the parties and the interveners was necessary to declare the ban unjustified. The approach allowed the Court to advance its understanding of Article 36 TFEU at limited cost, thus creating a precedent that the intention of the measures and hence the Member State could be considered. The Court invoked *Henn and Darby*,[162] a British case which introduced 'the abuse of rights' to the case-law defined as

[157] Para 24.

[158] Para 38.

[159] Report for the Hearing, p 2812 and judgment in Case 40/82, para 23 'In these circumstances, a certain pressure was put on the United Kingdom Government, by articles in the press and in other ways, to take action in order to reduce imports of poultry products from France.'

[160] Para 25.

[161] The French turkey producers sued the British government for the losses they had suffered, reaching a sizeable (£3.5 million) out-of-court settlement. S Weatherill and PR Beaumont, *EU Law*, 3rd edn (London, Penguin Books, 1999).

[162] Case 34/79, *Henn and Darby*, ECLI:EU:C:1979:295.

disguised restriction into Article 36 TFEU, explaining that 'the second sentence of Article 36 is designed to prevent restrictions on trade mentioned in the first sentence of that article from being diverted from their proper purpose and used in such a way as either to create discrimination in respect of goods originating in other Member States or indirectly to protect certain national products'.[163]

A precedent introducing the intention of the Member State into the meaning of Article 36 TFEU, as the Court was surely aware, would 'lead to questionable results'[164] where measures could be objectively justified but still unlawful under the Treaty. A newly created legal uncertainty would be obvious considering the abundant existing case-law to the contrary and Article 34 TFEU's explicit reference to the effects of the measures (cf. *Dassonville* formula). The Court did, however, rely on a precedent which ran contrary to *Newcastle Disease*, by considering the United Kingdom's restriction on the importation of pornography at stake in *Henn and Darby* which was justified on the grounds of public morality, a derogation also permitted by Article 36 TFEU. This was an important difference – the Member State, which could continue limiting the imports of obscene material on grounds of public morality, could not limit the imports of poultry on grounds of animal health. The analogy was questionable.[165]

Second, and more importantly, the Court ruled only on 'the 1981 measures' targeting the imports of Christmas turkeys, reserving judgment on the 'other points at issue'.[166] According to the Court it was:

> in the interest of a proper administration of justice that the Commission should be given an opportunity to lodge its reply, within a period to be fixed by the President of the Court, on the issues which are still outstanding, that the defendant should respond to this reply and that the interveners should be given the opportunity to present such observations as they think fit.[167]

Those issues were 1) the ban on imports of poultry products into Northern Ireland from other Member States, except Ireland and Denmark and 2) the United Kingdom's legislation which constitutes the basis of the measures taken with regard to both Great Britain and Northern Ireland, inasmuch as they embody an import licensing system. These were wide-ranging and more consequential than Christmas turkeys, questioning the legality of the national licensing system and challenging the regulatory power of the Member States to adopt national policies for the protection of human and animal health by controlling the imports of animal products.

The delay was unnecessary. On the first point, the Court followed the request of the intervening Irish government, which was in the process of defending its own policy on import bans in Case 74/82, *Commission v Ireland*. However,

[163] Para 36.
[164] In this sense see Oliver et al (n 24) 225.
[165] The Court had to go to great lengths to prove the protectionist intent by including the discussion of the context rather than only stating the effect along with the arbitrariness and the discriminatory nature of the measures.
[166] Title V of the judgment.
[167] Para 51.

the Commission initiated the infringement proceedings against Ireland in Case 74/82 only 15 days after initiating the proceedings against the United Kingdom. The Court could have easily joined the cases given that Ireland and Northern Ireland maintained the same policy. Advocate General Mancini delivered a Joined Opinion in the cases during the second proceedings, clearly noting the parallels.[168]

On the second point, the Court considered that it did not have sufficient information. The Commission concentrated on the 1981 measures and did not fully develop its arguments on the compatibility of the British import licensing system with Articles 34 and 36 TFEU. Procedurally, the Court could have simply dismissed part of the action and the claims because they were unproven. Delaying the final decision gave the Commission enough time to restart the dialogue with the United Kingdom and for the latter to reconsider its policy choices. Politically and economically, the Court saved Britain's 1981, 1982, and 1983 Christmases, while not entirely sabotaging the French or the Community's own festivities.

Cold Turkey (The Second Judgment)

Following the first judgment, the United Kingdom retracted the licensing system but maintained the rules according to which it could reinstate the ban at any point. It also changed its licensing system for the imports of eggs and egg products. The Court delivered the final judgment in January 1984, declaring the licensing system contrary to the Treaty. Northern Ireland could continue to carry out controls and, where necessary, restrict imports,[169] but could not categorically prohibit all imports of poultry products from Member States which permitted vaccination against the Newcastle Disease.[170] Contrary to England, Scotland and Wales, Northern Ireland could continue to apply its licensing system due to the particularity of its poultry flock.

In the judgment against Ireland, delivered on the same date, the Court considered that the Irish import ban was contrary to Article 34 EEC and, although not arbitrary, unjustified on grounds of animal health. However, the Irish licensing system was compatible with the free movement and necessary and proportionate to maintain animal health.[171]

[168] Joined opinion of Mr Advocate General Mancini delivered on 8 November 1983 in cases *Commission v United Kingdom of Great Britain and Northern Ireland* (Case 40/82) and *Commission v Ireland* (Case 74/82), ECLI:EU:C:1983:309.

[169] Importantly, the Commission accepted that Northern Irish import prohibitions introduced and kept in force since the 1960s (prior to EU accession) to protect animal health did not constitute arbitrary discrimination or a disguised restriction on trade between Member States within the meaning of the second sentence of Art 36 of the Treaty. The Commission challenged them because they were excessive and their negative effect on the free movement of goods in the Community was disproportionate to their objective of protecting health.

[170] Case 40/82, *Newcastle Disease* (final judgment), ECLI:EU:C:1984:33, para 19.

[171] Ireland has maintained its policy of slaughter in the event of an outbreak combined with the prohibition of vaccination and strict import controls since the 1930s with excellent results. See the Opinion of AG Mancini, p 307.

This marks an important point – the same licensing system derogating from free movement under the criteria of Article 36 TFEU could be both lawful and unlawful under the Treaty – the intent rather than the effect making the difference.

The Court highlighted 1) the fact of 'the particular case of Ireland,' and the characteristics of its poultry flock and 2) that 'the question whether or not national measures on animal health may include an import licensing system without infringing Article 36 of the Treaty cannot be answered uniformly in every case'. The reply to that question depended:

> upon the relationship in an individual case between, on the one hand, the inconvenience caused by the administrative and financial burdens imposed under such a system and, on the other hand, the dangers and risks for animal health resulting from the imports in question. In the present case, those dangers and risks may under certain circumstances outweigh the inconvenience alluded to.[172]

Table 6 An overview of the judgments in the *Newcastle Disease* dispute. The first column denotes the date of the judgment, the second the name of the case, the third the main claim of the Commission (the infringement of the Treaty), the fourth the disputed national measures restricting imports, and the fifth column the Court's decision about the compatibility of the disputed measures

Date	Case	Claim	Legislation at stake	Decision
15 July 1982	Case 40/82, *Newcastle disease* (first judgment) Lodged 4 February 1982	By prohibiting imports and adopting the contested system of import licences in the sector of poultry products, the United Kingdom has failed to fulfil its obligations under Article 30 of the Treaty (Article 34 TFEU).	The Animal Health Act 1981 and the Importation of Animal Products and Poultry Products Order 1980 (Statutory Instrument 1980, No 14), as amended by the Importation of Animal Products and Poultry Products (Amendment) Order 1981 (Statutory Instrument 1981, No 1238).	By applying measures which had the effect of preventing imports of fresh and refrigerated poultry products, including eggs (not intended for hatching) and egg products other than heat-treated egg products, into England, Wales and Scotland from any Member State other than Ireland and Denmark, the United Kingdom had failed to fulfil its obligations under the Treaty. Reserved judgment on the licensing ban and Northern Ireland.

(continued)

[172] Paras 50 and 51.

Date	Case	Claim	Legislation at stake	Decision
31 January 1984	Case 74/82, *Newcastle disease Ireland* (judgment) Lodged 19 February 1982	By adopting the import ban and the import licensing system referred to with respect to poultry carcasses, poultry eggs and poultry products, Ireland has failed to fulfil its obligations under Article 30 of the EEC Treaty.		The ban is incompatible with the Treaty. The licensing system is compatible with the Treaty.
31 January 1984	Case 40/82, *Newcastle disease* (second judgment) Lodged 4 February 1982		Animal Health Act 1981 and the Importation of Animal Products and Poultry Products Order 1980 (Statutory Instrument 1980, No 14), as amended by an order of 1981 (Statutory Instrument 1981, No 1238).	The licensing system contrary to the Treaty. Northern Ireland could continue to carry out controls and, where necessary, restrict imports but could not prohibit all imports into Northern Ireland of poultry products Northern Ireland could continue to apply its licensing system due to the particularity of its poultry flock.

F. UPHOLDING CONFLICTING INTERESTS: THE LONG TERM

Table 7 below presents an overview of judgments with the characteristics of three types of good judgment. As already observed in the free movement of persons (chapter five), these judgments are rare. Interesting differences emerge in the frequency by type over time.

The share of Type 1 judgments fluctuated extensively in the early decades of the common market, stabilising in the period between 1980 and 2005, and then falling steadily. Type 2 judgments are scarce; their share has been surprisingly stable over time. Type 3 judgments are the most frequent. Their share was especially high in the early 1960s, but decreased in the 1970s compared to the free movement of persons where Type 1 judgments continued to be the most frequent of the three.

Until the 1970s, the Court issued a limited number of free movement of goods judgments, which makes it hard to appraise and consequently theorise the phenomenon. Some judgments upholding conflicting interests overlap. The total share of the judgments upholding conflicting interests in the Table below does not equal the sum of its types.

The patterns in Table 7 confirm the expectation that judgments upholding conflicting interests should be the exception or confined to exceptional circumstances or periods of political or economic turmoil. The absence of a clear trend indicates that the major events and developments might be of limited importance in this area as compared to the free movement of people where the share of good judgment has stubbornly increased. It might also indicate a change in the enforcement priorities or that the law has settled.

Table 7 Overview of free movement of goods judgments upholding conflicting interests by type. The first column from the left indicates the five-year calendar period (e.g. 1960 means the period from 1 January 1960, to 31 December 1965, and 2020 the period since January 2020. This explains the low number of cases.). Column 2 provides the information of the number of free movement of goods judgments, which the Court decided in a given period (e.g. in the period from 2015–2020 the Court decided 137 cases / second row from the bottom). Columns 3–5 (from the left) contain the number of judgments upholding conflicting interests by type: *Non-sanctioning Europeanisation of national rules and policies*, *Deferential upholding of European rights against the state* and *Bounded undesirable interpretation*. The final three columns from the left indicate the share of free movement of goods judgments upholding conflicting interests in each period by type

Period (5 years)	Number of cases	Type 1	Type 2	Type 3	Type 1 (share)	Type 2 (share)	Type 3 (share)
1960	14	0	1	9	0%	7%	64%
1965	14	3	0	4	21%	0%	29%
1970	54	3	0	15	6%	0%	28%
1975	104	11	8	13	11%	8%	13%
1980	168	24	3	22	14%	2%	13%
1985	190	22	4	27	12%	2%	14%
1990	194	28	11	20	14%	6%	10%
1995	149	29	8	34	19%	5%	23%
2000	159	22	5	27	14%	3%	17%
2005	182	14	5	23	8%	3%	13%
2010	151	9	3	31	6%	2%	21%
2015	137	13	4	34	9%	3%	25%
2020	22	1	1	3	5%	5%	14%

Institutional developments, such as the changing composition of the Court, the augmented use of the chamber system, the collegiate decision-making model, the workflow, new policy and legislative priorities (from the market of goods to the digital market), and multilingualism potentially increase the likelihood of atypical justifications. External factors – such as deeply engrained traditions like food labelling or traditional modes of production, national resistance to open markets and outside competition, political aspects of economic protectionism, changing economic incentives and modes of consumption, historic rivalries, and conflicting visions of the internal market between the Member States – however, are impossible to discount as impervious. For instance, a large share of judgments limiting the adverse effects of the rulings for national regulatory autonomy (top row, first column from the right) coincides with the 'empty chair crisis' in the early 1960s. Chapter seven discusses a variety of these circumstances along with the free movement of persons judgments.

Part III

The Mechanisms of Good Judgment

7

The Court as a Context-Conscious Lawmaker

SUMMARY

CHAPTER SEVEN UNPACKS the mechanisms of good judgment, building on the conceptualisation of good judgment in chapter three and the analysis of free movement of persons and goods judgments in chapters five and six.

This chapter investigates the rationale behind three types of good judgment. It argues that good judgment typically reconciles incommensurable claims under the weight of non-legal factors. Good judgment is a conceptually and formally discrete methodology of the Court, distinct from the methodology of constitutional balancing, the reading down of statutes, judicial minimalism, legal diplomacy, Solomonic judgments, strategic behaviour, consequentialism, prudence, judicial horse sense, stone-by-stone decision-making or other metaphors associated with context-conscious judging. As such, good judgment is an indispensable optic for the understanding of judicial decision-making.

A. INTRODUCTION

The question of the mechanisms of good judgment pertains to when case characteristics or external factors motivate the Court's departure from a typical structure of justification and model law application; when and how do political or economic circumstances, the relevant personal characteristics of the applicants or subject matter (legal issues) of the dispute affect the probability of good judgment and when do they do this in a significant way rather than randomly or incidentally?

All accounts of context-conscious judging outlined in chapter two grappled with this question in different settings – most often in the decisions of the United States Supreme Court and ordinary national courts, but also those of international courts like the European Court of Human Rights. Their insights have infused the theorising of the Court's reasoning and behaviour, which is the starting point for the concept of good judgment, as developed in chapter three.

The idea that case characteristics determine the Court's framing of the case, its legal argument (justification) and outcome, operationalises the legal realists' intuition of judicial sensitivity, judicial situation sense or horse sense[1], and the more formalised model of judicial behaviour which is fast-thinking judging or the cognitive accounts of judging and the identity approaches[2]. Incrementalism's alternative explanation of judicial situation sense as an institutional and institutionalised tendency to muddle through confounds the internal and the external mechanisms of good judgment, focusing on the mechanism of bounded rationality underlying both.[3] The idea that judges respond to institutional or external circumstances most closely resembles the strategic rational model of judicial behaviour[4] and the separation of powers model.[5] The idea that international court judges adopt state friendly solutions or depart from their preferred policy outcome when fearing legislative override[6] or other forms of legislative retaliation and constraint[7] resonates with the structuralist account of decision-making which states that judges avoid direct and unnecessary confrontations with powerful political actors.[8] The theory of effective supranational adjudication refines this insight by emphasising the principled aspect of adjudication with judges striving for practically workable solutions without compromising the integrity of the legal system, the rule of law, the protection of individual rights, and institutional authority.[9] Importantly, the theory distinguishes between factors within the control of the courts and those within the remit of the contracting states.

In short, theory and empirical research suggest that the Court's treatment of legal rules 'somehow' hinges on case facts, the political climate, and underlying conflicts.[10] The three types of good judgment provide a tool to

[1] KN Llewellyn, *The Common Law Tradition: Deciding Appeals* (Boston, Little Brown Company, 1960).

[2] L Epstein, U Šadl and K Weinshall, 'The Role of Comparative Law in the Analysis of Judicial Behavior' (2021) 69 *The American Journal of Comparative Law* 689.

[3] MM Shapiro, *The Supreme Court and Administrative Agencies* (New York, Free Press, 1968).

[4] L Epstein and J Knight, 'Toward a Strategic Revolution in Judicial Politics: A Look Back, A Look Ahead' (2000) 53 *Political Research Quarterly* 625.

[5] O Larsson and D Naurin, 'Judicial Independence and Political Uncertainty: How the Risk of Override Affects the Court of Justice of the EU' (2016) 70 *International Organization* 377.

[6] Larsson and Naurin (n 5).

[7] MR Madsen, P Cebulak and M Wiebusch, 'Backlash against International Courts: Explaining the Forms and Patterns of Resistance to International Courts' (2018) 14 *International Journal of Law in Context* 197; E Voeten, 'Populism and Backlashes against International Courts' (2020) 18 *Perspectives on Politics* 407.

[8] MR Madsen, '"Legal Diplomacy" – Law, Politics and the Genesis of Postwar European Human Rights' in St-L Hoffmann (ed), *Human Rights in the Twentieth Century* (Cambridge, Cambridge University Press, 2010).

[9] LR Helfer and A-M Slaughter, 'Toward a Theory of Effective Supranational Adjudication' (1997) 107 *Yale Law Journal* 273.

[10] It also predicts that Courts will legalise this conflict as politically independent judicial actors preserving the authority of the law and institutional legitimacy.

unpack the conceptual legal 'somehow' in single cases and empirically across a series of cases. In this sense, chapters five and six offered two important insights. First, they illustrated how the relationship between the Court's arguments, interpretative solutions, and decisions about individual claims were linked with the characteristics of the applicants and the legal issues, the subject matter of the disputes, the implications for the respondent state governments or private persons that are parties to the case, the underlying economic conflicts, and political interests. Second, the chapters highlighted the patterns (differences and changes) in the Court's use of good judgment.

i. Main Findings

As shown in Figure 1, the share of good judgment in the free movement of goods case-law has gradually decreased (grey line), while the share of free movement of persons judgments has gradually increased (dark grey). Interestingly, the patterns have converged in the past two decades with the share of good judgment in both policy areas becoming comparable.

This chapter brings the insights from the analysis to the fore, investigating which case characteristics become pivotal and under what circumstances. To assess the significance of the relationships between three types of good judgment and the available relevant information about the parties or the applicants, the legal content of the case, and the institutional features collected in the process of legal annotation described in chapter four, the chapter uses simple (linear) regression analysis.

To recall, the information about the case refers to 1) the information about the applicants in the proceedings at the national level when the preliminary references procedure is applicable and the applicants in direct actions before the Court at the European Union level mostly in actions for annulment and the failure to fulfil obligations; 2) the application of the legal framework or the subject of the case, especially the legal issues that the Court addresses in the dispute; and 3) the institutional features, like the type of proceedings, the number of sitting judges or the composition of the bench. This difference arises from the differences in the two policy areas.

The information is legally relevant to the policy areas and the discussion of context-conscious judging, and can be collected and processed systematically. Practically, the analysis uses the information related to all judgments like the composition of the Court, the type of proceedings, the subject matter and legal classification and the more specific case information that research assistants can reliably infer from the text of the judgments like the gender of the applicants or the domicile of the legal persons.

The findings below, summarily presented here and further unpacked and juxtaposed in the following sections, shed light on the Court's sensitivity to the particularities of the disputes and support valid inferences about the effect of broader political and economic circumstances on the three types of good judgment. The findings are also interesting considering the four accounts of context-conscious judging outlined in chapter two, and the alternative types of context-conscious judging which uphold conflicting interests by following the prototype justification which are discussed in the following sections.

In sum, in the free movement of persons disputes, the gender of the applicants is broadly not a determining factor. It is similarly inconsequential whether the applicants are workers (economically active) or workers' family members.[11] There are however differences between the three types of good judgment. The Court more often reconciles incommensurate claims by deferentially upholding rights in disputes involving workers' family members, and by limiting the implications of an undesirable interpretation of European Union law when the applicants are economically active: a worker, active jobseeker, or involuntarily unemployed.

Figure 1 shows the share of good judgment in free movement of goods (grey line) and persons (dark grey) case-law. The share of good judgment in the free movement of goods case-law has significantly decreased since the early 1960s (grey line), while the share of free movement of persons judgments has gradually increased since the mid-1960s (dark grey). The share of good judgment has been similar in both areas since the mid-2000s. Figure 1 is based on Tables 3 and 7, presented in chapters five and six (final section)

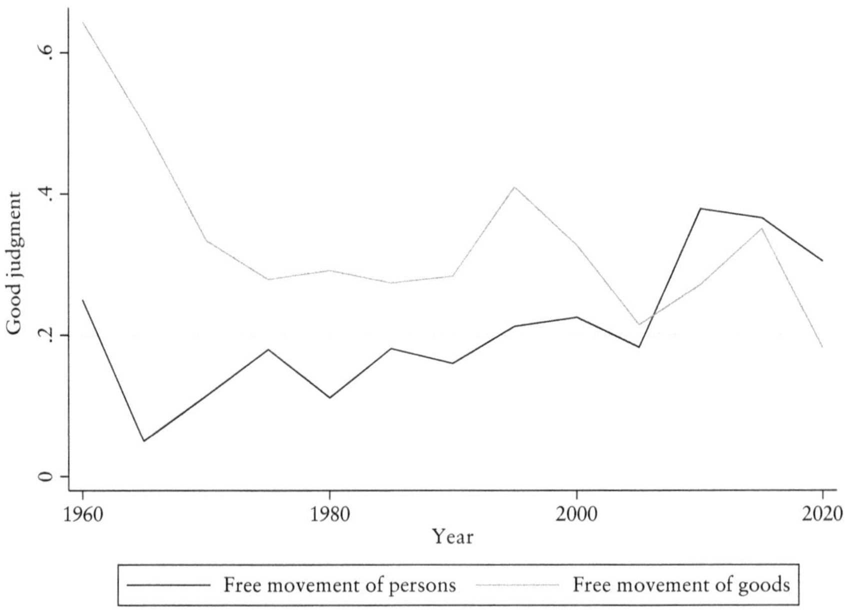

[11] Not statistically significant.

The subject matter of the case, understood as the rights or principles at stake or the legal issues discussed in the judgment, significantly increases the probability of good judgment in disputes about residence rights including family reunification and the residence of non-EU nationals and significantly decreases this probability when the free movement of persons disputes also concern provisions about European Union citizenship (Treaty based rights or questions about the Citizenship Directive 2004/38). Legal issues such as work-related or family-related benefits including social security or social assistance, equal treatment claims (nationality or residence based), and reserved professions (the public service exception) do not significantly affect the probability of good judgment.

Among the observed institutional features, the probability of good judgment increases when the Court sits in a larger formation (all judges sitting together before 2003 and in the Grand Chamber after the Treaty of Nice, which formally established the chamber system) and when two or more Member States submit their observations or intervene in the dispute before the Grand Chamber. The effect of Member State observations is greatest (more than doubling) when the Court scrutinises state policies without sanctioning them (the non-sanctioning Europeanisation of state policies). Member State observations in disputes decided in smaller formations do not significantly affect the probability of good judgment. The observed type of proceedings, i.e. the preliminary references or the infringement actions, are important; the probability of good judgment decreases in infringement cases, which are also infrequent, making up less than 13 per cent of the free movement of persons case-law.[12]

The patterns and the relationships are different in the free movement of goods judgments, which pose different legal challenges and involve different types of parties: most often (in 67 per cent of judgments) the litigants are legal persons challenging discriminatory or unjustified restrictions imposed by state governments on products crossing the border which are sold (product requirements) or marketed (selling arrangements) on the national territory. European institutions typically the Commission, are the applicants in 16 per cent of free movement of goods disputes and 15 per cent of judgments are rendered in the infringement proceedings against non-compliant Member States. In these disputes, the probability of good judgment decreases by a staggering 37 per cent. This is not true for other types of applicants, notably natural and legal persons.

Regarding the legal characteristics of disputes, questions as to whether a national measure constitutes a fiscal restriction or restricts trade have strong correlation with the increased probability of good judgment. The latter is also more likely when free movement of goods disputes overlap with other freedoms like the free movement of services or other policy areas of the European Union,

[12] The model includes time fixed effects, which eliminate the bias from unobserved factors that change over time but are constant over units (for instance, the subject matter of the disputes change, the number of judges and Member States involved increases, or the Commission's enforcement policy priorities shift).

most often agriculture or competition law (conditionally, it is more complex and potentially wider in scope). Finally, the Court will more often resort to good judgment when the dispute raises questions about the state or level of harmonisation. In contrast, good judgment is much less likely (22 per cent less likely) in disputes involving the interpretation of the Common Customs Tariff or questions related to the Customs Union more generally. While not often a

Figure 2 The probability of good judgment in free movement of persons case-law. The figure shows the effect of individual case characteristics and institutional features on the probability of good judgment. The personal characteristics of the applicants (worker, family members of a worker, and the gender of the applicant) have limited and statistically insignificant effects. Among the characteristics of the case related to the legal content of the dispute (middle bars / Case), European citizenship reduces whereas residence rights (rights to reside) increase the probability of good judgment. Among the institutional features (top bars / Court), infringement proceedings are negatively correlated while Grand Chamber is positively correlated with the probability of a good judgment. Member State observations (more than two Member States submitting observations) do not significantly affect the probability of good judgment when the Court does not deliberate in the Grand Chamber – in other words when it deliberates in Chambers of five or three judges, or in a large formation (prior to 2003). The probability of good judgment increases when Member States submit observations in disputes decided in the Grand Chamber.[13] The lighter shade indicates the effect, which is not statistically significant

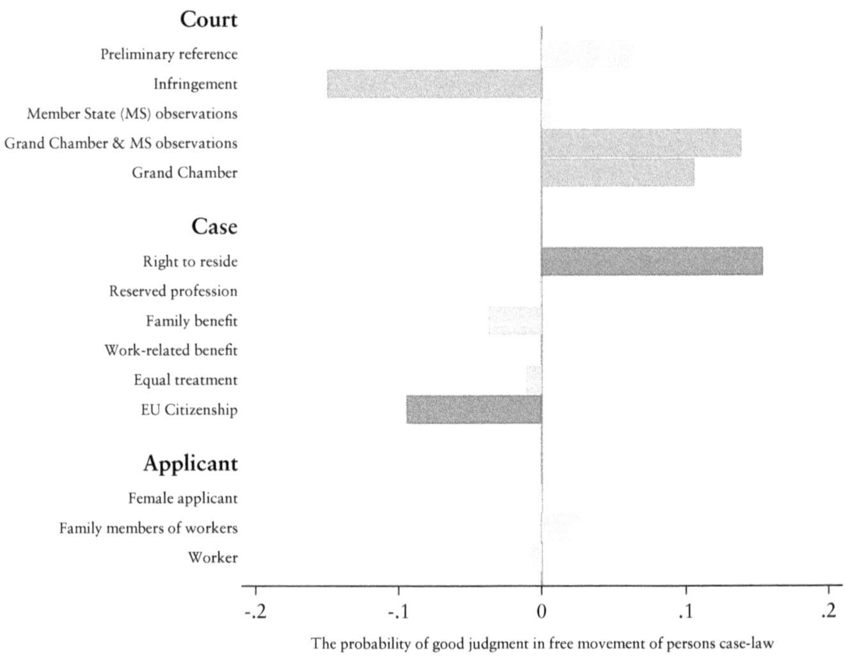

[13] Data on file with the author.

Figure 3 The probability of good judgment in free movement of goods case-law. The figure shows the effect of individual case characteristics and institutional features on the probability of good judgment. The characteristics of the applicants (natural or legal person or an EU institution) have limited effect, which is statistically significant only when the applicant is an EU institution (in which case the probability of good judgment decreases substantially). Among the characteristics of the case related to the legal content of the dispute (middle bars / Case), the disputes which concern trade and fiscal restrictions significantly increase the probability of good judgment, while the Common Customs Tariff significantly decreases the probability of good judgment. The probability of good judgment significantly increases when the dispute involves other freedoms and policy areas and when the Court establishes that the area is not harmonised. Among the institutional features (top bars / Court), the type of proceedings (infringement proceedings, preliminary reference proceedings) does not significantly affect the probability of good judgment. Member State observations (more than two Member States submitting observations) do not significantly affect the probability of good judgment when the Court does not deliberate in the Grand Chamber and instead deliberates in Chambers of five or three judges, or in a large formation (prior to 2003). The probability of good judgment increases when Member States submit observations in disputes decided in the Grand Chamber or generally in cases decided in the Grand Chamber.[14] The lighter shade indicates the effect, which is not statistically significant

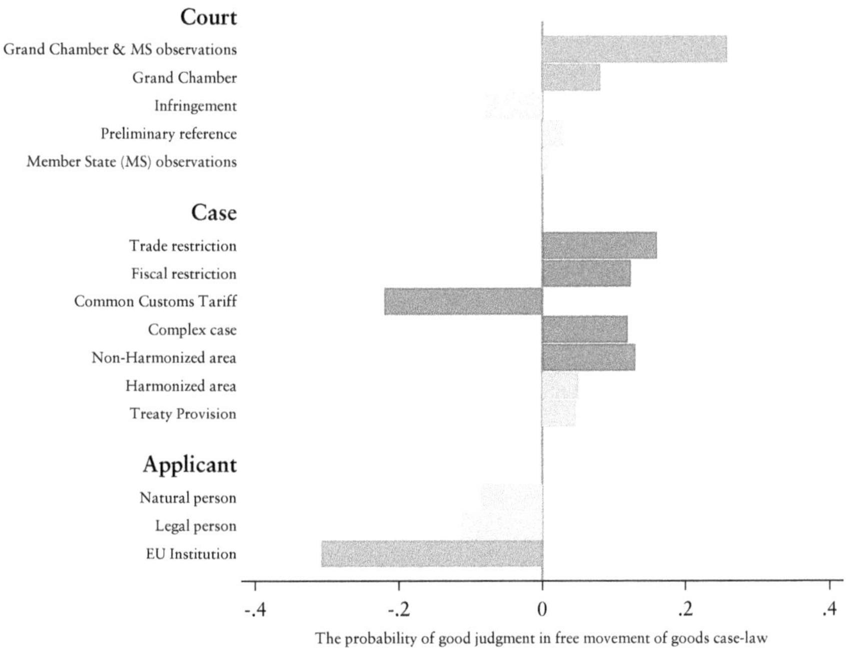

subject of scholarly analysis, every fifth judgment of the Court deals with the question of correct classification of products, including the seminal *Van Gend en Loos* case.

[14] Data on file with the author.

Unsurprisingly, Member State observations increase the probability of good judgment by a whopping 25 per cent when the Court either sits in the Grand Chamber or a large formation prior to 2003. Member State observations in smaller formations do not significantly affect the probability of good judgment. However, the Court is more likely to deliver a good judgment when sitting in a Grand Chamber, irrespective of the Member States' participation in the proceedings (the probability increases by 8 per cent in those cases). Member State observations have the most profound effect in the type of good judgment that is the non-sanctioning Europeanisation of national policies, arguably because the concrete outcome of the compatibility of national policy choices with European Union rules, standards, and values, has potentially wide-reaching implications. Finally, the Court is least likely to issue a good judgment in an infringement proceeding. Preliminary references have no significant effect.

ii. Unpacking the Findings: The Roadmap

In part ii, Section B below attempts to determine whether good judgment is case-motivated; concretely, it assesses which observed case characteristics affect which types of good judgment in both policy areas. Section B also considers and examines the findings of section A – namely, the Court's relative imperviousness to private applicants, selective responsiveness to legal issues, and strong correlation between the sitting formation and Member States' observations. It first finds that the economic and political context of the case and the implications of the rulings are often decisive; and second, that good judgment is not likely to be a consequence of the Court's working process and internal organisation. The Court is sensitive to the high stakes which a dispute of this nature presents to the Member States, the fragility of the political consensus of the national or European legislator, and the broader political climate. Hence, good judgment is a departure from the model justification, which is effectively context motivated.

Considering that the Court can tailor its justification to the context without departing from the model law application and typical justification, section C explores alternative forms of good judgment, notably the reframing of a dispute, the Court being allowed to decide on a less contentious legal problem than the case originally presents, the sending of mixed signals by simultaneously issuing more than one judgment on the same legal problem but with opposite case outcomes for the Member State, and rulings being delivered on explosive issues in cases that present lower than usual stakes in politically more opportune moments. Section D argues that the reading of the case-law in terms of the shifting relationships between rights, reasoning, outcomes, and methods of interpretation – i.e. through the lens of good judgment – and the theories of context-conscious judging, which suggest that the Court synchronises these relationships with the broader context of the disputes, creates a complete and nuanced understanding of adjudication, legal reasoning and judicial behaviour despite the limitations of the imperfect method and somewhat 'crude' conceptualisation of good judgment.

B. CASE-MOTIVATED GOOD JUDGMENT

Over 87 per cent of free movement of persons judgments and just under 82 per cent of free movement of goods judgments are issued in the preliminary reference procedure (Article 267 TFEU) where national courts and tribunals refer questions of interpretation and validity of European Union law in the context of concrete disputes. Article 94 of the Court's Rules of Procedure[15] regulates the content of the reference for a preliminary ruling, stating among other points that: 'In addition to the text of the questions referred to the Court for a preliminary ruling, the request for a preliminary ruling shall contain … a summary of the subject matter of the dispute and the relevant findings of fact as determined by the referring court or tribunal, or, at least, an account of the facts on which the questions are based'.[16]

A key characteristic of the procedure is the division of responsibilities between the Court and the national courts; the latter provide the facts about the dispute and the provisions of national law, the former hands down the European Union law. The description of facts about the applicants in the judgments varies. Very often, the national courts offer little in terms of context and other rudimentary information for disputes in the main proceedings, and tend to submit ambiguous preliminary questions.[17] The Court occasionally refuses the answer to the preliminary questions because the relevant facts of the dispute are unclear,[18] but at other times it might be inundated with detail.[19]

[15] Rules of Procedure of the Court of Justice of 25 September 2012 (OJ L 265, 29.9.2012), as amended on 18 June 2013 (OJ L 173, 26.6.2013, p. 65), on 19 July 2016 (OJ L 217, 12.8.2016, p. 69), on 9 April 2019 (OJ L 111, 25.4.2019, p. 73) and on 26 November 2019 (OJ L 316, 6.12.2019, p. 103).

[16] ibid. Art 94(a).

[17] A Wallerman Ghavanini, 'Sowing Wheat and Reaping Thorns: The Referring Court's (Lack of) Influence on the EU Court of Justice' paper presented at the ECPR Conference, 26 August 2020; U Šadl and A Wallerman, '"The Referring Court Asks, in Essence": Is Reformulation of Preliminary Questions by the Court of Justice a Decision Writing Fixture or a Decision-Making Approach?' (2019) 25 *European Law Journal* 416.

[18] An example is Case C-123/00, *Bellamy*, ECLI:EU:C:2001:214, para 23 and seq. The referring court inquired whether Arts 34 and 36 TFEU prevented the application of a national provision requiring specific description of a foodstuff on advertisements where the omission could mislead consumers. Mrs Bellamy omitted such information, but the referring court failed to specify the facts (and the nature of the omission). Mrs Bellamy explained that she used the term pasteurised whole fresh milk, which could be interpreted as giving a false impression that the milk was fresh (as opposed to pasteurised). The Commission stated that Mrs Bellamy used the term Breakfast Milk instead of legally mandated pasteurised whole fresh milk. The Court did not answer several questions. See also M Broberg and N Fenger, *Broberg and Fenger on Preliminary References to the European Court of Justice*, 3rd edn (Oxford, Oxford University Press, 2021) 281.

[19] Ole Due contributed this to the practice of some national courts of outsourcing the drafting of the references to the parties of the case. O Due, 'Danish Preliminary References' in D O'Keeffe and A Bavasso (eds), *Judicial Review in European Union Law* (Philadelphia, Wolters Kluwer, 2001).

Typically, the Court spells out its understanding of the facts in the judgment as a 'starting point for its 'useful' (i.e. specific) interpretation of the applicable provisions and principles of Union law'.[20] Reports for the Hearing are often rich in facts and Advocate General Opinions can often include revealing detail.

A case in point is *Dano*, which concerned Ms Dano's unsuccessful request to receive social benefits in Germany.[21] While it would be impossible to prove that Ms Dano's personal characteristics motivated the Court's decision to uphold the decision of the German authorities, it might be reasonable to assume that her circumstances were relevant to the case and contributed to shaping the Court's perception of the legal problem.[22]

The most interesting excerpt is footnote 5 of the Advocate's General Opinion which discusses the national court's preliminary reference of: 'The referring court also states that Ms Dano has been convicted for crimes against property and assets, receiving as maximum sentence a suspended two-year term of imprisonment. However, such factual statements do not, in my view, have any bearing on the answers to be given to the questions referred.'[23] This footnote is attached to a short description of Ms Dano's personal situation which identifies her as Romanian, uneducated ('attended school for three years in Romania and does not have any leaving certificate'), with poor German skills ('She understands German and expresses herself simply in German. On the other hand, she cannot write in German and her ability to read texts in the German language is only limited'), and no employment history ('She has not been trained in a profession and, to date, has not worked in Germany or Romania').[24] These facts feed directly into the benefit tourism discourse, indirectly expressing the opposition between the free movement of persons, based on solidarity and a high level of social protection, and the national desire to control free movement and public spending in order to prevent the abuse of a high level of social protection and solidarity.

Personal characteristics, which are the object of the present inquiry, intuitively matter more in the free movement of persons than in the free movement of goods disputes. This intuition resonates with the analysis of case-law showing that most of said disputes involve a conflict between individual citizens claiming their European free movement rights to social benefits and residence and

[20] K Lenaerts, K Gutman and JT Nowak, *EU Procedural Law* 2nd edn (Oxford, Oxford University Press, 2023) 252.

[21] Case C-333/13, *Dano*, ECLI:EU:C:2014:2358.

[22] See also A Lazović, 'Structuring Perception: How Structures of Practice Influence Decision-Making at the Court of Justice of the European Union' (PhD Thesis, European University Institute, 2023). The experimental evidence for the role of intuition is laid out by C Guthrie, JJ Rachlinski and AJ Wistrich, 'Blinking on the Bench: How Judges Decide Cases' (2007) 93 *Cornell Law Review* 1.

[23] Opinion of Advocate General Wathelet delivered on 20 May 2014 in Case C-333/13, *Elisabeta Dano and Florin Dano v Jobcenter Leipzig*, ECLI:EU:C:2014:341.

[24] ibid., para 34.

state administrations fending off their claims based on their personal and family status. Moreover, literature confirms that the identity of the applicant[25] affects both the interpretation and the case outcomes.[26]

i. The Applicants

Information about the applicant in the free movement of persons case-law includes their economic, family, and personal, status (gender). While no single detail definitively affects the likelihood of good judgment, the analysis of three types of good judgment shows that the Court is more likely to uphold individual free movement rights while leaving their application to the national court or administration (deferential upholding of rights) if the applicant is economically active i.e. a worker or a former worker actively seeking employment.[27]

A good example is the judgment in *Campana*.[28] The Court's interpretation stretched the meaning of the unemployment benefits in Regulation 1408/71 to include vocational training assistance in situations when an employed person was facing unemployment. This effectively converted the benefits into a preventive instrument for combating unemployment, and the Federal Employment Office (the Bundesanstalt) could therefore not deny them to the applicant. However, the Court first added that this interpretation was bound to situations where the applicants were unemployed or *actually* facing unemployment, then deferring the assessment to the national administration and courts: '(I)t is for the national authorities, subject to supervision by the competent courts, to assess in each individual case whether a person in employment who applies for assistance for vocational training may be deemed to be actually threatened by unemployment'.[29]

Deferring the assessment could logically follow from the division of tasks and jurisdiction between the Court and the national administrations more familiar with the factual situation. More likely it follows from the Court's aim to reassure the German government that the ultimate decision to award the newly qualified benefit rested with the national administrations and courts. In addition to the referring court's detailed description of the facts, this reading of the case is supported by the German government's argumentation, opposing the Court's

[25] Literature also refers to deserving migrants and citizens as rights holders. See C O'Brien, 'Civis Capitalist Sum: Class as the New Guiding Principle of EU Free Movement Rights' (2016) *Common Market Law Review* 937. Past literature has explored the concept of market citizenship, N Nic Shuibhne, 'The Resilience of EU Market Citizenship' (2010) 47 *Common Market Law Review* 1597.

[26] G Davies, 'Has the Court Changed, or Have the Cases? The Deservingness of Litigants as an Element in Court of Justice Citizenship Adjudication' (2018) 25 *Journal of European Public Policy* 1442.

[27] Data on file with the author.

[28] Case 375/85, *Campana*, ECLI:EU:C:1987:253.

[29] *Campana*, paras 12 and 13.

interpretation due to its far-reaching implications, especially its insistence on the literal interpretation,[30] stressing that any other interpretation 'would lead to considerable problems of delimitation since any measure of vocational training, schooling or general education has some relationship with unemployment in so far as it is capable of reducing the risk of future unemployment'.[31]

Critically, at the time of the application for assistance in 1981, the applicant born in 1941 had worked in the television repair business in Germany from 1964 until early 1977, in Italy from early 1977 to mid-1980, and had returned to employment in Germany from August 1980 onwards. These personal circumstances upheld the Court's impulse to protect the rights of migrant workers with documented employment history from facing unemployment in the second half of their working life, even in times of growing unemployment in the host state and the sensitive nature of the issues of social security and benefits for economically non-active migrants.

Similarly, the personal characteristics of an applicant correlate with a higher probability of good judgment if they are family members of workers. The Court's judgment in *Jia*[32] is an attempt to contain the extension of European Union law into national immigration rules. The case concerned the elderly Chinese parents-in-law of a self-employed migrant worker, a German national residing in Sweden. The retired couple entered Sweden separately on visitors' visas and, while in the country, applied for permanent residence on the grounds of financial dependency on the migrant worker. Their personal situation of complete dependency in later life, lawful entry, the exceptional nature of the situation (typically Member States are called to consider cases of spouses rather than parents-in-law[33]), the documented employment history of the nominated sponsor, and the fact that Ms Jia was 'not seeking to evade national immigration legislation illicitly'[34] were relevant considerations in the Court's re-interpretation of its prior unfavourable case-law (*Akrich*[35]) and

[30] Report for the Hearing, p 2391: 'The government of the Federal Republic of Germany proposes that the reply to the preliminary question should be in the negative, having regard to the wording of Arts 4 and 67 of Reg No 1408/71 and to the spirit, purpose and origins of the regulation.'

[31] Report for the Hearing, p 2392. Conversely, the Italian government (the country where Ms Campana had citizenship and which would therefore have been otherwise responsible for the payment of social security) insisted on a broad interpretation of the term unemployment benefit, which would also cover the assistance for the vocational training under the threat of future unemployment. At the time of the decision, Germany was struggling with high unemployment (around 8%, almost doubling since 1980 and tripling since the 1970s). See M Hellwig et al, 'Economic Policy in Germany: Was There a Turnaround?' (1987) 2 *Economic Policy* 105.

[32] Case C-1/05, *Yunying Jia v Migrationsverket*, ECLI:EU:C:2007:1.

[33] B Olivier and J Herman Reestman, 'Yunying Jia v Migrationsverket – Court of Justice of the European Communities: No Legal Residence Requirements for the Admission of Family Members with a Third-Country Nationality of Migrated Union Citizens. Grand Chamber Decision of 9 January 2007, Yunying Jia v Migrationsverket, Case C-1/05' (2007) 3 *European Constitutional Law Review* 463.

[34] *Jia*, para 31.

[35] Case C-109/01, *Akrich*, ECLI:EU:C:2003:491.

Directive 73/148 governing the residence for nationals of Member States prior to the Citizenship Directive.[36]

The context of the reference in *Jia* is an attempt on the part of the national court to clarify the condition of prior lawful residence which was at stake in *Akrich*, a ruling that could have been decided against the applicant on its facts (illegal residence, a conviction for criminal offences, a deportation order, and the abuse of free movement rights). Beyond the facts, however, *Akrich* allowed the Member States to impose the conditions of the first entry and residence of third country national family members.[37] To change course, the Court had to argue *Jia* on the facts and bring the situation within the scope of European Union law.

From the perspective of bounded undesirable interpretation, it is extremely relevant that the Court held in the main part of the judgment that European Union law governed the questions of prior lawful residence of third country nationals, trespassing on the Member State competence to autonomously regulate the first entry and residence of third country nationals related to European Union citizens. However, the Court also circumscribed the implications of this ruling by allowing the state to decide whether to make the residence permit of a third country national subject to the condition of lawful residence in the operative part of the judgment. Moreover, the Member States could independently decide which documents proved the relationship of dependency.

In disputes concerning the free movement of goods, good judgment has proven less likely in situations involving European institutions, notably the Commission, bringing infringement proceedings against non-compliant Member States. In contrast, whether the applicant is a natural or legal person, and the fact of the Commission's intervention in the proceedings (the submission of observations in the preliminary reference procedure) do not discernibly influence the probability of good judgment.[38]

To conclude, the very limited significance of the gender, family, and economic status of the applicants, as well as the irrelevance of whether the applicants are private parties, suggest that the Court is not overly-sensitive to the characteristics of private applicants in the free movement of persons disputes and even less sensitive to the status of private applicants in the free movement of goods disputes, and is therefore unlikely to uphold conflicting interests by means of good judgment. If the Court exercises its situation sense due to the applicant's personal characteristics, it does not systematically do so by departing from the model law justification. Like the Advocate General in *Dano*, the Court, more often than

[36] Dir 73/148/EEC of 21 May 1973 on the abolition of restrictions on movement and residence within the Community for nationals of Member States with regard to the establishment and the provision of services (OJ L172, 28.6.1973).

[37] E.g. this was the interpretation of the Dutch government which submitted the observations in the case.

[38] Data on file with the author.

not, deliberately and consciously attempts to acknowledge but set aside personal histories or details and focus on the broader implications of its interpretations.[39] Occasionally, the judgments give the impression of 'applying fairness to the facts,' like in *Jia* and *Campana*. Further indicative examples include the ruling in *Carpenter*, which concerned the residence permit of the spouse of a domestic service provider traveling abroad for work.[40] However, even in these cases, the unobserved factors, notably the broader political circumstances, which are unrelated to the applicant's personal circumstances might be influential.

From the perspective of the entire judgment, the personal characteristics of private applicants could nonetheless contribute to the Court's legal framing of the case which might in turn be shaped by the broader political or economic context. Their relevance might arguably increase in connection with the nature of the rights that the migrant workers or their family members, students, or other economically non-active migrants, notably retired persons claim from the host or the home state. The Court decided *Jia* in anticipation of the ruling in *Eind*, testing the political waters before making the next step in the discourse about the rules governing the entry of non-European family members of economically inactive migrants (discussed in section C).[41] In short, legal issues might be a weightier factor in the Court's decision-making process and justification if not for any other convincing reasons than the general validity and the precedential effect of the Court's interpretations under Article 267 TFEU.

ii. The Case

The information collected about the case, which captures the legal issues discussed in the judgment, is helpful when measuring and evaluating how and when the legal content of the case bears on the Court's reasoning and the case outcome. Because free movement of persons and goods judgments address two of the internal market's fundamental freedoms, the legal questions are complementary

[39] The question of whether the judges can in fact do so is different. For an interesting contribution to the debate on situation sense and prejudice, see J Zhuang Liu and X Li, 'Legal Techniques for Rationalizing Biased Judicial Decisions: Evidence from Experiments with Real Judges' (2019) 16 *Journal of Empirical Legal Studies* 630.

[40] Case C-60/00, *Mary Carpenter*, ECLI:EU:C:2002:434. The applicant's personal conduct and circumstances appeared key to the Court's ruling that the refusal of a residence permit was disproportionate: 'Although, in the main proceedings, Mr Carpenter's spouse has infringed the immigration laws of the United Kingdom by not leaving the country prior to the expiry of her leave to remain as a visitor, her conduct, since her arrival in the United Kingdom in September 1994, has not been the subject of any other complaint that could give cause to fear that she might in the future constitute a danger to public order or public safety. Moreover, it is clear that Mr and Mrs Carpenter's marriage, which was celebrated in the United Kingdom in 1996, is genuine and that Mrs Carpenter continues to lead a true family life there, in particular by looking after her husband's children from a previous marriage. In those circumstances, the decision to deport Mrs Carpenter constitutes an infringement which is not proportionate to the objective pursued.' Paras 44 and 45.

[41] Case C-291/05, R. N. G. *Eind*, ECLI:EU:C:2007:771.

and not immediately comparable in terms of the legal substantive or doctrinal dimensions. However, they address very similar underlying conflicts between the protection of national economic operators and workers and the benefits of competitive labour markets, between the economic and the social dimensions of the market, between the local and common interests, between autonomous and centralised policymaking, and between the democratic national and the bureaucratic supranational regulation. As emphasised in chapters five and six,[42] the legal issues of the cases just like the applicants in the free movement of persons cases have been changing. The analysis controls for time effects.

Over half of the free movement of persons disputes (60 per cent of judgments) concern social security or other benefits linked to free movement, from child support to tax deductions.[43] Around 12 per cent involve residence rights; over 17 per cent are about derived rights; around 27 per cent deal with equal treatment claims, of which most are based on nationality and residence rights; and 23 per cent of disputes link free movement rights and European Union citizenship. The share of European citizenship judgments is considerable given the short time span between the inauguration of European citizenship in the Treaty of Maastricht in 1992 and the first citizenship jurisprudence which emerged in the late 1990s. The legislative change, meaning the adoption of the Citizenship Rights Directive in 2004, undoubtedly contributed to the proliferation of case-law.[44]

Surprisingly, legal issues like work related benefits including pensions and unemployment benefits, reserved professions, public service exception, derived rights, and family related rights do not significantly affect the overall probability of good judgment. The probability of good judgment is lower in cases concerning the question of the European Union itself, probably because the more controversial cases are increasingly decided and classified as cases on social security benefits and the social security for migrant workers under the Regulation on Social Benefits. This affects core free movement rights of European Citizenship, which have become increasingly fragile in the past decade. As Shaw observes, European Union citizenship gives rise to questions about where exactly the edges of free movement lie.[45]

Most interestingly, the Court is 18 per cent more likely to reconcile competing interests by means of bounded undesirable interpretation for the respondent

[42] Tables 2 and 4.

[43] See also Table 2 in chapter five.

[44] Dir 2004/38/EC of the European Parliament and of the Council of 29 April 2004 on the right of citizens of the Union and their family members to move and reside freely within the territory of the Member States amending Reg (EEC) No 1612/68 and repealing Dirs 64/221/EEC, 68/360/EEC, 72/194/EEC, 73/148/EEC, 75/34/EEC, 75/35/EEC, 90/364/EEC, 90/365/EEC and 93/96/EEC (OJ L158, 30.4.2004), repealing and replacing previous piecemeal legislation regulating rights of individual categories of migrants such as students, workers, or economically inactive (e.g. retired) persons.

[45] J Shaw, 'Between Law and Political Truth? Member State Preferences, EU Free Movement Rules and National Immigration Law' (2015) 17 *Cambridge Yearbook of European Legal Studies* 247.

Member State when the case revolves around residence rights. As was true of the example discussed in the previous section (*Jia*), the Court's argumentation in *NA* is clarifying.[46] The case tackled residence rights of third country nationals who remained in the host state to care for minor Union citizens after a divorce and the departure of the Union citizen from that state.

The Court's interpretation of Article 13(2)(c) of the Citizenship Directive did not grant a divorced third-country national, who had also been a victim of domestic violence during the marriage, a separate right of residence in the host Member State because her abusive spouse had left the Member State before commencing the divorce proceedings.[47] However, she could remain in the Member State based on Article 12 of Regulation 1612/68 as a sole parent of a child of a former worker. Additionally, the Court specified that neither the minor European citizen nor her third country national parent could invoke Article 20 TFEU when the minor citizen did not exercise her right to move, unless the minor citizen had sufficient resources or attended school. In this case, the child and her carer could rely on Article 21 TFEU, subject to the decision of the referring court that they in fact satisfied those conditions.

The Court's interpretation in *NA* coincided with a constitutionally important moment (Brexit); the Court decided the case only a week after the British vote to leave the Union. The particularly sensitive subject of residence combined with immigration control guided the interpretation of Article 13(2) of the Citizenship Rights Directive and sought to confine the fact situation entirely to the ambit of legislation without compromising core citizenship rights under the Treaty.[48] Even if the facts of *NA* seem particularly distressing, the findings confirm that the Court has interpreted residence rights in ways that limited their implications for immigration policies.[49]

The free movement of goods opens up a different area of the internal market and, at first sight, raises the opposite, impersonal or even dispassionate discussion of doctrinal questions. The Treaty provisions on the abolition of customs, quantitative restrictions, fiscal charges, and all measures of equivalent effect, typically concern an economic interest attached to the free movement of goods rather than an individual right of free movement attached to the person.

[46] Case C-115/15, *NA*, ECLI:EU:C:2016:487.

[47] The Court was also aware that the Upper Tribunal (Immigration and Asylum Chamber), taking the view that the anticipated removal of NA's children from the United Kingdom would infringe their rights under Art 8 of the ECHR, upheld NA's action / request under that provision. See *NA*, para 21.

[48] The judgment could be read as the *arrêt d'espèce* (concrete case judgment). See D Sarmiento and D Jiménez-Valladolid, 'Half a Case at a Time: Dealing with Judicial Minimalism at the European Court of Justice' in M Claes et al (eds), *Constitutional Conversations in Europe: Actors, Topics and Procedures* (Cambridge, Intersentia, 2012).

[49] For the ways in which the Member States have actively and creatively used the legal inconclusiveness see also Shaw (n 45). This discussion continues in section C on context-motivated good judgment.

Obstacles to the free marketing, production, and trade in goods can, however, quickly and unexpectedly become unreasonable and passionate. This is illustrated by the case-law on the possible and de facto submitted justifications of national rules that are 'indefensibly protectionist and/or anachronistic and which have no sensible place in an integrating EU market'.[50]

An overview of the free movement of goods case-law shows that 50 per cent of cases concern the application of secondary legislation, and 26 per cent refer to the Treaty provisions. Over 15 per cent of judgments explicitly discuss free movement against the backdrop of the existence and scope of harmonisation. The most often raised legal issues concern classification under the Common Customs Tarif or Customs Union (22 per cent). These legal issues are closely followed by disputes in which the Court is called to classify national measures as restricting trade by prohibiting imports, and violating the standstill cause, or as imposing charges (21 per cent), and fiscal measures, including the charges with equivalent effect (18 per cent). An overwhelming majority of disputes (92 per cent) inquire about the application of free movement of goods regulations. Some (roughly 8 per cent of cases) touch on the Treaty provisions relating to agriculture (3 per cent), competition law (3 per cent), or other freedoms (1.5 per cent).

Overall, as shown in Figure 3 the legal issues raised in a dispute affect the probability of good judgment. In disputes about customs and nomenclature, this probability significantly decreases. In disputes where the Court establishes trade and fiscal restrictions, and where the European Union has not adopted harmonisation measures in the relevant area, this probability significantly increases.

Figure 3 unpacks the findings briefly explained above, demonstrating that the Court will opt for the deferential upholding of rights in disputes extending to other freedoms and policy areas, and where it cannot draw on the concrete legislative solutions and the political commitment indicative of harmonising legislation. The finding that the probability of non-sanctioning Europeanisation increases significantly in the absence of harmonising measures further supports this interpretation. Furthermore, the observation that the Court will soften negative interpretive outcomes for the responding Member State by confining or delimiting their implications for national regulatory autonomy in disputes about trade and fiscal restrictions, including measures with equivalent effect, resonates with the literature which suggests that the Court is sensitive to national political interests thus complementing the findings of the analysis in chapter six.

An additional indicator that a legal issue or subject matter of the case is not a neat, clearly-defined, strictly legal category but a highly contextual category

[50] S Weatherill, *Law and Values in the European Union* (Oxford, Oxford University Press, 2016) 398.

is the significant negative correlation between good judgment and questions related to the Customs Union and the application of the Common Customs Tariff. This echoes the most recent announcement that the Court has agreed to share its exclusive jurisdiction under Article 267 TFEU with the General Court in the domains of excise duties, the Customs Code and the tariff classification of goods under the Combined Nomenclature.[51] Among the reasons for this transfer of authority, the Court has stated that these areas 'are clearly defined and sufficiently separable from other areas covered by European Union law, are governed by a limited number of acts of secondary legislation and, as is apparent from the abovementioned statistics, rarely give rise to judgments of principle since, out of a total of more than 630 cases, only three were dealt with by the Grand Chamber of the Court of Justice during the period in question. Those areas have, furthermore, given rise to abundant case-law on the part of the Court of Justice, which should considerably limit the risks of divergences in the case-law'.[52]

Table 8 The probability of different types of good judgment depending on the legal issues raised in the disputes, allowing for time fixed effects. An empty cell means that the effect is not statistically significant. A below zero percentage means that the probability of a type of good judgment marked in the columns decreases by the type of legal issue discussed in the case marked in rows. A positive percentage means that the probability of a type of good judgment increases dependent on the legal issue discussed in the case

	Non-sanctioning Europeanisation of state policies	**Bounded undesirable interpretation**	**Deferential upholding of free movement rights**
Interaction of free movement with other freedoms and policy areas		8%	8%
Customs	−12%	−9%	
Absence of harmonising measures	15% (*Familiapress*)		4%
Trade restrictions		23% (*Danske Slagterier*)	
Fiscal restrictions (including the delimitation of fiscal restrictions from the questions of internal taxation)	−4%	17%	

[51] Art 2 of the proposed Reg of the European Parliament and the Council amending Protocol No 3 on the Statute of the Court of Justice of the European Union (Art 50(2) of the proposed Statute). https://curia.europa.eu/jcms/upload/docs/application/pdf/2022-12/demande_transfert_ddp_tribunal_en.pdf (accessed in December 2023), at p 5.

[52] ibid. at p 5.

The judgments in *Familiapress*[53] and *Danske Slagterier*,[54] discussed below, illustrate the relationship between good judgment and the concrete legal issues raised in disputes. *Familiapress* illustrates non-sanctioning Europeanisation in the absence of harmonising legislation; the judgment in *Danske Slagterier* combines elements of deferential protection of free movement rights and bounded undesirable interpretation for the Member State where they become liable for unjustified restrictions imposed on the free movement of goods. Both judgments are included in Table 7, which presents the overall findings.

In *Familiapress*, the Commercial Court in Vienna inquired whether the legislation prohibiting the sale of periodicals with prize puzzle competitions or games conflicted with Article 34 TFEU. Austrian Law on Unfair Competition, Article 9, barred free gifts and other press competitions in newspapers, which effectively banned the import and marketing of German newspapers. The Austrian government argued that the Law fostered press diversity by ensuring that small publishing houses did not lose out in the fierce market race for readers because they could not afford prizes and rewards.

The judgment is an interesting example of non-sanctioning Europeanisation because the Europeanisation of standards did not lead to a European solution.[55] In formal legal terms, the Court ruled that the Austrian Law imposed a restriction on the free movement of goods that could be justified by the overriding requirement of maintaining press diversity, provided that it complied with the principle of proportionality and the freedom of expression embodied in Article 10 ECHR.

This reasoning situates the Austrian law outside the ambit of European Union law because it is justified, while also insisting that in order to be justified, it must be proportionate and comply with human rights.[56] The latter requirement brings the Austrian law back within the ambit of European Union law, effectively stretching the European standard of human rights protection beyond the European Union's competence and the established case-law.[57] In other words, the Court could have examined whether the Austrian legislation was justified via public policy derogations under Article 36 TFEU and/or mandatory requirements, as in *Cassis de Dijon*, and it if was, uphold it within the ambit of European Union law. The question of whether a measure complied with the freedom of the press would cease to be a question of European Union law.[58]

[53] Case C-368/95, *Vereinigte Familiapress Zeitungsverlags- und vertriebs GmbH v Heinrich Bauer Verlag*, ECLI:EU:C:1997:325.

[54] C-445/06, *Danske Slagterier v Bundesrepublik Deutschland* ECLI:EU:C:2009:178.

[55] A Bavasso, 'Case C-368/95, Vereinigte Familiapress Zeitungsverlags- Und Vertriebs GmbH v. Heinrich Bauer Verlag, Judgment of 26 June 1997, ECR [1997] I-3689' (1998) 35 *Common Market Law Review* 1413, 1423.

[56] According to the case-law human rights apply as the general principles of European Union law (prior to the Treaty amendments and the adoption of the Charter).

[57] The standard established in ERT thus also applies to the mandatory requirements. For this reading see LFM Besselink, 'The Member States, the National Constitutions and the Scope of the Charter' (2001) 8 *Maastricht Journal of European and Comparative Law* 68, 79.

[58] F Jacobs, 'Human Rights in the European Union: The Role of the Court of Justice' (2001) 26 *European Law Review* 331.

From the perspective of good judgment, it is interesting that the Court coupled a laxer two-pronged proportionality test with detailed guidance on its application. The latter would correspond to a stricter three-pronged test, circumscribing the national court's discretion.[59] Lax tests compel the legislators to demonstrate a legitimate aim and the necessity of implementing the measures adopted, but typically exonerate them from a complex balancing exercise.[60] The Court's insistence on the balancing exercise is atypical, because it is entirely confined to the local market conditions and does not aim to install a generalisable European solution, instead settling on an Austria-specific option. The outcome of the judgment is debatable.

Practically, the national court could easily reconcile the Court's interpretation with the ruling of the Austrian Constitutional Court.[61] In a judgment which preceded the Commercial Court's preliminary reference in *Familiapress*, the latter emphasised that the information media were not mere goods but also an essential vector in the formation of the public opinion. According to that court, the legislation aiming to ensure the survival of small publishing houses by measures which prohibited certain forms of publicity was in the observance of the Austrian Constitution and Article 10 of the European Convention on Human Rights.[62]

Without harmonisation, political impetus, or guidance about how to handle the terrain of press diversity, media, or newspaper advertising, the Court confirmed that the European Union had a say in the matter as a matter of European Union law without divulging much more. Finally, it saw and seized the opportunity to tailor the *Cassis* formula and exercise a supervisory jurisdiction over national regulatory choices in areas where the adoption of relevant harmonising legislation lagged far behind.[63]

The dispute in *Danske Slagterier* was altogether different. The German court raised five questions about the basis and scope of State liability for the incorrect implementation of European Union law. The applicant, Danske Slagterier, an industry association of Danish slaughterhouses and pig farmers, claimed that

[59] T Tridimas, 'Constitutional Review of Member State Action: The Virtues and Vices of an Incomplete Jurisdiction' (2011) 9 *International Journal of Constitutional Law* 737.

[60] The Court conditionally accepted the Austrian justification, if the national court found that the prohibition was proportionate, elaborating multiple demanding criteria. The national court had to determine whether prize-offering newspapers in fact competed with small press publishers unable to offer comparable rewards, and whether the promise of winning a prize could in fact cause a shift in demand. This assessment would require a definition of the relevant market and the market shares of publishers; an evaluation of the extent to which, from the consumer's standpoint, the prize-offering disadvantaged small publishers, considering the factors likely to motivate consumers' purchase of newspapers, such as the advertising of the prize on the title page, the likelihood of winning, the value of the prize and so on.

[61] Decision of the Austrian Constitutional Court of 11 March 1994, OBI 1994, p. 151.

[62] The judgment is cited in the Advocate General's opinion in Case C-368/95, *Vereinigte Familiapress Zeitungsverlags- und vertriebs GmbH v Heinrich Bauer Verlag*, ECLI:EU:C:1997:325, para 27.

[63] In this sense, see S Weatherill, 'Recent Case Law Concerning the Free Movement of Goods: Mapping the Frontiers of Market Deregulation' (1999) 36 *Common Market Law Review* 51, 64.

Germany imposed an unlawful import ban on meat from uncastrated male pigs from 1993 to 1999. The ban caused the members of the association to lose at least DEM 280 million in revenue (equivalent to around 205 million Euros). By the time of the Court's ruling in *Danske Slagterier*, it was clear that Germany had failed to implement two directives harmonising the measures which the authorities of the Member States could take to detect a pronounced sexual odour in uncastrated male pigs,[64] and that the conditions and checks imposed on the slaughtered animals were excessive.

The Court held that the individuals harmed by the incorrect transposition and application of the directives could rely directly on the free movement of goods provisions (Article 34 TFEU) to claim damages from the State for the breach of Community law.

The Court, however, qualified this right and added important delimitations to the implication of its ruling. The applicants' right to damages under European Union law was, crucially, curtailed by German procedural rules. The Court saw no fault with the latter: it deemed a three-year time limit, which Germany imposed for bringing the proceedings in the interests of legal certainty, was reasonable and compatible with European Union law;[65] it ruled that the limitation period could run from the date on which the first injurious effects of the incorrect transposition occurred and further injurious effects were foreseeable, even if that date preceded the correct transposition of the directive; it held that the German legislation, which barred compensation when the individual wilfully or negligently failed to avert damages through alternative legal remedy (here deferring to the national court to ultimately decide), was unobjectionable from the European Union's law point of view. Concretely, the applicants showed negligence by waiting for the national court to refer preliminary questions or relying on the infringement proceedings pending before the Court of Justice. German procedural rules gave the applicants a reasonable recourse to a legal remedy, which they failed to pursue to their own detriment.

The limitation, interpretation, and the yielding to the procedural rules of a Member State would be unremarkable if the economic implications of the opposite outcome were not sizeable, if the outcome of the case for the litigants after a 16 year-long dispute was not largely negative,[66] and if the Court did not manipulate the technicalities of national procedures regardless of the outcome. Paradoxically, the otherwise much-criticised inroad into the national procedural

[64] Case C-102/96, *Commission v Germany*, ECLI:EU:C:1998:529.

[65] *Danske Slagterier*, paras 31–35.

[66] From the deferential protection of rights, the clear finding of liability for the breach of free novement rights and the dictum that individuals could rely on the direct effect of Art 34 TFEU, did ιot result in the corresponding liability of the State but hinged on the national court's findings that he applicants used the available remedies diligently. However, the Court importantly limited the cope of liability even if the national courts acknowledged the diligence of the applicants, possibly ɔ signal to the participating Member State governments and the broader legal audiences that the ability for incorrect implementation would never be excessive.

autonomy de facto exculpated the State. Germany incurred liability in principle, yet escaped consequences in practice through the Court's interpretation of the statute of limitations. A generous interpretation of the right was at odds with the less generous interpretation of the remedy.

To conclude, the legal issues, especially the qualification of national measures as trade or fiscal restrictions and measures of equivalent effect in the free movement of goods judgments, correlate with the probability of good judgment to a much higher degree than the main legal issues which the Court typically tackles in the free movement of persons judgments.

This analysis does not stand on its own, especially as it does not consider the effect of the established precedent over time or engage closely with case complexity. Nonetheless, the findings support the argument that the political and economic consequences of interpretations and outcomes steer the Court's sensitivity to the applicants' individual characteristics and the legal issues raised in a case. The next section examines the relative importance of procedural factors, including the observations of the Member States and the sitting formation, to further strengthen this conclusion. Incidentally, the Court sat in the Grand Chamber in *Danske Slagterier* and as a Full Court in *Familiapress* (the case being decided prior to the Nice Treaty).

iii. The Institution: Idiosyncratic Good Judgment

The Court's reasoning becomes the law (it has a de facto precedential effect); the authoritative decision about the validity, interpretation, or application of European Union law to the concrete facts puts an end to the dispute. The institutional features, such as the sitting formation, the type of procedure, and the Court's working method potentially affect both. These features are difficult to isolate, organise, and study. However, they are also comparable across the free movement of goods and persons case-law, contrary to the characteristics of the applicants and the subject matter of the case. Hence, comparisons can complement and elucidate the interpretation of the findings.

The analysis considers the effect of the preliminary references and the failure to fulfil obligations as two types of procedure that account for 96 per cent of free movement of goods and 99 per cent of free movement of persons judgments. It also takes into account the sitting formation, meaning whether the Court decides a case as the Full court, in the Grand Chamber post Nice or in a large formation prior to Nice, and the number of Member State observations or interventions.

To focus the argument, which is also necessary due to the limited data sources, the analysis excludes factors related to the Court's decision-making process, which literature has considered or demonstrated to be pertinent. These include the civil law origins, multilingualism, collegiate decision-making geared toward consensus, the working culture and multiculturalism, the interpersona dynamics and strategic behaviour of individual judges, the influence of the Court's president, the inter-institutional hierarchy created formally by the institutions of the vice presidents and the chamber presidents and informally between the cabinets due to language barriers or other forms of social capital, the changes in the Court's membership, chamber rotation, the role of the reporting judge, and personal (integrationist) preferences of judges.[67]

The overall findings imply that the type of procedure is not associated with a greater likelihood of any type of good judgment in the free movement of persons and goods case-law. The Court will, however, be less likely to deferentially uphold the rights of individuals in a judgment rendered in infringement proceedings (see Figures 2 and 3).

The probability of good judgment in the free movement of persons judgments, concretely the non-sanctioning Europeanisation and the bounded undesirable interpretation, increases when the Court sits in the Grand Chamber. The same is true for the non-sanctioning Europeanisation type of good judgment in the free movement of goods judgments.

Finally, Member State observations increase the probability of good judgment rendered by the Grand Chamber or a large formation by 26 per cent in the free movement of goods disputes, and by 14 per cent in the free movement of persons disputes, a finding that does not depend on the year of the judgment or the type of procedure. In contrast, Member State observations submitted in the free movement of goods or persons disputes decided by smaller formations do not affect the probability of good judgment in any way. This means that the participation of the Member States in legally or politically important cases compels the Court to uphold conflicting claims and protect conflicting interests. Admittedly, the direction, form, and limits of this relationship remain unclear.

[67] For legal literature and political science work that touch on these issues, see SSL Hermansen, 'Building Legitimacy: Strategic Case Allocations in the Court of Justice of the European Union' (2020) 27 *Journal of European Public Policy* 1215; L Azoulai, 'La Fabrication de La Jurisprudence Communautaire' in P Mbongo and A Vauchez (eds), *Dans la Fabrique du Droit Européen: Scènes, Acteurs Et Publics De La Cour De Justice Des Communautés Européennes* (Brussels, Bruylant, 2009); K McAuliffe, 'Behind the Scenes at the Court of Justice. Drafting EU Law Stories' in F Nicola and B Davies (eds), *EU law stories. Contextual and critical histories of European jurisprudence* (Cambridge, Cambridge University Press, 2017); H Rasmussen, 'Remedying the Crumbling EC Judicial System' (2000) 37 *Common Market L. Rev.* 1071; U Sadl et al, 'That's an Order! The Orders of the CJEU and the Effect of Article 99 RoP on Judicial Cooperation' paper presented to the Social Science Research Network 2020, SSRN Scholarly Paper ID 3715514 <https://papers.ssrn.com/abstract=3715514> (accessed 20 December 2020); U Šadl et al, 'Law and Orders: The Orders of the European Court of Justice as a Window in the Judicial Process and Institutional Transformations' (2022) 1 *European Law Open* 549; S Hermansen and D Naurin, 'Will Do? Selecting Judges on the Basis of Policy Preferences or Performance Indicators', https://www.semanticscholar.org/paper/Building-legitimacy%3A-strategic-case-allocations-in-Hermansen/448525a891605adcbf27bca2b01d675da99937fe; C Krenn, 'A Sense of Common Purpose: On the Role of Case Assignment and the Judge-Rapporteur at the European Court of Justice' in MR Madsen, F Nicola and A Vauchez (eds), *Researching the European Court of Justice: Methodological Shifts and Law's Embeddedness* (Cambridge, Cambridge University Press, 2022).

The findings call for additional analysis of the non-legal motivations, therefore focusing on the political or economic dimensions to establish that the unobserved institutional features and practices do not motivate departures from the model law application. This is even more important because scholars have offered inconclusive findings about the reasons for and the effect of the Member States' observations.[68]

The Court convenes the Grand Chamber in disputes that raise important legal questions and questions of principle.[69] The Court, however, decides on the chamber size only after it has received the observations from the Member States, meaning that legal importance / significance might not be the only and / or the most important factor. Moreover, the Member States might submit observations to contribute to the legal solution of the dispute rather than to force the Court to align its legal solution to their political or economic preferences.[70] The distinction between the legal and political elements is not clear-cut, and Member State governments keep law and politics simultaneously in mind.[71] Other literature, however, strongly suggests that the main reason for government participation in the procedure is not primarily legal and that the Court perceives this accordingly, that is, as a threat of legislative override in accordance with the strategic model of judicial behaviour.[72]

Regarding the Court's working method, the growing membership, increased workload, and other unobserved factors arguably add 'quirks' to the argument and the justification, increasing the risk of inadvertent justificatory inconsistencies.[73] At the same time, they have led to a further streamlining of routines and procedural practices, reinforcing the role of the administrative services, such as the Research and Documentation department.[74]

Moreover, the attention and the meticulousness with which the Court attends to the final texts of its judgments should make involuntary errors and slip-ups practically impossible. The starting point of the deliberation is a text drafted in the cabinet of the reporting judge, which is shared with the cabinets of all sitting judges. During deliberation, judges agree on the outcome and the main line of justification. After deliberation, all sitting judges can shape the justification

[68] CJ Carrubba, MJ Gabel and C Hankla, 'Judicial Behavior under Political Constraints: Evidence from the European Court of Justice' (2008) 102 *American Political Science Review* 435; CJ Carrubba and MJ Gabel, *International Courts and the Performance of International Agreements: A General Theory with Evidence from the European Union* (Cambridge, Cambridge University Press, 2015). The argument is controversial and subject to debate.

[69] Art 60 of the Rules of Procedure of the Court of Justice (RoP).

[70] Anecdotally, the Court does not place significant legal weight on observations, which are no longer translated into the working language of the Court. However, the Member States also deliver oral observations at the hearings in important cases.

[71] J Dederke and D Naurin, 'Friends of the Court? Why EU Governments File Observations before the Court of Justice' (2018) 57 *European Journal of Political Research* 867.

[72] Larsson and Naurin (n 5).

[73] U Šadl, 'Old Is New: The Transformative Effect of References to Settled Case Law in the Decisions of the European Court of Justice' (2021) 58 *Common Market Law Review* 1.

[74] Šadl et al (n 67).

by raising additional points or concerns. The final draft is subject to language editing, giving the justification a recognizable, standardised structure and style.

Although a standardised text production method delivers a standardised text, too many highly routinised and experienced 'cooks' under close supervision of a centralised unit might still spoil the standardised broth. It is highly unlikely, however, that they would do so repeatedly in a statistically significant way. Moreover, the probability would not vary according to policy area (the probability of good judgment in the free movement of persons cases increases by 14 per cent and the probability of good judgment in the free movement of goods increases by 26 per cent). Finally, the same institutional idiosyncrasies rarely reduce the frequency of good judgment in the free movement of goods case-law while increasing it in the free movement of persons case-law over the same period (Figure 3, noting especially the differences in the first and the last two decades under study). In sum, idiosyncratic good judgment is possible but unlikely in light of the analysis in chapters five and six, the findings presented in sections i. and ii. above, as well as the literature, which has highlighted the Court's role in settling bilateral political and economic disputes by means of juridification.[75]

C. CONTEXT-MOTIVATED GOOD JUDGMENT

The section draws on the analysis in section A to argue that economic and political (non-legal) considerations primarily motivate good judgment. Case and applicant characteristics have a varied and sporadic effect when considered in isolation but gain additional force when considered against the political and economic stakes of the dispute and the implications of the ruling. This insight is important because it nuances the arguments about the Court's unconditional commitment to free movement rights and the internal market, its reasons for deferring the law-making authority to the national courts and the legislators, and most generally, its appetite for integration.

First, the Court pays limited attention to the individual characteristics of the applicants, who can thus expect equal treatment under normal circumstances (on a positive note) and special treatment under exceptional circumstances. Second, the subject matter of the case is not a strictly legal category. The legal issues which significantly affect the probability of good judgment, like the qualification of national measures as measures of equivalent effect, or consideration of residence rights including family reunification, and which blatantly challenge State protectionism or demand financial solidarity with migrants are economically controversial and politicised. Permanent residence and the conditions

[75] See W Phelan, *Great Judgments of the European Court of Justice Rethinking the Landmark Decisions of the Foundational Period* (Cambridge, Cambridge University Press, 2019); Weatherill (n 50).

under which Member States can terminate residence rights, in particular, gave rise to prolonged debates and conflicts in the Council at the time of the adoption of the Citizenship Rights Directive. The protracted negotiation process of the Coordination of Social Security Regulation, reflected in the minutes of the Council and scholarly commentary, highlight the struggle between free movement and the national interest to confine social security to national territory (the territoriality principle).[76]

The Court deferentially upholds free movement rights in legally complicated disputes involving more than one freedom and policy area. In these instances, the Court defers the terms of application to the national courts and legislators, without relinquishing its promise of free movement. It moreover defers the protection of rights and scrutinises national measures and policies without sanctioning them in the absence of harmonising legislation.

This suggests that the Court might be practicing passive virtues, tuning them to the political will,[77] acting in line with the division of tasks inherent in Article 267 TFEU, or trying to avoid clear answers to politically charged and economically consequential questions. The latter interpretation is the most convincing given the finding that legal issues largely dissociated from major political conflicts significantly reduce the probability of good judgment, like disputes raising questions related to the customs union and Common Customs Tariff. It also echoes the historical shifts in the frequency of good judgment. As demonstrated in Figure 1, the frequency of good judgment in the free movement of goods case-law increased in the mid-1990s, possibly because of the Court's reversal of its prior jurisprudence on quantitative restrictions and the potential which the Member States saw in justifying trade restrictions against the backdrop of expanding Union's competences.[78] The share of good judgment has since been steadily decreasing, with a minor increase following the financial crisis (2007–2008). Free movement of goods and the customs union were Europe's economic priority, and the Member States gradually gave in to the European bargain: they would open their national markets to reap the economic gains of the Common market.

In contrast, the share of good judgment in the free movement of persons grew steadily until the late 1990s, increasing rapidly after the 2004 enlargement, peaking around the financial crisis and continuing until the migration crisis in 2015 and the Brexit referendum in 2016. Uncontroversially, these events strained the Member States' budgets and political tolerance for migration – even the movement of European citizens. Free movement became a contested issue

[76] Ch five, p 8. See also O Golynker, 'EU Coordination of Social Security from the Point of View of EU Integration Theory' (2020) 22 *European Journal of Social Security* 110.

[77] J Zglinski, *Europe's Passive Virtues: Deference to National Authorities in EU Free Movement Law* (Oxford, Oxford University Press, 2020).

[78] The ruling in joined cases C-267/91 and C-268/91, *Keck and Mithouard*, ECLI:EU:C:1993:905.

among European governments and stakeholders in the Member States after decades of flying below the radar of public attention.[79] Compared to the free movement of goods, this trend suggests that the Member States needed more convincing to accept the political and social costs of economic integration and not view the phenomenon as a potential threat to public security or a burden on the social security systems. The Council flatly rejected the Commission's proposal in the Citizenship Rights Directive to extend unconditional residence for European citizens from three to six months and shorten the qualification period for permanent residence to four years.

The following subsections engage with three instances of contextually motivated good judgment. At the outset it is important to stress that context sensitivity is a continuum and not a binary category, which the conceptualisation of good judgment considers and operationalises as three types of sensitivity and broad categories that accommodate the diversity of situations. The analysis in subsections i. – iii. demonstrates the levels or degrees of the Court's sensitivity, in particular to the political context, ranging from the recognition of high political, social and cultural stakes of the case, to the Court's honouring of a fragile political consensus or the will of the European legislator, to its oversensitivity to the political and electoral mood in the respondent state. These degrees of context sensitivity reflect the different degrees of the underlying rationale of good judgment, a combination of prudence, political savviness, and legal expertise. At one end of the spectrum is the Court's consideration of the desirability of the implications of its ruling, and its careful consideration to propose the most acceptable, legally permissible and justifiable interpretation. At its opposite end is the Court's acceptance of the political reality, its political savviness, and ultimate willingness to adapt the justification to the politically desired outcome of the case. In the former case, legal rules decide the case. In the latter, politics decides the case. Good judgment becomes both an empirically questionable strategy and normatively problematic.

i. Recognising the Stakes

The probability of good judgment increases in disputes which the Court decides in a larger formation or in the Grand Chamber, especially when Member State governments other than the respondent government participate in the proceedings. Legal salience and increased attention increase the stakes of the Court's interpretation and outcome.

Collins,[80] decided by the Full Court as the largest sitting formation, combines the challenging legal issue of social benefits, a reluctant Member State repeatedly

[79] Shaw (n 45).
[80] Case C-138/02, *Collins*, ECLI:EU:C:2004:172.

questioning the limits of free movement of persons, a claimant with a sketchy employment history and tenuous connection to the host Member State, the looming accession of Cyprus and the Eastern European states with a combined population of 75 million to the European Union (the Court decided the case in March 2004 and the Accession Treaties were signed on 1 May 2004), the imminent adoption of the Citizenship Rights Directive designed to further strengthen free movement rights adopted on 29 April 2004 with an open invitation from the referring tribunal to define the effect of free movement of persons and thus the European Union competence in the domain of social benefits.

The judgment is an emblematic example of good judgment where the Court resolved the immediate conflict between the applicant and the Social Security Commissioner by upholding the Secretary of State for Work and Pensions' refusal to grant the applicant the jobseeker's allowance and the Member State's policy to exclude applicants without strong links with its labour market from the benefits of free movement, while also extending the scope of equal treatment and European Union citizenship to the entire domain of financial benefits. The fact situation might be unique, but the underlying conflict is standard.

The Social Security Commissioner questioned whether the applicant was a worker for the purposes of Regulation 1612/68; if he was a worker, did he have a right to reside pursuant to Directive 68/360, and if not, did any principle or provision of European Union law require the payment of a social security benefit like income-based jobseeker's allowance?

Opinions on the last question conflicted. The United Kingdom and German governments argued fiercely that no provision or principle of European Union law required them to pay a benefit such as jobseeker's allowance to a person in the circumstances of Mr Collins[81] who did not work, habitually reside in the host state, or have an established link with its employment market. The Commission highlighted that Mr Collins was a citizen of the Union, lawfully resident in the United Kingdom as a jobseeker, and entitled to equal treatment under the Treaty in any situation governed by European Union law. According to the Commission, the allowance was a social advantage within the meaning of Regulation 1612/68 and within the material scope of Community law.[82] The United Kingdom's legislation tying the allowance to habitual residence was indirectly discriminatory given that United Kingdom nationals could fulfil this condition much more easily than non-nationals.

Recalling the discussion in sections i. and ii., the applicant's personal situation could have changed the stakes. Mr Collins arrived in the United Kingdom from the United States with a recently acquired Irish passport, seeking work, and claiming a jobseeker's allowance. The German government highlighted the applicant's tenuous link with the United Kingdom to distinguish the case from

[81] *Collins*, para 46.

[82] The Opinion of Mr Advocate General Ruiz-Jarabo Colomer delivered on 10 July 2003 in Cas C-138/02, *Brian Francis Collins*, ECLI:EU:C:2003:409.

Martinez Sala,[83] a judgment from sixteen years prior in which Germany was obliged to pay child benefits to a long-term economically inactive resident with Spanish nationality on the grounds that she was a European citizen.

The Court agreed, formalising Germany's argument of a genuine link requirement,[84] accepting that the United Kingdom could 'require a connection between persons who claim entitlement to such an allowance and its employment market'.[85] The Advocate General further reassured sceptics that a residence condition, 'intended to ascertain the degree of connection with the State and the links which the claimant has with the domestic employment market, may be justified in order to avoid what has come to be known as 'benefit tourism', where persons move from State to State with the purpose of taking advantage of non-contributory benefits, and in order to prevent abuses'.[86]

Collins confirmed that jobseekers' allowance fell within the scope of non-discrimination on the grounds of nationality and thus European Union law, reversing or at least upgrading previous case-law (*Lebon*, decided in 1987).[87] Access to the allowance nonetheless remained conditional on the veracity of the link which the applicant could prove, and the Member State could require by reference to habitual residence respecting the common European standard of proportionality. In sum, the Social Security Commissioner could condition Mr Collins's claim for the allowance on his habitual residence in the United Kingdom, but the proportionality of this condition would need to meet the common European standard.

Collins was a high stakes case, felicitously timed and skilfully executed, which strengthened free movement rights and the notion of European citizenship while calming resistance by accepting national employment policies of individual Member States.[88] The Court claimed European Union competence without acting on it in the concrete case.

The stakes in *Eind* seemed legally and politically higher. In addition to the Netherlands, where the dispute arose, five Member States and the European Commission submitted written observations. The case concerned the residence of third country family members of economically inactive European citizens and the useful effect (*effet utile*) of their free movement rights. The referring court sought to clarify whether European Union free movement

[83] Case C-85/96, *María Martínez Sala*, ECLI:EU:C:1998:217.

[84] For the argument that the genuine link criterion is 'moral,' implying that it gives the Member States greater possibilities to exclude certain groups of applicants from the welfare system than the argument of economic costs and financial strain on such system, see M Dougan, 'The Court Helps Those Who Help Themselves … The Legal Status of Migrant Work-Seekers under Community Law in the Light of the Collins Judgment' (2005) 7 *European Journal of Social Security* 7, 15.

[85] *Collins*, para 71.

[86] AG Opinion in *Collins*, para 75.

[87] Case 316/85, *Lebon*, ECLI:EU:C:1987:302.

[88] For the interpretation of *Collins* as a case in reconciliatory interpretation aligning primary law with legislation see K Lenaerts, 'How the ECJ Thinks: A Study on Judicial Legitimacy European Union Law Issue: Essay' (2013) 36 *Fordham International Law Journal* 1302.

law or national immigration rules applied in the situation where a European citizen reliant on social benefits returned to their home state with a family member, a national of a non-member country, from a Member State where that family member lawfully resided. For the government of the Netherlands, which actively pursued stricter immigration policy at the time of the proceedings, and likely for those of the intervening Member States, the issue was if and when European Union law rules on free movement could deny a Member State the authority over its own nationals, thereby potentially blocking national policy objectives.

Practically, the case concerned the residence permit of a twelve-year old Surinamese girl who joined her Dutch father in the Netherlands rather than pursuing the route of a marriage of convenience or other fraudulent use of free movement rights that the Dutch government tried to prevent or limit (notably the Belgian route, and the fictitious residence and employment contracts that the Dutch government tried to combat with stricter entry and residence requirements). The Dutch authorities insisted that the girl returned to Surinam to reapply for family reunification according to the Dutch immigration rules controlling the first entry of third country nationals to its territory.

The Court resolved the question by upholding the applicant's right to free movement and residence without rejecting the Dutch legislation or policy choice.[89] The Netherlands did not have to accept the residence permit issued by the United Kingdom as proof of Ms Eind's lawful residence under European Union law – in this sense, the European Union law did not cover the right of first entry or prior lawful residence. However, the authorities had to consider that Ms Eind was a family member of a Dutch national who exercised his free movement and citizenship rights, and was hence entitled to join her father in the Netherlands upon his return from the United Kingdom as a matter of free movement law and European citizenship provisions. Ms Eind would retain the residence right until she turned 21 and was a dependent of her father pursuant to Article 10(1)(a) of Regulation 1612/68 applied by analogy.

On the most contentious issue, the Court held that prior lawful residence of a third-country family member under the national law in the Member State of which the worker was a national did not bear on the determination of that national's right to reside in the latter State. The Netherlands did not, therefore, need to abandon its attempts to pursue a stricter immigration policy. The constitutional implications of *Eind* were groundbreaking; the practical consequences

[89] Interestingly, the crux of the matter was addressed in the *Akrich* ruling where the Court allowed the Member States to impose a prior lawful residence condition and thus effectively control the first entry of third country nationals. The Dutch ministry based the refusal of the permit on that ruling, and the Member States intervening in the proceedings, the Commission, the applicant and the Advocate General engaged with it. The Court does not mention *Akrich*, which it is called to clarify, at all. An interesting fact, potentially contributing to this silence, is that the national referring court disagreed with the Ministry's interpretation of *Akrich* (and possibly even expressing its disagreement with the policy change of the Dutch government).

were not.[90] After the ruling and combined with the ruling in *Jia*, discussed in section i. above, Ireland, Denmark, Finland, and the United Kingdom, banking on the Court's framing of the dispute, introduced the requirement of prior lawful residence in their legislation.[91]

The Court decided *Eind* in the Grand Chamber in December 2007, conscious of the political struggles related to the topic during the negotiation of the Citizenship Rights Directive which came into effect in mid-2006. The relationship between good judgment and salient cases touching on such issues is discussed below in Section ii.

ii. Honouring Fragile Consensus

The Court can show sensitivity to the European Union's policy choices or acknowledge the fragility of political consensus formulated in a legal act or provisions that the dispute raises. The political struggle over European Union legislation or the desirability of the adopted policy can continue in the courtroom, aptly illustrated by Germany's frustration over the Tobacco Advertising Directive.[92] The Court can also show sympathy for difficult national legislative solutions when examining national policies pursuing economic or social ends. In the former case, the Court honours the common European political consensus.[93] In the latter case, the Court acknowledges the difficult policy choices of a Member State legislator whilst harbouring doubts about the chosen means to pursue legitimate ends.

The judgment in *Scotch Whisky Association* illustrates the latter situation.[94] To reduce hazardous and harmful consumption of cheap alcohol in Scotland, the Scottish Parliament imposed a minimum unit price for alcohol (the Alcohol Act) in 2012, fixing the minimum price per unit of alcohol (MPU). According to the Act, the Scottish Government would assess the effect of the MPU within five years and the MPU would expire within six years unless the Parliament

[90] JB Bierbach, 'European Citizens' Third-Country Family Members and Community Law: Grand Chamber Decision of 11 December 2007, Case C-291/05, Minister Voor Vreemdelingenzaken En Integratie v. R.N.G. Eind The Return of the Member State National and the Destiny of the European Citizen' (2008) 4 *European Constitutional Law Review* 344.

[91] C Costello, 'Metock: Free Movement and "Normal Family Life" in the Union' (2009) 46 *Common Market Law Review* 587, 595.

[92] Dir 98/43/EC of the European Parliament and of the Council of 6 July 1998 on the approximation of the laws, regulations and administrative provisions of the Member States relating to the advertising and sponsorship of tobacco products, OJ L 213, 30.7.1998, pp 9–12. Case C-376/98, *Germany v European Parliament and Council*, ECLI:EU:C:2000:544.

[93] When the Council and the European Parliament agree to a legislative solution, the Court's loyalty to the legislative compromise would be interpreted as yielding to the legislative will. When the struggle is between the European Parliament and the Council, with the Council's position prevailing, the Court's upholding of the compromise would be interpreted as yielding to the political will.

[94] Case C-333/14, *Scotch Whisky Association*, ECLI:EU:C:2015:845.

decided otherwise (the sunset clause). During the notification procedure, the European Commission raised the issue of compatibility with Article 34 TFEU, holding that the public policy exception under Article 36 TFEU could not justify the restrictions. The Scotch Whisky Association (the applicant) initiated judicial review.

The referring court asked whether a minimum retail price of alcoholic beverages complied with the Single Common Organisation of Agricultural Products (CMO), and Articles 34 and 36 TFEU. It furthermore inquired into how to review the proportionality of the Scottish measures and what evidence to consider. The dispute attracted the interest of six Member State governments, Norway, and the EFTA Surveillance Authority. Pan-European alcohol trade bodies representing European spirit producers, like spiritsEUROPE, and Comité européen des entreprises vins representing European wine producers mobilised in support of the applicants.[95]

The Advocate General concluded that the Scottish rules amounting to price fixing were contrary to Article 34 TFEU, examining the possibility of justification under public health exception under Article 36 TFEU, and in this context, their proportionality. He suggested a stricter three-pronged proportionality test but deferred the balancing (the third prong) to the national courts, emphasising the discretion of the State regarding the protection of public health, the complexity of the assessments, the uncertainty about the effects of the measure, and – referring to the six-year sunset clause – its experimental and fixed-term nature. While he considered the MUP appropriate to reduce alcohol consumption, he wondered whether higher taxes would not attain this objective more effectively.

The Court, sitting in a five-judge formation, agreed with the Advocate General that the Scottish measures undermined the CMO, but suggested a laxer two-pronged proportionality test of legitimate aim and necessity. Through the lens of context-motivated non-sanctioning of state policies, the judgment intrudes deep into the realm of national non-economic choices, which seems excessive because the adopted measures were undoubtedly pursuing a legitimate aim; the parties agreed, and the respondent government offered ample evidence documenting that the Act was not explicitly or tacitly protectionist.[96] The review is also excessively deferential to the national court and indirectly to the Scottish legislator, asking them to consider alternatives like excise duties.[97] Given the undisputed existence of a less restrictive and more efficient alternative with additional advantages, the Court's deferential attitude is not

[95] O Bartlett and A MacCulloch, 'Evidence and Proportionality in Free Movement Cases: The Impact of the Scotch Whisky Case' (2020) 11 *European Journal of Risk Regulation* 109.

[96] *Scotch Whisky*, paras 37-38.

[97] The judgment can also be read and criticised as a balancing exercise between free movement of goods and public health (rule – exception – proportionality analysis). A Alemanno, 'Balancing Free Movement and Public Health: The Case of Minimum Unit Pricing of Alcohol in Scotch Whisky' (2016) 53 *Common Market Law Review* 1037.

legally convincing or necessary politically. It is safe to conclude that the Court's sensitivity to fragile political consensus accompanied by massive economic implications for the politically powerful applicants who actively blocked the legislators' policies on the national level motivated the justification.

The Scottish legislator adopted the disputed measures with great difficulty facing formidable resistance of a powerful industry. Its attempts to combat harmful and hazardous scientifically documented consumption of cheap alcohol, especially among the economically unprivileged population, persistently met with fervent opposition and political manoeuvres of the alcohol producers to delay implementation, mitigate the effects, and prevent the extension of the policy to the whole territory. The Scottish legislator thus also faced a vociferous anti-MUP position which emerged as the dominant industry voice in the legislative debate.[98] The references to the national legislative debate and the mobilisation of the alcohol industry behind the applicant support the interpretation that the Court's intention to uphold the fragile political equilibrium motivated its reluctance to speak the final word on proportionality and deliver an unambiguous ruling. The judgment simultaneously recognises the legitimacy of the aim, the in principle necessity of the selected means (the MPU), and the existence of less restrictive alternatives (taxation) in one breath. The latter favours the alcohol industry and free movement, the former the national legislative consensus and public health.

In the aftermath of the judgment, the Supreme Court of the United Kingdom upheld the Scottish system of minimum pricing as proportionate under European Union law.[99] On the critical issue of whether taxation would have achieved the same objectives as minimum pricing in combatting the problematic levels of drinking, thereby reducing alcohol-related mortality, hospitalisation and other forms of alcohol-related harm, the Supreme Court deferred to the government and the legislator. It held that; '(t)hat was a judgment which it was for them to make, and their right to make it militates strongly against intrusive review by a domestic court'.[100]

In *Scottish Whisky Association*, the Court upheld the fragile political consensus and a sincere attempt on the part of the national legislator to combat a public health crisis, even if by sub-optimal means from the European Union perspective.

The Court also honoured the political will of the European legislator, notably the Council, expressed during the legislative procedure. While it would be unreasonable to expect the judges to tune in to the Council meetings, a debate

[98] B Hawkins and MCI van Schalkwyk, 'Politics and Fantasy in UK Alcohol Policy: A Critical Logics Approach' *Critical Policy Studies* 1. (Published online in May 2023).

[99] *The judgment of the Supreme Court of the United Kingdom, ([2017] UKSC 76), available at https://www.supremecourt.uk/cases/docs/uksc-2015-0177-judgment.pdf; eg paras 9, 15, 46 and 48.

[100] ibid., para 63.

on legislative acts such as the Citizenship Rights Directive seeking to codify the Court's case-law would not escape its attention.

X. v Belgium[101] illustrates the Court's reluctance to reopen the question of residence for third-country national family members of Union citizens who departed from the host State, even if the personal situation of the applicant is dire. X., a third-country national victim of domestic violence could retain the right of residence in a host Member State, but only if the divorce followed the departure of the sponsor Union citizen within a reasonable timeframe and X. remained financially self-sufficient going forward.

X. tapped into a fragile consensus reached in the Citizenship Rights Directive about permanent residence, the requirement of sufficient resources, the rights of family members who are not European citizens, and the retention of residence when they no longer form a family unit with the European citizen. During the legislative procedure, the Council flatly rejected the European Parliament's and the European Economic and Social Committee's insistence on the increased and explicit protection of vulnerable family members,[102] particularly victims of domestic violence. The reluctance to revive the debate could have contributed to the Court's upholding of individual rights and the validity of Article 13(2) of the Citizenship Rights Directive requiring the victims of domestic violence to demonstrate sufficient resources, even if those choices were inconsistent with the choices made in other legislative acts.[103]

iii. Adjusting to the Climate

The Court can uphold conflicting interests by tailoring the justification and the outcome to the political climate or even the electoral mood, the popular will or political pressure. The upholding of conflicting claims and the protection of opposing interests by means of good judgment in such adverse political situations tests the rationale of good judging. In this radical and empirically rare situation, the sensitivity to the political circumstances carries substantive, if not decisive, weight.

Historically, the clearest example of context-conscious non-sanctioning Europeanisation of national policies is the decision in *Commission v the United Kingdom*. It was a First Chamber judgment without any Member State

[101] Case C-930/19, *X. v Belgium*, ECLI:EU:C:2021:657.

[102] See ch five, p. 57.

[103] In *X.*, the problem arose regarding Dir 2003/86 on family reunification, granting autonomous residence permits to third-country nationals who could retain residence after the dissolution of the family unit with the lawfully resident third-country national subject only to proof of the existence of acts of domestic violence. Under Art 15(4) of that Dir, national law could determine the conditions for the autonomous residence permit, and specified no requirement of financial self-sufficiency of the beneficiary. The Court held the spouses of Union citizens and the spouses of third country nationals were not in a similar situation.

interventions. The Court delivered a state-friendly interpretation of Regulation 883/2004,[104] Article 4, which stated that the persons covered by the Regulation enjoyed the same benefits and had the same obligations as nationals under the legislation of any Member State. It also sought to subject the practice of the United Kingdom's authorities to the European standards with a discussion of proportionality, to dodge the full discussion of non-discrimination, sever the case from European Union citizenship, frame the ruling narrowly to the confines of the Commission's claims and European competence in the coordination of social security, and thus restrict the interpretation to the circumstances of the situation at hand. By not increasing the number of judges during the proceedings, the Court might have wanted to signal that the ruling, not rendered by the Grand Chamber, did not unequivocally and finally settle the issue.[105]

Commentators noticed that justification was only very loosely held together, entertaining doomsday scenarios for European citizenship, European solidarity, and a European Union with a social face. The reaction showed that the Court did not control its context; in politically charged situations, good judgment and the normative authority lose persuasive force. Simple legal questions about the interpretation of a secondary law provision in matters outside European Union competence gain unprecedented symbolic meaning – they become politically consequential. The answers can only be political and politicised, meaning they are inescapably used for political ends.[106]

The case has a long and conspicuous procedural history. The Commission commenced a dialogue with the United Kingdom in 2008, issued a reasoned opinion pursuant to Article 258 TFEU in 2011, and brought the proceedings in 2014. On 20 February 2016, Prime Minister David Cameron, announced that the United Kingdom Government would formally recommend to the British people that the United Kingdom should remain a member of a reformed European Union and that the referendum would be held on 23 June 2016. The Court waited until June 2016 to rule in the case.

The Commission challenged the United Kingdom's 'habitual residence test,' a rule imposed on those who claimed a child benefit and a child tax credit under its Social Security Contributions and Benefits Act from 1992 and the Tax Credits Act from 2002. The test, it argued, added a condition and linked it to family benefits (Article 3(1)(j) of Regulation 883/2004); it was discriminatory and hence also unlawful, because United Kingdom nationals automatically met it

[104] Reg (EC) No 883/2004 of the European Parliament and of the Council of 29 April 2004 on the coordination of social security systems (OJ 2004 L 166, p. 1).

[105] Art 60(3) of the Rules of Procedure states that the formation to which a case has been assigned may, at any stage of the proceedings, request the Court to assign the case to a formation composed of a greater number of Judges.

[106] On the distinction see J Ferejohn, 'Judicializing Politics, Politicizing Law' (2002) 65 *Law and Contemporary Problems* 41.

whereas other European citizens had to demonstrate they satisfied the conditions for lawful residence including the proof of financial self-sufficiency under the Citizenship Rights Directive.

In practice, the claimants had to fill out a claim form and provide data on the lawfulness of residence to be subjected to subsequent checks by the authorities responsible for granting the benefit. The claimants only had to offer proof of lawful residence on United Kingdom territory in specific cases. To conduct the checks, the administrative department responsible for the benefits would consult the Department for Work and Pensions, which would then determine if a person claimed social assistance and was thus (in)eligible for the benefit. If the question of lawful residence was impossible to settle on the basis of the information provided by the Department for Work and Pensions, the authorities would conduct an individual assessment of personal circumstances, including the history of the person's social security contributions, and whether they were actively seeking work with a genuine possibility of employment.[107]

The Court acknowledged that the residence checks were indirectly discriminatory by requiring a justification under the test of proportionality, only to entertain the proposition that the protection of public finances was in principle a legitimate objective irrespective of whether public finances were in any way under threat. However, the Court added that the checks had to meet the requirements set out in the Citizenship Rights Directive, clawing back on the State administrations' discretion to impose and implement them without scrutiny.[108]

Previously, the Court allowed the Member States to deny social assistance to economically inactive European citizens.[109] In *Commission v United Kingdom*, it extended this stance to the so-called classic social security benefits.[110] This distinction is important; the Member States retain competence in social assistance matters but social security is tied to free movement and is thus a matter of European Union law that cannot be discriminatory. Ceding the regulatory competence to a Member State is a rare occurrence in European Union law, inviting interpretations of the judgment as a lost political gamble.[111]

Another far-reaching implication for citizenship rights was the Court's re-reading of its previous case-law, especially the reading of so-called

[107] *Commission v United Kingdom*, para 53.

[108] Para 81. Member States may verify if Union citizens and their family members meet the residence conditions under Article 14(2) of Dir 2004/38 only in specific cases, 'where there is a reasonable doubt as to whether a Union citizen or his family members satisfy the conditions set out in those articles.' They could not do so systematically.

[109] Notably Case C-140/12, *Peter Brey*, ECLI:EU:C:2013:565 and Case C-333/13, *Dano*, ECLI:EU:C:2014:2358.

[110] H Verschueren, 'Recent Case before the Court of Justice of the European Union' (2017) 19 *European Journal of Social Security* 71.

[111] Most critically, C O'Brien, 'The ECJ Sacrifices EU Citizenship in Vain: Commission v. United Kingdom' (2017) 54 *Common Market Law Review* 209.

rights-opening judgments like *Grzelczyk* and *Bidar*,[112] as cases that accepted the United Kingdom's justification of the protection of public finances:

> In that regard, it is clear from the Court's case-law that the need to protect the finances of the host Member State justifies in principle the possibility of checking whether residence is lawful when a social benefit is granted in particular to persons from other Member States who are not economically active, as such grant could have consequences for the overall level of assistance which may be accorded by that State (see to this effect, in particular, judgments of 20 September 2001 in Grzelczyk, C-184/99, EU:C:2001:458, paragraph 44; of 15 March 2005 in Bidar, C-209/03, EU:C:2005:169, paragraph 56; of 19 September 2013 in Brey, C-140/12, EU:C:2013:565, paragraph 61; and of 11 November 2014 in Dano, C-333/13, EU:C:2014:2358, paragraph 63).[113]

The judgment in *Commission v United Kingdom* gives insight into what happens to the law when the Court exercises good judgment. It becomes unsettled because the Court is not a legislator who can impose sunset clauses to weather storms; the Court cannot compel Member States to execute a 'correct' interpretation of European Union law as it had itself envisaged or hoped. The most critical reading of *Commission v United Kingdom* would suggest that the non-sanctioning Europeanisation of state policies might be too obviously political to meet the criterion of good judgment and its underpinning rationale of judicial prudence, legal savoir faire and political savviness. It would also suggest that the Court could have opted for other alternatives of context-conscious judging but misread the context. These options are discussed in the following section.

D. ALTERNATIVE TOOLS OF CONTEXT-CONSCIOUS JUDGING

The analysis of good judgment rests on the assumption that courts are mindful of societal implications when solving legal disputes, leveraging interpretive tools and procedural means that rules allow but do not always require; they are context conscious. So far, the discussion has conceptualised and explored judicial context consciousness or sensitivity through the prism of conflicting interests and subtle, yet detectable, departures from typical justification and model law application. From this perspective, good judgment emerged as conceptually and empirically distinct from legal diplomacy, judicial minimalism, incrementalism, strategic citations of precedent, deference, horse sense, reformulation of preliminary questions, majoritarian activism, reading down of statutes (prudential avoidance), or tacit overruling. The conceptualisation of good judgment encompasses these alternatives of context sensitivity techniques when they defy model law application. However, when these alternative tools

[112] N Nic Shuibhne, 'Limits Rising, Duties Ascending: The Changing Legal Shape of Union Citizenship' (2015) *Common Market Law Review* 889.
[113] Para 80.

of context-conscious judging fly under the radar of good judgment given their conceptualisation and the corresponding methodology (annotation of characteristics as argued in chapter four), they call for a separate discussion.

Legal scholarship and political science studies have mostly used the concepts cited above to highlight the relative autonomy of the law and judicial institutions from political, economic, and social life, and, in the European Union context, to elucidate the origins and the expansion of the Court's influence over the integration process and its political power, aka. the success of European supranational adjudication.[114] Witnessing a growing political resistance and backlash against international, European and other supranational courts, recent literature has reconceptualised the same tools as resilience techniques which courts use to maintain and defend their legal authority.[115]

This literature is helpful in two important respects. First, it theorises the Court as a relational actor: its relationship with the European legislator (notably the Member States in the Council), individual Member State governments, as well as with the national Supreme, Constitutional, and ordinary national courts. It also sheds light on the question of judicial legitimacy, and the capacity of law to absorb socio-political arguments to formalise real life relationships into legal relationships: the power of neutralisation and universalisation. Second, it highlights the consequences of the Court's relative autonomy and its struggle to maintain legitimate authority and hence the effectiveness of supranational adjudication for legal outcomes and the decision-making process; in other words, it establishes the framework in which to explain case outcomes and judicial reasoning in their broader context.

The first checklist of effective supranational adjudication by Helfer and Slaughter included tuning in to the audiences, demonstrating neutrality and autonomy from political interests, incremental construction of doctrines, quality of reasoning, judicial dialogue, and form of opinions as controllable general factors that courts, including the Court, employed to increase their effectiveness. Empirical and conceptual studies have progressively been adding to and fine-tuning the checklist, occasionally formulating the questions of international and supranational adjudication within a new framework of institutional legitimisation and authority. The puzzle, which this literature sought to solve, was: under which conditions and with what tools, excluding swords and purses – a problem most acute in non-state settings – can courts fulfil their mandates and elicit respect for and compliance with the law they make? The most pertinent contributions to the debate complement the analysis of good

[114] Reference to n 41 in ch 2, citing relevant literature.

[115] S Caserta and P Cebulak, 'The Limits of International Adjudication: Authority and Resistance of Regional Economic Courts in Times of Crisis' (2018) 14 *International Journal of Law in Context* 275; KJ Alter, LR Helfer and M Rask Madsen, 'How Context Shapes the Authority of International Courts' in KJ Alter, LR Helfer, M Rask Madsen (eds) *International Court Authority* (Oxford, Oxford University Press, 2018).

judgment by demonstrating the link between non-legal motivations and judicial tools, both theoretically and empirically.

Scholars have singled out concrete techniques of reasoning, like comparative legal reasoning mobilising the case-law of peer courts and the jurisprudence of authoritative national courts, restrictive interpretation of the rules of standing and jurisdiction, narrow focus on concrete legal aspects of complex disputes, reformulation of preliminary questions, timing of the rulings to a favourable context, or other avoidance techniques allowing the Court to decide half a case at a time (judicial minimalism)[116] so as to build the house of European Union law stone-by-stone (judicial incrementalism).[117] Some examples are explored below.

i. Reframing Disputes

The Court can reframe a dispute by reformulating preliminary questions, dismissing parts of the action, joining preliminary questions, or dismissing them as obsolete in light of previous answers. In so doing, it can anchor the dispute in the legal rule, a general principle, or a Treaty provision or legislation which avoids a direct political confrontation and upholds conflicting claims in response to fact or non-legal situations by following a typical form of justification.

Heylens illustrates how the Court can reframe disputes by reformulating the preliminary question, and thus decide on a potentially far-reaching but commonly acceptable and accepted principle.[118] Lille Olympic Sporting Club appointed George Heylens, a Belgian national, to coach its professional football team. The President of the Club asked the Minister for Youth and Sport to recognise Heylen's Belgian education diploma as equivalent to a French diploma. The Minister consulted the Equivalence Committee and, upon receiving a final negative opinion, rejected the request. Heylens continued his coaching duties and was subsequently criminally prosecuted for wrongful assumption of a title.

The criminal tribunal questioned the competence of the Committee, and formulated the following question before the Court: 'Does the requirement that a person wishing to exercise a gainful occupation as a trainer with a sports team must hold a French diploma or a foreign diploma recognised as equivalent thereto by a committee whose rulings do not state the reasons on which they are based and against whose decisions no specific legal remedy is available constitute a restriction on freedom of movement for workers as defined by Articles 48 to 51 of the EEC Treaty, in the absence of any directive applicable to

[116] Sarmiento and Jiménez-Valladolid (n 48).

[117] K Lenaerts, 'EU Citizenship and the European Court of Justice's 'Stone-by-Stone' Approach' (2015) 1 *International Comparative Jurisprudence* 1.

[118] Case 222/86, *Heylens*, ECLI:EU:C:1987:442.

that occupation?'.[119] In other words, the French court was unsure whether the administrative practice conflicted with the provisions of the Treaty governing the free movement of workers.

France defended its system of the recognition of diplomas, arguing that the applicant could appeal against the negative ministerial decision and that the recommendations of the Committee were not binding on the Minister. It proposed that the Court should interpret the free movement provisions as allowing the Member State to condition the exercise of the occupation as a trainer on the recognition of his diploma by the administrative authorities where the decisions taken by the latter with regard to the recognition of equivalence could be subject of 'an action brought before a court having jurisdiction to review its merits'.[120]

The Commission proposed a reply to the question which would limit the discretion of the Member States regarding the recognition of diplomas, using a reasoning reminiscent of the *Cassis de Dijon* terminology of mutual recognition. Concretely, the Commission held that the Member State's refusal, 'without stating the reasons therefor, to recognise the equivalence of a diploma issued in a Member State, in circumstances making it impossible, without express objective evidence, for the holder of the diploma to exercise in the Member State of refusal a given activity as an employee whereas he may engage in such activity on the strength of that diploma in the Member State in which it was issued to him,'[121] was unlawful and contrary to the free movement of workers. However, since a remedy to challenge the ministerial decision was available under French administrative law, the lack of a special remedy against the preparatory measure constituted by the opinion of an Equivalence Committee which is responsible for carrying out a prior examination of applications for the grant of equivalence was not contrary to the requirements of the Treaty.

The Advocate General rephrased the question, because the French court had arguably inquired about a non-existing problem. The opinions of the Committee were not binding therefore, according to the Advocate Geneal, the 'real' question was whether, 'as a result of the Community rules on the movement of persons, national decisions affecting the rights given to migrants must comply with a number of minimum requirements, including the duty to give an express statement of reasons?'.[122] His response was that the free movement of workers should be interpreted as prohibiting national rules or administrative practices which allowed unreasoned refusals to recognise the equivalence of a football trainer's diploma issued by another Member State thus preventing its holder from exercising their profession.

[119] The facts are reconstructed, and the citations are excerpts from the Report for the Hearing.
[120] *Heylens*, Report for the Hearing, p 4100.
[121] *Heylens*, Report for the Hearing, p 4104.
[122] Opinion of the Advocate General Mancini in Case 222/86, *Heylens*, ECLI:EU:C:1987:304, para 3

The Court reformulated the question tacitly: 'question put by the national court essentially seeks to establish whether, if in a Member State access to an occupation as an employed person is dependent upon the possession of a national diploma or a foreign diploma recognised as equivalent thereto, the principle of the free movement of workers laid down in Article 48 of the Treaty requires that it must be possible for a decision refusing recognition of the equivalence of a diploma granted to a worker who is a national of another Member State by that Member State to be made the subject of judicial proceedings, and that the decision must state the reasons on which it is based.' According to the Court, the Treaty required that a decision refusing to recognise the equivalence of a diploma 'must be made subject of judicial proceedings in which its legality under Community law can be reviewed, and for the person concerned to ascertain the reasons for the decision'.[123]

The Court's reformulated question and the answer to it redirected the dispute from the contentious topic of unlawful administrative practices and the underlying obligation of the Member States to facilitate free movement by recognising diplomas and qualifications, to the question of procedural guarantees and the much less contentious principle of remedies and judicial review. The Court qualified the request, adding that the remedy must be reviewable under European Union law.

The outcome did not invalidate the administrative practice of the respondent state, as French law already provided a sufficient remedy, and at the hearing, the applicant admitted knowing that such an action against a negative decision by the Minister was possible. The Court's interpretation of declaration of the practice as lawful was, in principle, unsatisfactory for the individual applicant and future applicants because the available remedy could only lead to the annulment of the Ministerial decision and not to a positive decision reversing the Committee's opinion. This potential dissatisfaction for Mr Heylens was much mediated by the Equivalence Committee's reconsideration of its recommendation and the Minister for Youth and Sports' ultimate decision to recognise his Belgian diploma as equivalent to the French certificate of sports master, first class, during the proceedings.

The broader context rather than the legal question primarily guided the Court's reply. The Court did not enter into the issue of the requirement of motivation for the Ministerial decision and did not rule on the compatibility of the practice with the principles of free movement i.e. on the substance of non-discrimination and access to employment, instead focusing on the procedural requirement of justification: European Union law required a remedy when the administration refused to recognise a diploma. The European legislator struggled to harmonise titles and diplomas, and the Court's action could not offer ersatz rules. However, it could address discriminatory, untransparent,

[123] *Heylens*, Operative Part.

and potentially arbitrary administrative practices which, in the absence of harmonisation, restricted free movement indirectly through reformulation and 'reading between the lines' rather than openly and confrontationally. A procedural demand that decisions had to be reviewable with respect to European Union law was a context-conscious step towards the Europeanisation of administrative practices in the domain of the recognition of diplomas.

ii. Mixed Signals

The Court can resourcefully contain the implications of its judgments by issuing more than one judgment simultaneously.[124] The judgments send a mixed signal to the parties of the case and the broader audience, the first advancing an expansive and state autonomy threatening interpretation of European Union law, the second demonstrating that the Member States set the terms of its application in concrete cases (discretion).[125] Only the examination of both judgments reveals the Court's potential sensitivity to the broader political and economic implications of the ruling for the respondent government and the Member States, expressed inter alia by their participation in and arguments submitted during the proceedings.

An example of mixed signals is the judgments in the *Lair*[126] and *Brown* cases,[127] which the Court delivered on the same day. Lair was a French national residing in Germany where she first worked regularly as a bank clerk and then intermittently in various jobs, punctuated by periods of unemployment and retraining. After three years in Germany, she enrolled at the University of Hannover to study languages and literature and applied for a student maintenance and training grant. Her application was unsuccessful because she 'was not engaged in an occupational activity' in Germany for at least five years, meaning that she did work consistently and contribute to the German social security system by paying taxes and social security contributions which sustained the German system of student maintenance and training grants.

Brown was a dual French English national who completed his baccalauréat in France and then moved to the United Kingdom to study engineering at Cambridge. Prior to enrolment, he completed an eight month 'pre-university industrial training' in Edinburgh. 'On various grounds based on national law',

[124] On the procedural aspect of delaying the judgments in individual cases on vexing legal issues see the reconstruction of the Sunday Trading saga in H-W Micklitz, *The Politics of Judicial Co-Operation in the EU: Sunday Trading, Equal Treatment and Good Faith* (Cambridge, Cambridge University Press, 2005).

[125] Sending mixed signals differs from the method of creating instant precedents by deciding two disputes simultaneously and using the decision in the first to justify the decision in the second and vice versa. For the latter see S Dothan, *Reputation and Judicial Tactics: A Theory of National and International Courts* (Cambridge, Cambridge University Press, 2014).

[126] Case 39/86, *Sylvie Lair*, ECLI:EU:C:1988:322.

[127] Case 197/86, *Steven Malcolm Brown*, ECLI:EU:C:1988:323.

the Scottish Education Department refused the award of student allowance consisting in a means-tested maintenance grant and the payment of means independent tuition fees.[128]

The disputes raised a contentious issue which required careful consideration: the financing of economically inactive persons and the abuse of generous welfare systems in areas of retained competence.

The Court drew a fine line between the cases to shed light on these issues. In *Lair*, it ruled that the five-year period was an unjustified restriction of free movement rights. Member States could not discriminate between national and foreign students regarding the provision of assistance for training and university studies which covered registration and other fees, notably tuition fees. The Member States could furthermore not refuse a maintenance and training grant to a former worker who left the labour market to study. Maintenance grants were deemed social assistance, due if there was 'a link between the previous occupational activity and the studies in question'.[129] Finally, the Member State could not make the right to social advantage conditional upon a minimum period of prior occupational activity on its territory.

The Court acknowledged the concerns of the German, Danish, and United Kingdom governments who claimed that the rules governing student maintenance grants avoided the abusive use of free movement rights, stating that European Union law excluded situations 'where it may be established on the basis of objective evidence that a worker has entered a Member State for the sole purpose of enjoying, after a very short period of occupational activity, the benefit of the student assistance system in that State'.[130] Nonetheless, the ruling implied that Lair and all future applicants in her position could claim assistance, threatening to unleash a wave of dissatisfaction and political opposition from Member States.[131]

On the same day, *Brown* reassured the Member State governments who had lost their case in *Lair*, that they were not losing control over student maintenance grants and social assistance. The Court accepted the United Kingdom's argument that the applicant was a student, and his employment subsidiary was to be undertaken primarily for the purpose of the study. To reinforce the nexus between the judgments, the Court referred to *Lair* in *Brown*[132] on the point that maintenance grants were social advantages which foreign students who could establish a link between their previous occupational activity in that state and proposed studies could claim on the same terms as national students.

[128] *Brown*, para 4.
[129] *Lair*, Operative Part.
[130] *Lair*, para 43.
[131] Report for the Hearing, p 3215. The United Kingdom in *Brown* insisted that 'If maintenance payments of the nature accorded to workers were extended to students undergoing vocational training there would be in consequence a serious risk of profound distortion in patterns of study in the Community'.
[132] *Brown*, paras 25–27.

The context of the decisions was an explosive question of the abuse of free movement rights, of faux short-term employment to ground claims to maintenance grants, and the overlap of free movement with educational and social policy, which at the time of the rulings fell squarely within the Member States competence. While the cases raised near-identical issues, which the Court had to resolve consistently, they could be distinguished on their facts.

In both cases, the Court ruled that maintenance grants, as opposed to tuition fees, fell outside the scope of European Union law but that the Member States had to treat former workers and prospective students equally, irrespective of nationality, if they could establish a link with the host Member State. Brown could not claim maintenance allowance for his studies because he was not a worker, and his employment relationship in the host State for a period of eight months was ancillary. Lair, on the other hand, was a former worker in the true sense of the term.

Lair and *Brown* assimilated the question of maintenance grants under European Union law while signalling deference to the concerns of individual Member States about the abusive use of free movement rights and the exploitation of their generous in the case of Denmark student welfare systems. Historically, both judgments were an exercise in incrementalism rather than deference.[133]

iii. Low Stakes

The judgments in *Decker*[134] and *Kohll*[135] illustrate that the Court can deliver a far-reaching and unsettling interpretation of European Union law in disputes with low economic stakes for the responding Member State, and by waiting for the political stakes to decrease.

Decker concerned a request submitted by a Luxembourgish citizen insured in Luxembourg for the reimbursement of the cost of spectacles with corrective lenses. The applicant purchased a pair of spectacles from an optician in Belgium, on a prescription from an ophthalmologist established in Luxembourg. The Caisse de Maladie des Employés Privés refused the reimbursement request because the applicant failed to obtain prior authorisation. Such authorisation was not necessary for purchases made in Luxembourg. On the same day, the Court also delivered a judgment in *Kohll*. This latter case concerned a restriction of the free movement of services linked to the reimbursement of an orthodontist's bill incurred in Germany without prior authorisation from Luxembourg

[133] Ruling in *Bidar* reversed the Lair-Brown case-law. See C Barnard, 'Case C-209/03, R (on the Application of Danny Bidar) v. London Borough of Ealing, Secretary of State for Education and Skills' (2005) 42 *Common Market Law Review* 1465.

[134] Case C-120/95, *Nicolas Decker*, ECLI:EU:C:1998:167.

[135] Case C-158/96, *Raymond Kohll*, ECLI:EU:C:1998:171.

where Kholl was insured. As in *Decker*, such authorisation was not necessary for orthodontic services solicited in Luxembourg. The Advocate General joined the cases for the purposes of his opinion.[136] The Court issued two separate judgments without any cross-references, although Judge Ragnemalm was the reporting judge in both cases.

The cases raised a succinct question about whether Luxembourgish rules on prior authorisation unjustifiably restricted free movement of goods (*Decker*) and services (*Kohll*), and whether budgetary concerns were valid reasons for import restrictions. However, they also unleashed the possibility that the Court could liberalise patient mobility under free movement rules, despite the European Union's lacking competence in health care and social security.[137] The competence question and the financial aspects of social security and cross border medical care increased the salience of the case. The governments of France, the United Kingdom, the Netherlands, Germany, Belgium, Spain, and Luxembourg submitted observations. Previously, the Court avoided clear-cut reasoning on the topic of public expenditure for social security even if their primary objective was protection and promotion of public health.[138] In *Decker*, it seemingly 'grasped the nettle'.[139]

Mr Decker and the Commission argued that the system of prior authorisation restricted the free movement of goods. The Member States argued that the disputed rules merely governed the conditions for the reimbursement of medical expenses without affecting imports. The Court observed that the disputed rules impeded free movement because they encouraged persons insured under Luxembourg's social security scheme to purchase their spectacles from, and have them assembled by, opticians established in Luxembourg rather than in other Member States. The same was true in the context of dental treatment.

The compatibility of national measures with the prohibition of quantitative restrictions and measures of equivalent effect (Article 34 TFEU) hinges on two questions: first, whether a measure falls under the scope of Article 34 TFEU; and second, whether Article 36 TFEU derogations provided in the Treaty or mandatory requirements elaborated by the Court can justify it. As commentators note, as the scope of Article 34 TFEU expands, the main weight of the case shifts to the validity of the submitted justification.[140] This was the case in *Decker*.

The government of Luxembourg and the Member States who submitted observations insisted that the aim of preserving the financial balance of the

[136] Joined opinion of Mr Advocate General Tesauro in Case C-120/95, *Decker*, and Case C-158/96, *Kohll*, ECLI:EU:C:1997:399.

[137] The competence in social security matters is not a shared competence.

[138] Case 238/82 *Duphar*, ECLI:EU:C:1984:45.

[139] S Enchelmaier in P Oliver et al, *Oliver on Free Movement of Goods in the European Union* (Oxford, Hart Publishing, 2010) 193.

[140] N Nic Shuibhne, *The Coherence of EU Free Movement Law: Constitutional Responsibility and the Court of Justice* (Oxford, Oxford University Press, 2013).

social security system was a mandatory requirement, and could thus justify the restrictive measures. The Court repeated its established line of jurisprudence, stating that aims of a purely economic nature could not justify a barrier to the fundamental principle of the free movement of goods, but that 'the risk of seriously undermining the financial balance of the social security system may constitute an overriding reason in the general interest capable of justifying a barrier of that kind'.[141] While reassuring in principle, Luxembourg lost the case because it could not prove such a risk.

On first inspection, the implications for Member States who would soon be facing similar requests from their citizens purchasing cross-border services were considerable. However, two aspects decisively lowered the elevated political and economic stakes. First, the Court referred to the submission of the government of Luxembourg, which openly admitted in reply to a question from the Court, that a flat rate reimbursement of the cost of spectacles and corrective lenses purchased in other Member States had no effect on the financing or balance of the social security system.[142] Second, the political tide was about to turn. The Treaty of Amsterdam, which expanded the European Union competence to adopt measures with the aim of ensuring a high level of human health protection,[143] was signed on 2 October 1997. The Court decided *Decker* and *Kohll*, lodged in 1995 and 1996, on 28 April 1998.[144]

The *Decker* and *Kohll* rulings elicited forceful reactions. The German Minister of Health argued that they undermined the German health system and posed a threat to its sustainability, highlighting that they conflicted with Member State preferences, and thus called for Treaty amendment.[145] In reality, though, little changed on the ground: the judgments pertained to a pair of spectacles and children's orthodontic treatment in the context of Luxembourg's rather particular healthcare system.

E. APPRAISAL

Before drawing the final conclusions and lessons from the analysis, a short appraisal is required. Chapter three conceptualised good judgment as a distinct

[141] *Decker*, para 39.

[142] *Decker*, para 40.

[143] According to Art 129 (1) of the Treaty of Amsterdam, the European Union action could complement national policies for improving public health, preventing human illness and diseases, and obviating sources of danger to human health. The European Union could adopt measures to achieve these objectives (Art 129(4)).

[144] The preliminary references arrived at the Court with a one-year time lag, in 1995 and 1996 respectively.

[145] D Sindbjerg Martinsen, 'Conflict and Conflict Management in the Cross-Border Provision of Healthcare Services' (2009) 32 *West European Politics* 792.

mode of context-conscious judging which 1) upholds conflicting claims and protects competing interests, 2) particularly in response to the facts and the broader circumstances of the dispute, and 3) typically results in subtle but detectable departures from model law application. It identified three types of departures. Chapter four elaborated the methodology to investigate such departures systematically in two policy areas; the free movement of persons (1091 judgments) and the free movement of goods (1538 judgments). The analysis in chapters five and six offered two important insights, 1) demonstrating how the factual and legal characteristics of disputes, as well as the political or economic circumstances in which the disputes arose, translated into different forms of justification, elucidating the relationship between rights, arguments, interpretative choices and outcomes, and 2) highlighting the differences in the Court's use of good judgment over time and policy areas. This chapter investigated the mechanisms of good judgment, inquiring into the weight of case characteristics and non-legal factors, and arguing that good judgment was context- rather than case-motivated.

Good judgment is a heuristic tool which imposes a particular approach and methodology on the legal materials and sources. The reading of the case-law in terms of the shifting relationships between rights, reasoning, outcomes, and methods of interpretation sheds a different light on adjudication, legal reasoning, and judicial behaviour. At the same time, this lens oversimplifies case-law to selected parameters, with each of them imposing a limited range of values / outcomes. This might be in stark contrast to the myriad ways in which adjudication unfolds in real life, and the variety of tools that judges use to uphold the law, institutional legitimacy, rights, and societal values. Second, the approach imposes a specific reading on cases, which potentially decontextualises important legal developments, concepts, doctrines, and procedural tools, treating them in isolation from the immediate legal context of justification in which they appear and as separate from the narratives of legal development in which they are logically embedded. Third, the statistical analysis is overly simplistic, imposing a formalistic understanding of the law and the Court's sensitivity to case facts, legal problems, and non-legal circumstances.

The method and the conceptualisation of good judgment, which are necessary for its operationalisation, are imperfect. The interpretation of the findings in chapter seven recognises this and draws on the legal analysis in chapters five and six, as well as the legal literature to support general claims about the circumstances in which the Court will more likely uphold conflicting interests and defy the structure of ideal justification and the model law application. Legal scholars raise eyebrows in disbelief when confronted with stark generalisations and categorical claims about the Court's law-making and the law that it makes. At the same time, they construct general narratives about the Court's law-making and the law that it makes with limited support from the judgments and by overemphasising carefully curated details. The findings do not challenge the normative critique of the Court's reasoning or deny that the Court will reach predictable and surprising outcomes, that it can marshal convincing and feeble reasons for its decisions – using literal, systemic, and purposive interpretation without further thought – abide by precedent or overrule it tacitly, and yield to the political climate or stand tall in the face of political pressure. As such, they are an ideal counterpart to legal studies and the studies of judicial behaviour.

8

Conclusion

A. THE ARGUMENT

GOOD JUDGMENT IN common parlance describes a combination of knowledge, experience, analytical skill, and gut feeling, used to make sound choices under uncertainty. It is a desirable quality of individuals, which typically compels trust and high regard. Good judging in supranational adjudication refers to a court's awareness of the audiences, the demonstrated autonomy from political interests, incremental style of decision-making, quality of legal reasoning, dialogue with other supranational tribunals, and the form of judicial opinions.[1] It is a quality, which typically underwrites effectiveness, understood as the power of courts to compel a party to a dispute to the courtroom, argue against the plaintiff's claim, and comply with the resulting judgment.[2]

In this book, I grappled with two questions: 'What is good judging? How can we study it empirically?' and omitted one question: 'Is good judging per se a good idea?'.

I used the term good judgment to describe one element of good judging that the literature has not sufficiently explored, but which I considered key to the understanding of the supranational courts: judicial decisions, which depart from the structure of typical justification and model law application to uphold conflicting claims and protect conflicting interests in response to extra-legal demands and implications. I did not want to imply that good judgment was a desirable quality – that it was good, but used it metaphorically and as a heuristic device to investigate the interplay of law and its broader context, and the manifold ways in which case facts and other characteristics of disputes, along with their political and economic circumstances, keep trickling into legal reasoning and case outcomes. Good judgment offered me a new lens to observe and explain the decision-making and the role of the European Court of Justice – a court known for its effectiveness, considerable political influence on the process of European integration through law, and non-negligible legal authority as

[1] LR Helfer and A-Marie Slaughter, 'Toward a Theory of Effective Supranational Adjudication' (1997) 107 *Yale Law Journal* 273, 308.
[2] ibid, 283.

well as a court whose judgment has been considered good by all standards of good judging and whose judgments have also been criticised as instances of bad judgment.

My main argument is that the Court upholds conflicting interests when the political and economic stakes are sufficiently high, varying by policy area and historical period. In other words, politics has shaped the Court's reasoning and outcomes and thus, European Union law. The insight that the Court has always responded to political and economic conflict by upholding conflicting claims nuances the arguments that the Court has become increasingly deferential, selectively activist, and rights restrictive.

My starting point was four perspectives on judging, developed by legal scholars and political scientists, which all suggest that courts decide concrete disputes with societal implications in mind – that they are context-conscious. Together, these perspectives, highlighting various aspects of the judicial decision-making process, offered a rich and nuanced conceptual background and research strategy. They are described in chapter two.

The consequentialist legal-argumentative position conceptualises context-conscious judging as judicial prudence, or wisdom. When the indeterminacy of language allows for more than one valid and justifiable interpretation, judges use prudence to select the interpretation, which best furthers the values of the legal system / produces the most desirable consequences. The incrementalist framing considers context-conscious judging as a survival instinct of courts as political actors trying to 'muddle-through' akin to the administrative agencies. Compared to the consequentialist position, which treats courts as rational decision-makers applying valid rules to concrete facts to solve a dispute (declare a winner and a loser), and judicial reasoning as a series of syllogisms leading to a logical conclusion, incrementalism relaxes the demands of rationality and rational justification, allowing for non-binary outcomes (two winners and no loser scenario). The structural approach considers context-conscious judging as a professional outlook, which focuses on legal practice of rationalisation, and a series of strategies that judges as legal professionals use to reproduce the belief in the neutrality and universality of law – the two key facets of the force of law and lawyers. Finally, the strategic behavioural model suggests that judges act rationally and deliberately to enforce their policy or personal preferences against the internal (legal rules etc) and external (legislative override etc) constraints.

The literature about the Court's decision-making describing the judicial strategies, which enabled the Court to reconcile legal principles with political demands, directly inspired my conceptualisation of good judgment as a separate mode of context-conscious judging upholding opposing claims – protecting individual free movement rights, yielding to the vital political and economic interests of respondent states, sustaining the functioning of the internal market and the coherence of European Union law by a series of far-reaching concepts and doctrines – often all in one single justification.

I hypothesised three scenarios, which would be visible as subtle departures from the model law application, formulating them as three types of good judgment: the Court can censure Member State policies but adopt Member State friendly outcomes (*Non-sanctioning Europeanisation of national policies*); it can limit unfavourable outcomes and interpretations so as to reduce their practical effect (*Bounded undesirable interpretation*); and it can uphold free movement rights while conditioning and deferring key terms of their application to the national courts and administrations (*Deferential upholding of European rights*). Thereby, the Court ideally ensures individual rights protection, workable solutions, legally correct outcomes, and the effectiveness of its rulings.

This conceptualisation was a deliberate and the most consequential choice, which I justified in chapter three. I made this choice, among other reasons, to operationalise context-consciousness for the empirical examination of the case-law and produce a comprehensive picture of the effect of case facts, institutional factors, and external circumstances on legal reasoning and case outcomes. To scale the legal analysis, I decided to collect all available information about the judgments in two significant areas of the internal market, central to the process of European integration and often calling for diplomatic solutions – free movement of persons and goods, using case annotation. Case annotation involved a close reading of selected judgments according to detailed guidelines, notably coding protocols, or codebooks, to map the parts of the Court's justification (selected legal characteristics). These permitted me to identify the departures from the typical structure of justification and associate them with case characteristics (selected information about the subject matter of the dispute and the applicant). The relationships would further allow me to explain the departures and theorise the Court's decision-making.

The literature about the Court, while inspiring, was unhelpful in operationalising the theory for the empirical analysis, with legal literature not having advanced much beyond promising empirical research agendas, and with most political science literature considering only case outcomes. Crucially, there was no ready-to-use data about the relevant parts of justification – the Court's use of purposive interpretation, deference, proportionality analysis, no classification of judgments as doctrinally significant, and no categorisation of outcomes about the compatibility of disputed national measures with European Union law or the entitlement of individual applicants to free movement rights to reside, enjoy a social security benefit, health care, or a tax advantage, no closer categorisation of legal issues like whether the case concerned trade restrictions, fiscal charges, mutual recognition, and no attempt to systematically measure the implications of the judgment for national regulatory autonomy. I had to collect and organise the information about the characteristics of the applicants like gender, nationality, or whether the applicants were workers, economically active, legal or natural persons, foreign or domestic traders. The information about the institutional features, like the sitting formation, the type of procedure, and the number of participating Member States in the proceedings, was available from the official sources like Eurlex or Curia, but not organised in a dataset.

This work was accomplished by a handful of doctoral students at the European University Institute in Florence between 2017 and 2022, under the so-called Coding Project, who hand coded 1538 free movement of goods and 1091 free movement of persons judgments decided from 1957 to 2022.

Using the collected information about legal characteristics, I identified the judgments upholding conflicting interests, based on the predicted interaction of the legal characteristics relevant to the analysis of three types of good judgment. Combined with legal analysis of reasoning and case outcomes, descriptive statistics of patterns and trends, and regression analysis, I could establish when the three types of good judgment were motivated by case characteristics including institutional features, or broader non-legal circumstances. The methodology and the research strategy are laid out in chapter four.

Chapters five dealing with the free movement of persons and six dealing with the free movement of goods situated good judgment in the legal framework of Treaty articles, landmark rulings and key legislative instruments (e.g. the Citizenship Rights Directive), highlighting the resistance to free movement, the national instincts to advantage the domestic products, screen off the national markets from outside competition, and control free movement rights, political debates and compromise behind concrete legislative solutions. The chapters also illustrated the types of good judgment on selected emblematic judgments in the context of these debates. Each concluded with a brief presentation of the patterns: while the share of good judgment in the free movement of goods case-law has gradually decreased, the share of free movement of persons judgments has gradually increased. The patterns have converged in the past two decades, meaning that the share of good judgment in both policy areas has become comparable (around 20 per cent with occasional surges of a particular type of good judgment).

In chapter seven, I probed into significant relationships between selected characteristics of the applicants, legal issues, and institutional features and good judgment, showing 1) that the Court pays limited attention to the individual characteristics of the applicants like gender or whether they are private or legal persons; 2) that legal issues which significantly affect the probability of good judgment, like the consideration of residence rights including family reunification are economically controversial and politicised and 3) that the participation of Member State governments in cases decided by the Grand Chamber almost doubles the probability of good judgment compared to the cases decided by the Grand Chamber without the participation of the Member States. Member State observations submitted in cases decided by smaller formations or the type of proceedings (infringement actions or preliminary references) do not significantly affect the probability of good judgment. Good judgment is unlikely a consequence of the Court's working process and internal organisation. Hence the Court upholds conflicting claims primarily in response to the external non-legal factors.

The findings led me to explore these relationships by returning to the basic assumptions, the definition of good judgment, as well as to the theoretical perspectives on context-conscious judging. Given that context sensitivity is a continuum, and that good judgment is a combination of prudence, political savviness, and legal expertise, I formulated three scenarios on different points of this continuum. At one end was the Court's consideration of the desirability of the implications of its ruling, and its prudence to propose the most acceptable legally permissible and justifiable interpretation. At its opposite end was the Court's recognition of the political reality, its political savviness, and the willingness to adopt a politically desired outcome by muddling through, strategically yielding to external demands. I captured these situations by analysing individual judgments corresponding to these categories of contextually motivated good judgment: the recognition of high political and social, including cultural stakes of the case, the Court's honouring of a fragile political consensus or the will of the European legislator, and its oversensitivity to the political / electoral mood in the respondent state.

Conscious of the argument that the Court can tailor the rules to their societal context in myriad ways, I also engaged with three instances where the Court upheld conflicting interests without departing from the typical structure of rational justification. First, I showed how the Court reframes the dispute by reformulating preliminary questions, dismissing parts of the action, joining preliminary questions, or considering them obsolete in light of previous answers. Thereby, it could anchor the dispute in the legal rule, a general principle, Treaty provision or legislation, which avoids a direct political confrontation. Second, I demonstrated how the Court resourcefully contains the implications of its judgments by issuing more than one judgment simultaneously, sending a mixed signal to the parties of the case and the broader audience, the first judgment advancing an expansive and state autonomy threatening interpretation of European Union law, the second demonstrating that the Member State can set the terms of its application in concrete cases (discretion). Only the examination of both judgments reveals the Court's potential sensitivity to the broader political and economic implications of the ruling for the respondent government and the Member States, expressed inter alia by their participation and the arguments submitted during the proceedings. Third, I examined the situation where the Court delivers a far reaching and unsettling interpretation of European Union law in disputes with low economic stakes for the responding Member State, waiting for the political stakes to decrease.

In sum, good judgment is only one possible but vital window in the Court's context-conscious decision-making, explaining its political success, the scholarly critique, the incremental development of European Union law, and the profusion of preliminary references seeking to clarify the established jurisprudence. All keep the Court busy and relevant.

B. CONTRIBUTION

The book contributes to the existing analysis of the Court's decision-making and internal market case-law conceptually, doctrinally, methodologically, and theoretically.

Benjamin Cardozo wrote that '[m]etaphors in law are to be narrowly watched, for starting as devices to liberate thought, they end often by enslaving it.'[3] I constructed the concept of good judgment as a metaphor to liberate my own thinking about courts and internal market case-law. Regarding the former, I often felt that the exalted portraits of judging and judicial responsibility often authored by judges unnecessarily mystified and glorified adjudication, obstructing rather than illuminating the law-politics interplay, replacing the interesting detail with a vague rhetoric of prudence, situation sense, or wisdom. What happens to justification, individual rights, and the division of competence when European judges make wise value choices or prudently reconcile competing principles? Judicial minimalism, deference, constitutional balancing, reading down statutes, and legal diplomacy were unhelpful in answering this question empirically, informed by facts and legal text.

Regarding the free movement case-law, I tried to understand the Court's role and contribution to the internal market through the perspective of disputes and conflicting claims, by reading primary sources alongside the scholarly analyses and commentary. This proved a good intuition. Developing a codebook and testing it on a pilot sample of landmark and randomly selected judgments proved that textbook doctrinal understanding of free movement of goods captured only a small piece of the legal arguments, legal issues, claims, and factual situations playing out in the free movement disputes.

Good judgment and legal characteristics are a conceptual toolbox to capture the practice of courts against the background of doctrinal categories. It completes our knowledge about the Court as a legal actor using legal arguments to uphold free movement rights by – at times – unorthodox use of procedural possibilities and justification.

Methodologically, the book scales legal analysis based on the legal characteristics of judgments in two policy areas. I thought and argued a lot about the benefits of empirical methodology to answer legal questions and reexamine the existing legal categories and established beliefs about European institutions, notably the Court, as key players in European integration. This book was an excellent opportunity and a unique challenge to put my research agenda into an empirical research strategy: collect data, annotate the judgments, develop concepts that capture the legally relevant and interesting factual / societal phenomena, analyse them systematically, and learn from the findings. This book

[3] Cited in T Alexander Aleinikoff, 'Constitutional Law in the Age of Balancing' (1987) 96 *The Yale Law Journal* 943.

was also an occasion to connect my interest in the Court and internal market law with my study of legal argumentation, judicial behaviour and theories of European integration, weaving the insights to construct a bridge between the disciplines separated by assumptions, approaches, and vocabulary.

Theoretically, I wanted to develop an empirically informed portrait of supranational adjudication, which can complement the models of judicial behaviour and the normative critique of the Court's interpretive methodology as legitimate / illegitimate policymaking with a methodical assessment of its actual implications for individual free movement rights and state regulatory autonomy. As the findings show, the Cout often limits the implications for the latter when expansively interpreting Treaty rules. Critique of interpretation does not capture the nuance of interpretive outcomes, and yields an unnecessarily narrow or harsh view of the Court, perpetuated by entrenched concepts (judicial activism, neoliberal turn) and approaches (hermeneutics).

C. IS GOOD JUDGMENT A GOOD IDEA?

I can no longer avoid the inevitable question, is good judgment a good idea, and if, under what historical, political, economic, and social circumstances? My answer to this question is short and underwhelming, deriving from two insights of literature on legal reasoning and supranational adjudication.

As MacCormick remarks, unorthodox judgments work as a surprise. When Solomon reaches for the child to divide it between two women claiming to be the child's mothers, the true mother screams out and surrenders her right. Solomon's sonorous wisdom looking at the particularity of the situation and intuiting the just and correct decision, has added the air of mystique to the act of judging for millennia to come. When the Court limits the temporal effects of a judgment considering extensive negative economic implications for the respondent state, the State expecting a major blow adjusts its discriminatory policy as a lesser evil. However, the biblical case is not part of a bureaucratic routine.[4] The Court's good judgment will not work as a standardised instrument of judging.

The analysis showed that the Court used good judgment sparingly, using bounded undesirable interpretation most often in the free movement of goods in the early years of integration, and resorting to the deferential protection of individual rights in the free movement of people after the financial and the migration crisis. Adjusting the mode of context-conscious decision-making to the problem at hand and increasingly using good judgment in periods of exceptional political contestation or economic strife is undoubtedly good judgment,

[4] N MacCormick, *Rhetoric and the Rule of Law: A Theory of Legal Reasoning* (Oxford, Oxford University Press, 2005) 79.

which preserves the Court's authority and the values of the legal system. As Hart observed, courts can accomplish striking legal developments in fundamental societal matters because of the great prestige they gather from their unquestionably rule-governed operations over the vast and central areas of law.[5]

The second insight from the literature is that courts do not control their context. International courts can do everything that the normative theory expects from a legitimate judicial institution but their rulings will not elicit compliance.[6] This increases the likelihood that courts, striving for authority and compliance, will resort to servile judgments, issuing undemanding remedies or vague rulings which respondent states and referring national courts will willingly 'implement'. They will expose themselves as easily politicised actors, neutral and non-partisan institutions in rhetoric only. Political scientists have considered the perils of judicial politicisation. For legal scholars, its legal aspects are more interesting: politicised courts might fail to protect individual rights and compromise the values of the legal system.

The answer to the question and the lesson for the seventh decade of European supranational adjudication is that our political actors should yield to hard-won judicial authority and uphold judicial independence of our courts just as much as the Court has always been willing to uphold the hard-won political bargain of our political actors and yield to the needs of our economic system. Courts cannot exercise good judgment in political systems ruled by bad judgment.

[5] HLA. Hart, *The Concept of Law*, 3rd edn (Oxford University Press, 2012) 154.

[6] KJ Alter, LR Helfer and MR Madsen, 'How Context Shapes the Authority of International Courts', *International Court Authority* (Oxford, Oxford University Press, 2018) 29.

Bibliography

Albors-Llorens A, 'The Alcohol (Minimum Pricing) (Scotland) Act 2012 and the Collision between Single-Market Objectives and Public-Interest Requirements' (2017) 76 *The Cambridge Law Journal* 25

Albors-Llorens A, Barnard C and Leucht B, *Cassis de Dijon: 40 Years On* (London, Bloomsbury Publishing, 2021)

Aleinikoff TA, 'Constitutional Law in the Age of Balancing' (1987) 96 *The Yale Law Journal* 943

Alemanno A, 'Balancing Free Movement and Public Health: The Case of Minimum Unit Pricing of Alcohol in Scotch Whisky' (2016) 53 *Common Market Law Review* 1037

Alexander Lazović, 'Structuring Perception: How Structures of Practice Influence Decision-Making at the Court of Justice of the European Union' (PhD Thesis, European University Institute 2023)

Alexy R, 'On the Structure of Legal Principles' (2000) 13 *Ratio Juris* 294

Alter KJ, *The European Court's Political Power: Selected Essays* (Oxford, Oxford University Press, 2009)

Alter KJ, Helfer LR and Madsen MR, 'How Context Shapes the Authority of International Courts', *International Court Authority* (Oxford, Oxford University Press, 2018)

Alter KJ and Meunier-Aitsahalia S, 'Judicial Politics in the European Community: European Integration and the Pathbreaking Cassis de Dijon Decision' (1994) 26 *Comparative Political Studies* 535

Armstrong KA, 'Governing Goods: Content and Context' in Damian Chalmers and Anthony Arnull (eds), *The Oxford Handbook of European Union Law* (Oxford, Oxford University Press, 2021)

Arnull A, 'What Shall We Do on Sunday?' (1991) 16 *European Law Review* 112

Aschwanden R et al, 'Moving Mountains: The Protection of the Alps' in A-K Wöbse and P Kupper (eds), *Greening Europe* (Berlin, De Gruyter, 2022)

Azoulai L, 'La Fabrication de La Jurisprudence Communautaire' in P Mbongo and A Vauchez (eds), *Dans la Fabrique du Droit Européen: Scènes, Acteurs Et Publics De La Cour De Justice Des Communautés Européennes* (Brussels, Bruylant, 2009)

——, 'The Retained Powers' Formula in the Case Law of the European Court of Justice: EU Law as Total Law' (2011) 4 *European Journal of Legal Studies* 178

Barnard C, 'Case C-209/03, R (on the Application of Danny Bidar) v. London Borough of Ealing, Secretary of State for Education and Skills' (2005) 42 *Common Market Law Review* 1465

——, The Substantive Law of the EU, 7th edn (Oxford, Oxford University Press, 2022)

Bartl M and Lawrence JC (eds), *The Politics of European Legal Research: Behind the Method* (Cheltenham, Edward Elgar Publishing, 2022)

Bartlett O and MacCulloch A, 'Evidence and Proportionality in Free Movement Cases: The Impact of the Scotch Whisky Case' (2020) 11 *European Journal of Risk Regulation* 109

Baum L, 'C. Herman Pritchett: Innovator with an Ambiguous Legacy' in N Maveety (ed), *The Pioneers of Judicial Behavior* (Ann Arbor, University of Michigan Press, 2003)

Bavasso A, 'Case C-368/95, Vereinigte Familiapress Zeitungsverlags- Und Vertriebs GmbH v. Heinrich Bauer Verlag, Judgment of 26 June 1997, ECR [1997] I-3689' (1998) 35 *Common Market Law Review* 1413

Bengoetxea J, *The Legal Reasoning of the European Court of Justice: Towards a European Jurisprudence* (Oxford, Clarendon Press Oxford, 1993)

Bengoetxea J, MacCormick N and Moral Soriano L, 'Integration and Integrity in the Legal Reasoning of the European Court of Justice' in G De Búrca and J Weiler (eds), *The European Court of Justice* (Oxford, Oxford University Press, 2001)

Besselink LF, 'The Member States, the National Constitutions and the Scope of the Charter' (2001) 8 *Maastricht Journal of European and Comparative Law* 68

Bierbach JB, 'European Citizens' Third-Country Family Members and Community Law: Grand Chamber Decision of 11 December 2007, Case C-291/05, Minister Voor Vreemdelingenzaken En Integratie v. R.N.G. Eind The Return of the Member State National and the Destiny of the European Citizen' (2008) 4 *European Constitutional Law Review* 344

Blauberger M, 'With Luxembourg in Mind ... the Remaking of National Policies in the Face of ECJ Jurisprudence' (2012) 19 *Journal of European Public Policy* 109

Blauberger M and Schmidt SK, 'The European Court of Justice and Its Political Impact' (2017) 40 *West European Politics* 907

Bobek M, *Comparative Reasoning in European Supreme Courts* (Oxford, Oxford University Press, 2013)

Bobic A and Dawson M, 'Making Sense of the "Incomprehensible": The PSPP Judgment of the German Federal Constitutional Court' (2020) 57 *Common Market Law Review* 1953

Bourdieu P, 'The Force of Law: Toward a Sociology of the Juridical Field' (1986) 38 *Hastings LJ* 805

Brekke SA et al, 'The CJEU Database Platform: Decisions and Decision-Makers' (2023) 11 *Journal of Law and Courts* 389

Broberg M and Fenger N, *Broberg and Fenger on Preliminary References to the European Court of Justice,* 3rd edn (Oxford, Oxford University Press, 2021)

Brook O, 'Politics of Coding: On Systematic Content Analysis of Legal Text' in M Bartl, P Cebulak, and J Lawrence (eds), *Behind the Method: The Politics of European Legal Research* (Cheltenham, Edward Elgar Publishing, 2022)

Brown C, 'Case C-112/00, Eugen Schmidberger, Internationale Transporte Und Planzüge v. Austria' (2003) 40 *Common Market Law Review* 1499

Buck M and Schmidt KJ, 'Special Section: Technical Infrastructures, Transnational Protest Movements and the Use of Counter-Expertise' (2022) 30 *NTM Zeitschrift für Geschichte der Wissenschaften, Technik und Medizin* 271

De Búrca G, 'Rethinking Law in Neofunctionalist Theory' (2005) 12 *Journal of European Public Policy* 310

Burley A-M and Mattli W, 'Europe Before the Court: A Political Theory of Legal Integration' (1993) 47 *International Organization* 41

Calabresi G and Melamed AD, 'Property Rules, Liability Rules, and Inalienability: One View of the Cathedral' (1972) 85 *Harvard Law Review* 1089

Carruba CJ, Gabel M and Hankla C, 'Understanding the Role of the European Court of Justice in European Integration' (2012) 106 *American Political Science Review* 214

Carrubba CJ, Gabel M and Hankla C, 'Judicial Behavior under Political Constraints: Evidence from the European Court of Justice' (2008) 102 *American Political Science Review* 435

Carrubba CJ and Gabel MJ, *International Courts and the Performance of International Agreements: A General Theory with Evidence from the European Union* (Cambridge, Cambridge University Press, 2015)

Caserta S and Cebulak P, 'The Limits of International Adjudication: Authority and Resistance of Regional Economic Courts in Times of Crisis' (2018) 14 *International Journal of Law in Context* 275

Conway G, *The Limits of Legal Reasoning and the European Court of Justice* (Cambridge, Cambridge University Press, 2012)

Cornelissen R, '50 Years of European Social Security Coordination' (2009) 11 *European Journal of Social Security* 9

Costello C, 'Metock: Free Movement and "Normal Family Life" in the Union' (2009) 46 *Common Market Law Review* 587

Curry A, 'Germany Celebrates a Half Millennium of Beer' National Geographic (2016) <https://www.nationalgeographic.com/travel/article/germany-celebrates-500-years-of-german-beer-reinheitsgebot-purity-law>

Davies G, 'Activism Relocated. The Self-Restraint of the European Court of Justice in Its National Context' (2012) 19 *Journal of European Public Policy* 76

——, 'Legislative Control of the European Court of Justice' (2014) 51 *Common Market Law Review* 1579

——, 'Has the Court Changed, or Have the Cases? The Deservingness of Litigants as an Element in Court of Justice Citizenship Adjudication' (2018) 25 *Journal of European Public Policy* 1442

——, 'Free Movement, the Quality of Life and the Myth That the Court Balances Interests' in P Koutrakos, N Nic Shuibhne, and P Syrpis (eds), *Exceptions from EU Free Movement Law: Derogation, Justification and Proportionality* (Oxford, Hart Publishing, 2016)

De Witte B and Imamovic Š, 'Opinion 2/13 on Accession to the ECHR: Defending the EU Legal Order against a Foreign Human Rights Court' (2015) 40 *European Law Review* 683

De Witte F, 'Sex, Drugs & EU Law: The Recognition of Moral and Ethical Diversity in EU Law' (2013) 50 *Common Market Law Review* 1545

Dederke J and Naurin D, 'Friends of the Court? Why EU Governments File Observations before the Court of Justice' (2018) 57 *European Journal of Political Research* 867

Derlén M and Lindholm J (eds), *The Court of Justice of the European Union: Multidisciplinary Perspectives, vol 10* (London, Bloomsbury Publishing 2018)

Dezalay Y and Madsen MR, 'The Force of Law and Lawyers: Pierre Bourdieu and the Reflexive Sociology of Law' (2012) 8 *Annual Review of Law and Social Science* 433

Dornbusch HD, *Prost!: The Story of German Beer* (Boulder, Brewers Publications, 1998)

Dothan S, *Reputation and Judicial Tactics: A Theory of National and International Courts* (Cambridge, Cambridge University Press, 2014)

Dougan M, 'The Court Helps Those Who Help Themselves … The Legal Status of Migrant Work-Seekers under Community Law in the Light of the Collins Judgment' (2005) 7 *European Journal of Social Security* 7

Düsterhaus D, 'Eppur Si Muove! The Past, Present, and (Possible) Future of Temporal Limitations in the Preliminary Ruling Procedure' (2017) 36 *Yearbook of European Law* 237

Enchelmaier S, 'Free Movement of Goods: Evolution and Intelligent Design in the Foundations of the European Union' in P Craig and G de Búrca (eds), *The Evolution of EU Law* (Oxford, Oxford University Press, 2021)

Epstein L and Jacobi T, 'The Strategic Analysis of Judicial Decisions' (2010) 6 *Annual Review of Law and Social Science* 341

—— and King G, 'The Rules of Inference' (2002) *The University of Chicago Law Review* 1

—— and Knight J, *The Choices Justices Make* (Washington, Sage, 1998)

——, 'Toward a Strategic Revolution in Judicial Politics: A Look Back, A Look Ahead' (2000) 53 *Political Research Quarterly* 625

——, Šadl U and Weinshall K, 'The Role of Comparative Law in the Analysis of Judicial Behavior' (2021) 69 *The American Journal of Comparative Law* 689

—— and Waterbury NW, 'Judicial Behavior', *Oxford Research Encyclopedia of Politics* (Oxford, Oxford University Press, 2020)

European Commission (Press Release, 30. June 2009), 'The Return of the Bendy Cucumber: "Wonky" Fruit and Vegetables Back on Sale from 1st July'

Ferejohn J, 'Judicializing Politics, Politicizing Law' (2002) 65 *Law and Contemporary Problems* 41

Frankenreiter J and Livermore MA, 'Computational Methods in Legal Analysis' (2020) 16 *Annual Review of Law and Social Science* 39

Galanter M, 'The Radiating Effects of Courts' (1983) in K Boyum and LM Mather (eds) *Empirical Theories about Courts* (New York, Longman, 1983)

Garben S, 'Case C-73/08, Nicolas Bressol and Others, Céline Chaverot and Others v. Gouvernement de La Communauté Française' (2010) 47 *Common Market Law Review* 1493

Golynker O, 'EU Coordination of Social Security from the Point of View of EU Integration Theory' (2020) 22 *European Journal of Social Security* 110

Guthrie C, Rachlinski JJ and Wistrich AJ, 'Blinking on the Bench: How Judges Decide Cases' (2007) 93 *Cornell Law Review* 1

Halberstam D, 'Understanding National Remedies and the Principle of National Procedural Autonomy: A Constitutional Approach' (2021) 23 *Cambridge Yearbook of European Legal Studies* 128

Hall MA and Wright RF, 'Systematic Content Analysis of Judicial Opinions' (2008) 96 *California Law Review* 63

Cokelaere H, 'How a Fight over an Alpine Pass Turned into an EU-Wide Political Headache' POLITICO (7 September 2023)

Hartley, Trevor C., *The Foundations of European Union Law: An Introduction to the Constitutional and Administrative Law of the European Union,* 8th edn (Oxford, Oxford University Press, 2014)

Hawkins B and van Schalkwyk MC, 'Politics and Fantasy in UK Alcohol Policy: A Critical Logics Approach' *Critical Policy Studies* 1

Helfer LR and Slaughter A-M, 'Toward a Theory of Effective Supranational Adjudication' (1997) 107 *Yale Law Journal* 273

Heinisch R, 'Austria: Confronting Controversy' in E Zeff (ed), *The European Union and the Member States. Cooperation, Coordination, and Compromise* (Boulder, Lynne Rienner Publisher, 2001

Hellwig M and others, 'Economic Policy in Germany: Was There a Turnaround?' (1987) 2 *Economic Policy* 105

Hermansen S and Naurin D, 'Will Do? Selecting Judges on the Basis of Policy Preferences or Performance Indicators'

Hermansen S, 'Building Legitimacy: Strategic Case Allocations in the Court of Justice of the European Union' (2020) 27 *Journal of European Public Policy* 1215

Hart HLA, *The Concept of Law,* 3rd edn (Oxford, Oxford University Press, 2012)

Hojnik J, 'Free Movement of Goods in a Labyrinth: Can Buy Irish Survive the Crises?' (2012) 49 *Common Market Law Review* 291

Holmes OW, 'The Path of the Law' (1897) 10 *Harvard Law Review* 457

Hutcheson Jr JC, 'Judgment Intuitive: The Function of the Hunch in Judicial Decision' (1928) 14 *Cornell Law Quarterly* 274

IRU, 'Speed up Brenner Negotiations, IRU Says to European Commission President' <https://www.iru.org/news-resources/newsroom/speed-brenner-negotiations-iru-says-european-commission-president>

Jacob M, *Precedents and Case-Based Reasoning in the European Court of Justice: Unfinished Business* (Cambridge, Cambridge University Press, 2014)

Jacobs F, 'The Role of the European Court Of Justice in the Protection of the Environment' (2006) 18 *Journal of Environmental Law* 185

—— F, 'Human Rights in the European Union: The Role of the Court of Justice' (2001) 26 *European Law Review* 331

Kahneman D et al, 'A Survey Method for Characterizing Daily Life Experience: The Day Reconstruction Method' (2004) 306 *Science* 1776

Kelemen RD, *Eurolegalism: The Transformation of Law and Regulation in the European Union* (Harvard, Harvard University Press, 2011)

Kilpatrick C and Scott J (eds), *New Legal Approaches to Studying the Court of Justice: Revisiting Law in Context* (Oxford, Oxford University Press, 2021)

King G et al, *Designing Social Inquiry: Scientific Inference in Qualitative Research* (Princeton, Princeton University Press, 2021)

Krenn C, 'A Sense of Common Purpose: On the Role of Case Assignment and the Judge-Rapporteur at the European Court of Justice' in MR Madsen, F Nicola and Krippendorff K, *Content Analysis: An Introduction to Its Methodology*, 4th edn (Washington, Sage, 2019)

Kumm M, 'Internationale Handelsgesellschaft, Nold and the New Human Rights Paradigm' in M Poiares Maduro and L Azoulai (eds), *The Past and Future of EU Law The Classics of EU Law Revisited on the 50th Anniversary of the Rome Treaty* (London, Bloomsbury Publishing, 2010)

Lane R and Nic Shuibhne N, 'Case C-281/98, Roman Angonese v. Cassa Di Risparmio Di Bolzano SpA' (2000) 37 *Common Market Law Review* 1237

Lasser M De S.-O.-L'E, *Judicial Deliberations: A Comparative Analysis of Transparency and Legitimacy* (Oxford, Oxford University Press, 2009)

Larsson O and Naurin D, 'Judicial Independence and Political Uncertainty: How the Risk of Override Affects the Court of Justice of the EU' (2016) 70 *International Organization* 377

Lenaerts K, 'How the ECJ Thinks: A Study on Judicial Legitimacy' (2013) 36 *Fordham International Law Journal* 1302

——, EU Citizenship and the European Court of Justice's 'Stone-by-Stone' Approach, (2015) 1 *International Comparative Jurisprudence Pages* 1

——, Gutman K and Nowak JT, *EU Procedural Law*, 2nd edn (Oxford, Oxford University Press, 2023)

Lindblom CE, 'The Science of "Muddling Through"' (1959) 19 *Public Administration Review* 79

——, 'Still Muddling, Not yet Through' (1979) 39 *Public Administration Review* 517

Liu JZ and Li X, 'Legal Techniques for Rationalizing Biased Judicial Decisions: Evidence from Experiments with Real Judges' (2019) 16 *Journal of Empirical Legal Studies* 630

Llewellyn KN, *The Common Law Tradition: Deciding Appeals* (Boston, Little Brown Company, 1960)

Lock T, 'Is Private Enforcement of EU Law through State Liability a Myth? An Assessment 20 Years after Francovich' (2012) 49 *Common Market Law Review* 1675

MacCormick N and Summers RS, *Interpreting Statutes: A Comparative Study* (London, Routledge, 2016)

——, *Rhetoric and the Rule of Law: A Theory of Legal Reasoning* (Oxford, Oxford University Press, 2005)

Madsen MR, '"Legal Diplomacy" – Law, Politics and the Genesis of Postwar European Human Rights' in S-L Hoffmann (ed), *Human Rights in the Twentieth Century* (Cambridge, Cambridge University Press, 2010)

——, 'The Protracted Institutionalization of the Strasbourg Court: From Legal Diplomacy to Integrationist Jurisprudence' (2011) 2 *The European Court of Human Rights between Law and Politics* 43

——, Cebulak P and Wiebusch M, 'Backlash against International Courts: Explaining the Forms and Patterns of Resistance to International Courts' (2018) 14 *International Journal of Law in Context* 197

——, Nicola F and Vauchez A (eds), *Researching the European Court of Justice: Methodological Shifts and Law's Embeddedness* (Cambridge, Cambridge University Press 2022)

Maduro LMPP, *We the Court: The European Court of Justice and the European Economic Constitution* (Oxford, Hart Publishing, 1998)

Mair S, 'Kahn in Luxembourg: A Prolegomena to the Cultural Study of EU Law' (2023) 24 *German Law Journal* 735

Mancini F, 'The Making of a Constitution for Europe' (1989) 26 *Common Market Law Review* 595

Martinsen DS, 'Conflict and Conflict Management in the Cross-Border Provision of Healthcare Services' (2009) 32 *West European Politics* 792

——, *An Ever More Powerful Court? The Political Constraints of Legal Integration in the European Union*, 1st edn (Oxford, Oxford University Press, 2015)

Martinsen DS and Blauberger M, 'The Court of Justice of The European Union And The Megapolitics of Posted Workers' (2021) 84 *Law and Contemporary Problems* 29

McAuliffe K, 'Behind the Scenes at the Court of Justice. Drafting EU Law Stories' in F Nicola and B Davies (eds), *EU Law Stories. Contextual and critical histories of European jurisprudence* (Cambridge, Cambridge University Press, 2017)

Micklitz H-W, *The Politics of Judicial Co-Operation in the EU: Sunday Trading, Equal Treatment and Good Faith* (Cambridge, Cambridge University Press, 2005)

Murphy WF, *Elements of Judicial Strategy* (New Orleans, Quid Pro Books, 2016)

Nic Shuibhne N, *The Coherence of EU Free Movement Law: Constitutional Responsibility and the Court of Justice* (Oxford, Oxford University Press, 2013)

——, 'Limits Rising, Duties Ascending: The Changing Legal Shape of Union Citizenship' (2015) 52 *Common Market Law Review* 889

——, 'The Resilience of EU Market Citizenship' (2010) 47 *Common Market Law Review*

——, 'Derogating from the Free Movement of Persons: When Can EU Citizens Be Deported?' (2006) 8 *Cambridge Yearbook of European Legal Studies* 187

Nicola F and Davies B (eds), *EU Law Stories* (Cambridge, Cambridge University Press, 2017)
O'Brien C, 'The ECJ Sacrifices EU Citizenship in Vain: Commission v. United Kingdom' (2017) 54 *Common Market Law Review* 209
——, *Unity in Adversity: EU Citizenship, Social Justice and the Cautionary Tale of the UK* (London, Bloomsbury Publishing, 2017)
——, 'Civis Capitalist Sum: Class as the New Guiding Principle of EU Free Movement Rights' (2016) 53 *Common Market Law Review* 937
Due O, 'Danish Preliminary References' in D O'Keeffe and A Bavasso (eds), *Judicial Review in European Union Law* (Philadelphia, Wolters Kluwer, 2001)
Oliver P, 'Cases C-46/93 and C-48/93, Brasserie Du Pêcheur v. Germany, and The Queen v. Secretary of State for Transport Ex Parte Factortame, [1996] ECR I-1029; Case C-392/93, The Queen v. Her Majesty's Tre' (1997) 34 *Common Market Law Review* 635
——, *Oliver on Free Movement of Goods in the European Union* (Oxford, Hart Publishing, 2010)
Olivier B and Reestman JH, 'Yunying Jia v Migrationsverket – Court of Justice of the European Communities: No Legal Residence Requirements for the Admission of Family Members with a Third-Country Nationality of Migrated Union Citizens. Grand Chamber Decision of 9 January 2007, Yunying Jia v Migrationsverket, Case C-1/05' (2007) 3 *European Constitutional Law Review* 463
Paunio E, *Legal Certainty in Multilingual EU Law: Language, Discourse and Reasoning at the European Court of Justice* (London, Routledge, 2016)
Peczenik A, 'A Theory of Legal Doctrine' (2001) 14 *Ratio Juris* 75
Pe'er G and others, 'Action Needed for the EU Common Agricultural Policy to Address Sustainability Challenges' (2020) 2 *People and Nature* 305
Pelc KJ, 'The Politics of Precedent in International Law: A Social Network Application' (2014) 108 *The American Political Science Review* 547
Pescatore P, *The Law of Integration: Emergence of a New Phenomenon in International Relations, Based on the Experience of the European Communities* (Amsterdam, A W Sijthoff, 1974)
Phelan W (ed), *Great Judgments of the European Court of Justice Rethinking the Landmark Decisions of the Foundational Period* (Cambridge, Cambridge University Press, 2019)
Pritchett CH, 'Divisions of Opinion Among Justices of the U. S. Supreme Court, 1939–1941' (1941) 35 *The American Political Science Review* 890
Rasmussen H, *On Law and Policy in the European Court of Justice: A Comparative Study in Judicial Policymaking* (Leiden, Brill, 1986)
——, 'Remedying the Crumbling EC Judicial System' (2000) 37 *Common Market Law Review* 1071
Reich N, 'Francovich Enforcement Analysed and Illustrated by German (and English) Law' in A Jakab and D Kochenov (eds), *The Enforcement of EU Law and Values: Ensuring Member States' Compliance* (Oxford, Oxford University Press, 2017)
Reinhorn LJ, 'Butter Mountains and Wine Lakes' (2007) 94 *Economics Letters* 197
Rudden B, 'Consequences' (1979) 24 *The Juridical Review* 193
Šadl U, 'Old Is New: The Transformative Effect of References to Settled Case Law in the Decisions of the European Court of Justice' (2021) 58 *Common Market Law Review* 1
—— et al, 'That's an Order! How the Quest for Efficiency Is Transforming Judicial Cooperation in Europe (2023) 61 *Journal of Common Market Studies* 58
—— et al, 'Law and Orders: The Orders of the European Court of Justice as a Window in the Judicial Process and Institutional Transformations' (2022) 1 *European Law Open* 549
—— and Wallerman A, '"The Referring Court Asks, in Essence": Is Reformulation of Preliminary Questions by the Court of Justice a Decision Writing Fixture or a Decision-Making Approach?' (2019) 25 *European Law Journal* 416
—— and F Tarissan, 'The Relevance of the Network Approach to European Case Law: Reflection and Evidence' in C Kilpatrick and J Scott (eds), *New Legal Approaches to Studying the Court of Justice* (Oxford, Oxford University Press, 2020)

—— and S Hermansen, 'The European Court of Justice, an Able and Unwilling Lawmaker: Evidence from 920 Free Movement of Persons Judgments' in M Dawson, E Muir, and B DeWitte (eds), *Revisiting Judicial Politics in the European Union* (Cheltenham, Edward Elgar Publishing, 2024)

Sankari S, *European Court of Justice Legal Reasoning in Context* (Paris, Europa Law Publishing, 2013)

Sarmiento D and Jiménez-Valladolid D, 'Half a Case at a Time: Dealing with Judicial Minimalism at the European Court of Justice' in M Claes et al (eds), *Constitutional Conversations in Europe: Actors, Topics and Procedures* (Cambridge, Intersentia, 2012)

Scharpf FW, 'The European Social Model' (2002) 40 *Journal of Common Market Studies* 645

Schauer F, 'Precedent' (1987) 39 *Stanford Law Review* 571

——, 'Do Cases Make Bad Law' (2006) 73 *University of Chicago Law Review* 883

——, *Thinking Like a Lawyer* (Harvard, Harvard University Press, 2009)

Schmidt SK, *The European Court of Justice and the Policy Process: The Shadow of Case Law* (Oxford, Oxford University Press, 2018)

Schubert GA, 'The Study of Judicial Decision-Making as an Aspect of Political Behavior' (1958) 52 *American Political Science Review* 1007

Schütze R, '"Re-Constituting" the Internal Market: Towards a Common Law of International Trade?' (2020) 39 *Yearbook of European Law* 250

——, *European Union Law* (Oxford, Oxford University Press, 2021)

Segal JA and Spaeth HJ, *The Supreme Court and the Attitudinal Model* (Cambridge, Cambridge University Press, 2002)

Shapiro M, *Courts: A Comparative and Political Analysis* (Chicago, University of Chicago Press, 1981)

Shapiro M, *The Supreme Court and Administrative Agencies* (New York, Free Press, 1968)

Shaw J, 'Between Law and Political Truth? Member State Preferences, EU Free Movement Rules and National Immigration Law' (2015) 17 *Cambridge Yearbook of European Legal Studies* 247

Simon HA, 'Theories of Bounded Rationality' (1972) 1 *Decision and Organization* 161

Snell J, 'General Principles in Free Movement Law: Applicability and Application' in K S. Ziegler, P J. Neuvonen, and V Moreno-Lax (eds), *Research Handbook on General Principles in EU Law* (Cheltenham, Edward Elgar Publishing, 2022)

Somek A, *Individualism: An Essay on the Authority of the European Union* (Oxford, Oxford University Press, 2008)

Spamann H and Klöhn L, 'Justice Is Less Blind, and Less Legalistic, than We Thought: Evidence from an Experiment with Real Judges' (2016) 45 *The Journal of Legal Studies* 255

Spaventa E, 'The Classic Freedom? The Free Movement of Goods: Old Doctrines, New Cases and Contemporary Reflections' in S Garben and I Govaere (eds), *The Internal Market 2.0* (Oxford, Hart Publishing 2021)

Stein E, 'Lawyers, Judges, and the Making of a Transnational Constitution' (1981) 75 *American Journal of International Law* 1

Stone Sweet A, *The Judicial Construction of Europe* (Oxford, Oxford University Press, 2004)

—— and Brunell TL, 'The European Court and the National Courts: A Statistical Analysis of Preliminary References, 1961–95' (1998) 5 *Journal of European Public Policy* 66

Thym D, 'The Elusive Limits of Solidarity: Residence Rights of and Social Benefits for Economically Inactive Union Citizens' (2015) 52 *Common Market Law Review* 17

Tongeren F van, 'Standards and International Trade Integration: A Historical Review of the German "Reinheitsgebot"' in JFM Swinnen (ed), *The Economics of Beer* (Oxford, Oxford University Press, 2011)

Tridimas T, 'Constitutional Review of Member State Action: The Virtues and Vices of an Incomplete Jurisdiction' (2011) 9 *International Journal of Constitutional Law* 737

Van Cleynenbreugel P, 'Procedural Autonomy as Integration-Reinforcement. The Court of Justice of the European Union and National Procedural Choices' in W Werner and L Gruszczynski (eds), *Deference in international courts and tribunals. Standard of review and margin of appreciation* (Oxford, Oxford University Press, 2014)
Van Empel M, 'Centrafarm Revisited: A Few Comments on Cases 102/77 and 3/78' (1979) 16 *Common Market Law Review* 251
Van Gerven W, 'Of Rights, Remedies and Procedures' (2000) 37 *Common Market Law Review* 501
van Gestel R and Micklitz H-W, 'Revitalizing Doctrinal Legal Research in Europe: What about Methodology?' (2013) *EUI Working Papers*
Van Nuffel P and Afanasjeva S, 'The Posting of Workers Directive Revised: Enhancing the Protection of Workers in the Cross-Border Provision of Services' (2019) 2018 *European Papers: A Journal on Law and Integration* 1401
Vauchez A, 'The Transnational Politics of Judicialization. Van Gend En Loos and the Making of EU Polity' (2010) 16 *European Law Journal* 1
——, 'Keeping the Dream Alive: The European Court of Justice and the Transnational Fabric of Integrationist Jurisprudence' (2012) 4 *European Political Science Review* 51
——, 'When Scholarship Matters: Theory-Building and Theory Effects in the EU Polity Context' (2020) *iCourts Working Paper Series, No. 200, IMAGINE Paper no. 7, 2020* 1
Verschueren H, 'Preventing "Benefit Tourism" in the EU: A Narrow or Broad Interpretation of the Possibilities Offered by the ECJ in Dano?' (2015) 52 *Common Market Law Review* 363
——, 'Recent Case before the Court of Justice of the European Union' (2017) 19 *European Journal of Social Security* 71
Voeten E, 'Populism and Backlashes against International Courts' (2020) 18 *Perspectives on Politics* 407
Wallerman AG, 'Can Two Walk Together, except They Be Agreed?: Preliminary References and (the Erosion of) National Procedural Autonomy' (2019) 44 *European Law Review* 159
Wallerman AG, 'Sowing Wheat and Reaping Thorns: The Referring Court's (Lack of) Influence on the EU Court of Justice' (ECPR Conference, 26 August 2020)
Weatherill S, 'Recent Case Law Concerning the Free Movement of Goods: Mapping the Frontiers of Market Deregulation' (1999) 36 *Common Market Law Review* 51
——, *Law and Values in the European Union* (Oxford, Oxford University Press, 2016)
——, *The Internal Market as a Legal Concept* (Oxford, Oxford University Press, 2016)
—— and Beaumont PR, *EU Law*, 3rd edn (London, Penguin Books, 1999)
Weiler JHH, 'The Transformation of Europe' (1991) 100 *The Yale Law Journal* 2403
——, 'To Be a European Citizen-Eros and Civilization' (1997) 4 *Journal of European Public Policy* 495
——, 'Epilogue: Judging the Judges–Apology and Critique' in M Adams et al (eds), *Judging Europe's judges: The legitimacy of the case law of the European Court of Justice* (London, Bloomsbury, 2013)
Wilkinson MA, *Authoritarian Liberalism and the Transformation of Modern Europe* (Oxford, Oxford University Press, 2021)
Zglinski J, *Europe's Passive Virtues: Deference to National Authorities in EU Free Movement Law* (Oxford, Oxford University Press, 2020)

Index

NB – page locators in **bold** denote information found in tables and those in *italics* refer to information in figures.

www.ingramcontent.com/pod-product-compliance
Ingram Content Group UK Ltd.
Pitfield, Milton Keynes, MK11 3LW, UK
UKHW020844290926
15470UKWH00004B/1535

9 781509 96812